First Edition

Distributed simultaneously in Canada by Clarke, Irwin & Company
Limited, Toronto and Vancouver

Library of Congress Catalog Card Number: 72-90701
Standard Book Number: 0-525-05365-4
E. P. Dutton & Co., Inc., 201 Park Avenue South, New York, N.Y. 10003

American Indian Art: Form and Tradition

Walker Art Center
Indian Art Association
The Minneapolis Institute of Arts

E. P. Dutton & Co., Inc. New York 1972

Lenders to the Exhibition

The American Museum of Natural History, New York
The Brooklyn Museum, New York
Ralph T. Coe, Kansas City, Missouri
Cranbrook Institute of Science, Bloomfield Hills, Michigan
Earle De Laittre, Minneapolis
Carl S. Dentzel, Los Angeles
The Denver Art Museum
Field Museum of Natural History, Chicago
The Heard Museum, Phoenix
E. Adamson Hoebel, St. Paul
Joslyn Art Museum, Omaha
Logan Museum of Anthropology, Beloit College, Wisconsin
Lowie Museum, University of California, Berkeley
Milwaukee Public Museum
The Minneapolis Institute of Arts
Minnesota Historical Society Museum, St. Paul
Museum of Cultural History, University of California, Los Angeles
Museum of New Mexico, Santa Fe
Museum of Northern Arizona, Flagstaff
The Museum of Primitive Art, New York
Museum of the American Indian, Heye Foundation, New York
National Museum of Man, Ottawa
National Museum of Natural History, Smithsonian Institution, Washington, D.C.
Nebraska State Historical Society, Lincoln
The W. H. Over Dakota Museum, University of South Dakota, Vermillion
Peabody Museum, Harvard University, Cambridge
Peabody Museum, Salem, Massachusetts
Philbrook Art Center, Tulsa, Oklahoma
Royal Ontario Museum, Toronto
The Science Museum of Minnesota, St. Paul
Mr. and Mrs. Morton I. Sosland, Shawnee, Kansas
Southwest Museum, Los Angeles
The State Historical Society of Wisconsin, Madison
The Taylor Museum of the Colorado Springs Fine Arts Center, Colorado
Betty Toulouse, Santa Fe, New Mexico
The University Museum, University of Pennsylvania, Philadelphia
Walker Art Center, Minneapolis
Woolaroc Museum, Bartlesville, Oklahoma

Contents

Forewords
Martin Friedman — 5
Ron Libertus — 6
Anthony M. Clark — 7

Enriching Daily Life: The Artist and Artisan
Andrew Hunter Whiteford — 9

Tribal People and the Poetic Image: Visions of Eyes and Hands
Gerald Vizenor — 15

Of Traditions and Esthetics
Martin Friedman — 23

Rock Art
David Gebhard — 27

Men and Nature in Pueblo Architecture
Vincent Scully — 35

Iroquois Masks: A Living Tradition in the Northeast
William N. Fenton — 43

Woodland Indian Art
Robert E. Ritzenthaler — 49

Plains Indian Art
Ted J. Brasser — 55

Indian Art in the Southwest
Frederick J. Dockstader — 63

Indian Arts of the Intermontane Region
Richard Conn — 71

Heraldic Carving Styles of the Northwest Coast
Bill Holm — 77

Asiatic Sources of Northwest Coast Art
Ralph T. Coe — 85

Eskimo Sculpture
Dorothy Jean Ray — 93

Catalogue of the Exhibition (with illustration references) — 117

Bibliography — 148

Cover illustration: *1* Pawnee painted ceremonial drum   cat no 654

Foreword

Martin Friedman

This book, and the exhibition that preceded it show the range and distribution of forms and "object types" that characterize traditional Indian art. Many of the objects shown were produced before contact with white men. Most of the oldest works on view date from the beginning of the 19th century and some of the recent pieces — pottery and kachina carvings, for example — illustrate the persistence of certain visual traditions.

The major object types — pottery, basketry, hide painting, carved figures, masks, shields, pouches, painted hides and other distinct forms — can be characterized as intertribal, and some even occur in widely separated areas of the North American continent. Masks, for example, are found in Eskimo cultures, along the Northwest Coast, in the Southwest Pueblo societies, in upper New York and New England and, to a lesser extent, in the Southeast. Spread across the continent by trade and conquest, these basic object types took on individual form and design inflection in each region and also incorporated some of the designs and materials from white cultures without losing their intrinsic Indian character. In looking at groups of related objects from various societies, a sequence of painted hides or a cluster of shields, we perceive the universal character and inventiveness of Indian art — a collective expression which still permitted individual variation.

In preparing this book, the intention was that it serve not only as a catalogue of the exhibition, but that it function as a survey of current attitudes and information on many aspects of Indian art and culture. In this spirit, we have invited a number of distinguished specialists to contribute essays. These represent the diverse opinions of ethnographers, museum curators, an architectural historian, and a poet. No attempt has been made to cover systematically every style-type or geographic area of Indian art production; rather, we have asked these specialists to write about their particular areas of interest. Some of the essays, speculative in nature, deal with esthetic attitudes; others describe with great precision various stylistic manifestations and object-types associated with Indian art; still others stress the strong relationship of Indian art to daily and ritual life. This book is designed for use not only by the general public but by students of Indian art and culture, and is intended as a reference to supplement the distinguished books and catalogues on Indian art now in print.

Foreword

Ron Libertus

At a time when Indian groups and individuals throughout the nation are searching for identity through redefinition of cultural values, the power and beauty of the works of art in this exhibition can only serve as a catalyst in the quest for knowledge of the traditions of our people.

For Indian people, the exhibition reflects a reawakening of pride: for the non-Indian, it is the beginning of an educational process. Unfortunately our educational processes move slowly and the works of art must be labeled with names and terms that are not Indian, but the inventions of white historians and anthropologists. Indicative of this are the semantic blunders in many of the words for Indian names, most obvious of all the word "Indian" itself. More specific are the words Ojibwa and Chippewa, used interchangeably for the Indian people of Minnesota. In each tribal language the Indian knows of himself simply as "the people." In this area, the word for "the people" is Anishinabe. The Ojibwa or the Chippewa exist in the minds of the dominant society while the Anishinabe exist in the souls of "the people."

The Indian has long been denied individuality and has been, essentially, a romanticized creation of white society's imagination. Today the Indian is in theory what he has never been allowed to be in fact, a synthesis of himself.

A less than cordial relationship between Indian society and the dominant society has been caused by these conflicts in attitudes and by intolerance, and half-truths and stereotypes have been created by persistent generalizations.

Indian people feel that they came from the earth in the mythical past, and their existence must be in harmony with the earth. Indian art strongly reflects these feelings and it may provide an experience that will serve to create harmony once again with the earth and with all of society. Then perhaps, we can correctly speak of Indian art in the terms of "the people."

Indian Art Association

The Indian Art Association, a newly formed group, was developed to represent a variety of Indian views in the organization of the exhibition and its related programs, and includes, American Indian Movement, American Indian Student Association, Department of Indian Studies, University of Minnesota, Indian Advisory Council, Indian Upward Bound, S.T.A.I.R.S., Upper Midwest American Indian Center, Urban American Indian Center.

Foreword

Anthony M. Clark

When I was a child in suburban Philadelphia, Indians were close, but very far. The Wissahickon Gorge was a few miles from my home. An uncut and beautiful piece of the Eastern Woodlands, it seemed absolutely primeval to an exploring child, who could find arrowheads in it and sit with the huge, grandly placed statue of its most famous chieftain, communing unseen for hours. At home, there was a print of Benjamin West's PENN'S TREATY WITH THE INDIANS and I was told which man my ancestor was, how humane the Treaty was, how West had compared the Apollo Belvedere to an Indian brave.

Archeologists are sure that man came to America from Asia, and can be accounted for in the region where our present exhibition takes place in the eleventh and tenth millenia B.C. Our exhibition is very incomplete: the earliest works of art we show are well after the establishment of Europeans in America. In this later period a number of American Indian cultures flourished (for example the Northwest Coast tribes), splendidly continued (the Southwest tribes), or resisted and responded in new ways and with new means — brilliant, tragic, or worse. The Woodland peoples, the various Eastern and Southeastern tribes in whose lands I have lived (here, in Pennsylvania and in New England) were to be either set apart or victims of genocide.

When the Greek traders and colonists came to Italy in ancient times (not much later than the beginnings of the American Woodland cultures), they handled things much better than the European colonists arriving in America. The pagan Greeks did not have the same violent and rather narrow religion that the Europeans brought, nor were they far more literate than, nor technologically far different from, the humans they faced. The Americas that the Renaissance and Baroque Europeans pillaged still lived in cultures beautifully and expertly developed, but within the Stone Age and neolithic forms which the ancient Greeks knew and found. The Greeks gave the names of their deities to the Italic gods they met, and they could do so, for theirs was still a close religious cousinhood. Had Greeks of 900 B.C. met native Americans of 1500 A.D. they would also have found cousins, would have recognized the horned priests, the hearths, the underground kivas, the clans, the sacred springs, the weather deities, the goddess of the North Star, the stock and stones and sacred heights. Herodotus in America would have given a better and more sympathetic account of American religious beliefs and human customs than we have yet gotten.

The place in America I would most like to have known in its prime is the sacred and political center of Cahokia, near St. Louis (ca 1000 A.D.). The many mounds erected over a half-millenium, the plazas, the great palisade, make this center — which may have been the sacred city of half the United States — one of the sublime creations of man.

In the present exhibition we see the material culture of those who really knew how to live on our continent. To know more about them — and surely to find clues about the prospects of all of us today (and tomorrow) — I recommend the readings listed in the Bibliography of this catalogue.

ed. note: Mr. Clark's suggested readings appear in the Bibliography and are indicated by an asterisk*.

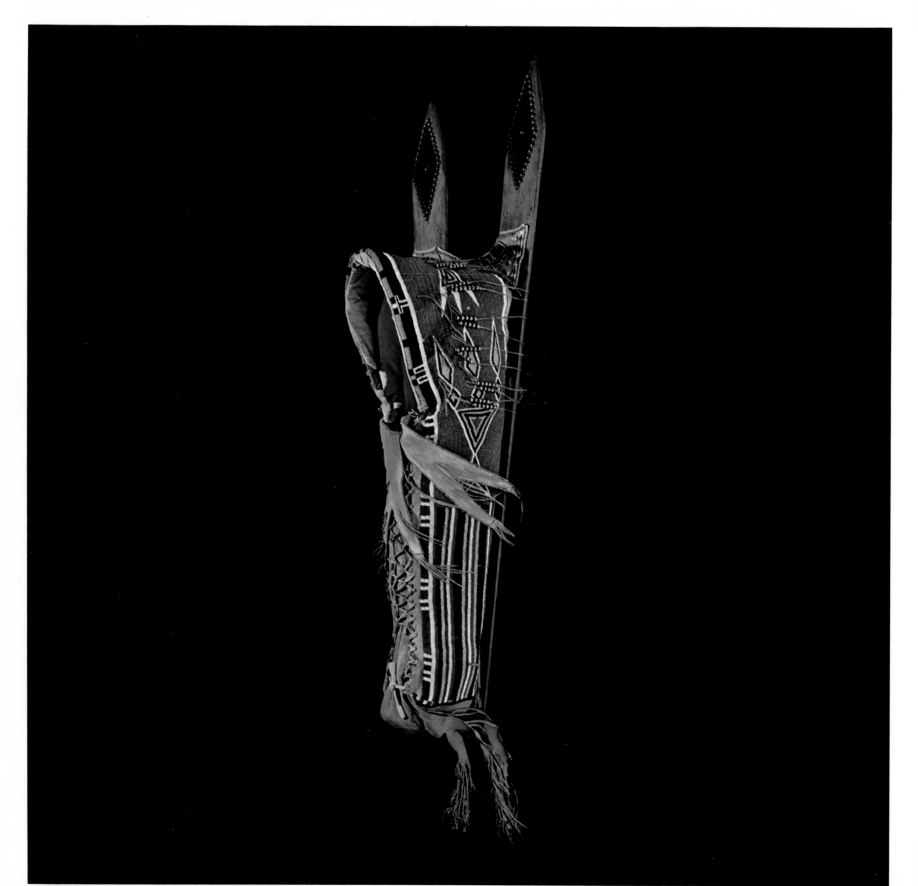

2 Kiowa beaded baby carrier

Enriching Daily Life: The Artist and Artisan

Andrew Hunter Whiteford

Is the visitor to an exhibition more likely to see the beauties of form and color in a Tlingit mask if he knows that it represents a mythical bird and was one of many used in elaborate dance dramas recounting events in a complex mythology? Will such information intensify his interest and deepen his response as he encounters the great carved mask in the isolation of an art gallery? Or will such information dilute and confuse the encounter so it becomes more difficult for him to *see* the mask and to appreciate and evaluate it? There is really no argument! It must be recognized that different kinds of experiences in "appreciation" have equal validity regardless of their diversity, and almost all such experiences combine esthetic, emotional and cognitive responses. The processes of recognition, identification, explication and comparison can be very satisfying but it is a kind of satisfaction which is possible only with the possession of knowledge. On the other hand there is a different kind of excitement and pleasure for which "non-knowledge" may be a requisite: the sudden view of something new and different, or the experience of coming upon a familiar object in a strange light or a peculiar perspective. New perceptions emerge and new sensations are experienced which are unlikely to occur if we are concerned only with classification and analysis. The person likely to derive the greatest enjoyment from an art exhibition is one who possesses ethnological/historical background information and also training in esthetics, but who is able to shift from one to the other and, better yet, to turn it all off on certain occasions as he views the materials on display.

What about the object on view? Is it to be regarded as an object of fine art only if it produces sensations of enjoyment in everyone, or in anyone, or in a select few, or just in the curator? This problem extends far beyond the concern for materials from another culture but it is germane here because exhibitions display many items used by Indians in their daily lives, utilitarian things which generally have been relegated to the non-art category of craft objects. The art historian Douglas Fraser made a clear distinction between art and crafts: only "objects of paramount importance," generally associated with "high spiritual values" can be regarded as art; secular and utilitarian objects produced by "slow, repetitive" processes such as weaving, are classified as crafts or "lesser arts."[1] He indicates also that, in the main, art is created by men, crafts are produced by women. Feder agrees with this distinction between art and craft:

> "We can admire the fine workmanship of a basket made by a California Indian, the countless hours involved in making a solidly beaded Sioux dress, the fine, even lines painted on a Pueblo pot; but their technical excellence does not necessarily mean artistic excellence . . . Although we can appreciate this skill and admire its results it is only those works which have an emotional impact on the viewer that are included here (as art). Usually, but not always, they were intended for use in some religious capacity."[2]

Both Fraser and Feder recognize that the Indians themselves did not make such distinctions and in our society today, as we experience the rapidly shifting scene in the arts and a vigorous renascence of crafts, the line between them seems to become increasingly obscure. Some scholars simply eliminate the dividing line and accept the ethnologist Herskovits's definition: "In the widest sense . . . art is to be thought of as any embellishment of ordinary living that is associated with competence and has describable form."(3) The advantage of such an all-encompassing definition is that it dilutes the insoluble question, "What is art?," while leaving it open for discussion and allowing us to proceed directly to contemplation of the practice and function of esthetic activities and products — of whatever sort. We can then recognize that the mystical and mysterious designs men painted on their shields (fig. 54) were utilitarian in that they served a specific purpose; we can also admire the designs and imagine that the artists felt the pleasures of esthetic creativity in painting them. These same things are also true of the complex geometric patterns women painted on rawhide boxes and parfleches. That one type of painting is realistic, religious, and male-produced, while the other is geometric, secular — although it may have religious connotations we do not know about — and female-produced does not suffice to put them in different categories. If we insist upon separating them, we are led to the disparaging conclusion that Indian men created sacred art; women only manufactured mundane crafts.

In most traditional Indian societies, in common with most of the rest of the world, men were generally the religious leaders, the ones most actively engaged in relationships with the supernatural. Most ritual objects were produced by men but women participated in many phases of religion and were sometimes leaders. What is significant is the extent to which the supernatural permeated every aspect of life. Women were affected as much as men and the concept of a secular life set apart from the supernatural hardly existed.

> "According to their beliefs, supernatural power permeated every phase of Cheyenne being: peace, war, hunting, courtship, art and music. To this day, such seemingly ordinary items as beaded tipi decorations are properly made only after certain ceremonies have been performed. The decorations themselves carry spiritual blessings for those who live or camp in the tipi."(4)

Because the direct relationship between art and the supernatural is discussed in other parts of this catalogue, materials dealt with here are not primarily — so far as we know — of a religious nature. These secular objects constitute the great bulk of material culture generally called crafts — objects produced primarily by women and not ordinarily considered worthy of exhibition in art museums. The catalogue of a recent major exhibition of American Indian art included, among the 158 pieces selected for illustration, fewer than ten objects made by women (four of these were made for tourist sale) and less than twenty which might have been used by women. (5)

Some of the non-religious things used in daily life are made by men. Hopi men spin and weave the textiles (fig. 140) for women's dresses and even bridal robes, and they also weave colored sashes and embroider designs on ceremonial garments. Some Pueblo and Navajo men are silversmiths, and prepare skins and make the implements for garden work. On the Rio Grande some men cooperate with women in the painting of pottery (fig. 6).

3 Pueblo (Santa Clara) burnished black jar   cat no 807

4 Mandan painted buffalo robe   cat no 463

5 Sioux carved horn spoons   cat nos 665, 666

6 Pueblo (San Ildefonso) painted pot by Maria and Julian Martinez   cat no 799

In the 19th century, Plains men made roaches and feather headdresses and painted tipis and robes with records of their exploits (fig. 4), which were sometimes religious but more often related to prestige. Here, and in the Prairie villages, they made bone and horn implements (fig. 5) and weapons of wood. A similar division of labor and production was found through the Lakes area and into the Northeast where both men and women worked on the construction of birchbark canoes, the men generally adding the decorations. Raw materials for baskets were sometimes gathered or prepared by men, but the weaving was always done by women. On the West Coast women made baskets and men made dugouts and other equipment for fishing. Many other utilitarian items were made by men, but such production contributed very little to a man's social position or to his status as a hunter or warrior.

For women the situation was very different. In all tribes a large part of a woman's time was spent producing the materials needed for the maintenance of the family's daily life. Though many of these activities were mundane and routine, women brought into existence a wealth of crafts to enrich their lives, enhance their prestige, and provide them with the satisfaction of esthetic creativity. Everything except the most temporary utensils was created with care and embellished with decoration. In most tribes a woman's reputation, and to some extent her social position, depended upon recognition of her skills and creativity. It was important to be capable in the ordinary tasks of cooking and gardening but prestige was derived from eminence in beading, painting, quill and ribbon appliqué work, weaving and pottery making. Some women were more skilled than others and they enjoyed the admiration of their peers — and probably their envy as well.

Young girls generally learned the arts from their mothers and also took instruction from other women, usually relatives, who were known for special skills. Such learning provided recreation and effective social relationships, for work was often carried on among a gathering of friends who enjoyed each other's company. In such groups success was immediately rewarded with praise, and errors or deviations were quickly corrected. Among the Cheyenne, and possibly other Plains tribes, there were women's craft guilds that invited only the most skilled beadworkers to meet with them to decorate tipi-linings and other important objects. Everyone in the tribe recognized the great craftswomen, and some Pueblo potters have achieved fame far beyond their tribe. Maria Martinez of San Ildefonso (fig. 6) is known for the fine pottery she and her relatives (male and female) produce; Nampeyo, the Tewa potter was responsible for the renascence of Hopi pottery (fig. 178); Lucy Lewis of Acoma Pueblo and many others are esteemed for their fine products. Tribal styles tend to be conservative and distinct but each woman had her own special designs and old-timers can look at a Menomini beaded bag and identify the bordering "otter trail" design as the work of a particular beadworker. A woman did not wear such beaded bags but when her husband took his place in the ceremonial circle everyone present knew who had made his new costume piece and the wife enjoyed the admiration as much as he did.

In the Plains, where personal pride and vanity were essential to being a great warrior, men's elegantly fringed shirts and leggings were decorated by the women with elaborate beadwork (fig. 7) or shining bands of porcupine quills (fig. 146). Women also painted the "sunburst" designs (fig. 155) on robes for men and traditional "box-patterns" on their own robes. These designs are consistent with the geometric motifs employed by women throughout the Plains and brought to culmination on the rawhide boxes and parfleches (fig. 168).

Delicate linear patterns were painted on white buckskin clothing by Naskapi women and the loom-woven beadwork of the Lakes area was angular and geometric. The technique of textile weaving also tended to produce angular geometric patterns, as is evident in Navajo rugs and blankets (fig. 8), and woven mats in other areas. Geometric motifs were carried over into the complex ribbon appliqué work of the Lakes and Prairie areas (fig. 117). Even the finger-woven textiles, which provided somewhat more freedom than loomed fabrics, generally had geometric patterns, as in the woven bags of the Lakes area (fig. 9). The hemp bags of the Plateau area are clearly geometric and the complex Chilkat blankets (fig. 118) of the Northwest Coast reveal few curves and almost never have realistic designs.

The fabulous variety of baskets produced by Indian women from Alaska to Florida ranged from the most simple, utilitarian paddle-shaped seedbeaters to exquisite specimens designed to sell for the mundane purpose of producing immediate income. In California, beaded and/or feather-covered masterworks (fig. 114) were frequently offered as gifts to friends or ceremonially destroyed. Angular geometric patterns were most easily produced in basket techniques such as the plaited splintwork common east of the Mississippi and in the complex imbricated coiling of the tribes along the Cascades (fig. 72). Even the fine twined baskets Tlingit women decorated with false embroidery are geometric, as are the beautifully woven twined baskets with colored overlay from Oregon and California. In these latter cases the process did not dictate the design, because the delicate, complex techniques could have produced any kind of form, geometric or organic. The designs on the coiled baskets made in California (fig. 115) and in the Southwest (fig. 112) tend to be radial and concentric — almost always geometric and usually angular.

Pottery decoration is generally geometric, in spite of the fact that it is much more difficult to paint a balanced pattern of geometric forms on a curved surface than to apply a loose, asymmetric figure. Angular forms are common but curvilinear elements (fig. 177) are more typical, sometimes combined in complex overall patterns and often taking on stylized floral and bird forms. Some curvilinear patterns are also created in basketry in spite of the restrictions imposed by certain techniques. Pima spirals, Mission coiled snakes, Chitimacha meanders (fig. 111) and Hopi "whirlwind" designs are outstanding examples.

Floral patterns are strongly represented in the decorations of the Northeast area where a "double-curve" motif has traditional roots and is found throughout the work of the Eastern Algonkians. Bead and quillwork here has a delicate, balanced quality expressed in the lace-like beaded decoration of the

7 Sioux buckskin shirt   cat no 353

8 Navajo fourth phase chief blanket   cat no 117

Iroquois and in Huron floral patterns embroidered in moosehair. As the floral styles spread to the West they became luxuriantly naturalistic among the Ojibwa and Cree and eventually affected the Blackfeet of the Northern Plains and the Nez Perce and other tribes of the Plateau area. The Sauk-Fox, Potawatomi and Prairie tribes such as the Oto developed a distinctive style which is more formalized and symmetrical.

9 Winnebago woven twine bag   cat no 23

10 Thalton beaded cloth "octopus" bag, Northern Athabascan

Animal and human forms are relatively rare in the art created by women, and their inclusion in some designs made in recent years generally reflects the tastes of white tourists. Birds of various kinds are often painted on Pueblo pottery and Hopi baskets depict stylized kachina figures. Papago baskets and some from California depict figures of men, dogs and horses and these are also worked into the coiled baskets of the Western Apache (fig. 112). Mythical feathered serpents are painted on pottery at San Ildefonso and the thunderbird and underwater panther appears on the textile bags of the Lakes area. Occasionally, human figures are worked in quill or beadwork, but they are rare, recent, or copies of men's painting.

Whatever the basic motifs employed, the range of designs is enormous; the variety is clear evidence that Indian women exercised creative imagination to a remarkable degree. There was no slavish copying but careful selection, arrangement and creation to produce designs within an accepted style but constantly new and different. The esthetic pleasure derived from such challenges seems clear, and the "feed-back" from creativity was immediate, direct, and personally rewarding. The sheer pleasure of creation has been documented dramatically in the patterns Ojibwa women bit into pieces of thin birchbark for no purpose but the enjoyment of looking at them and sharing with each other. A similar case seems to be the rawhide boxes of the Sauk with elaborately painted patterns that are lost when the rawhide is folded and sewn into box form; apparently making the painting was an end in itself.

Women's crafts have survived amazingly well in some tribes and have become major sources of family income. In recent years Indian women have begun to produce creative silverwork, and painters and sculptors are emerging in the younger generation. Whether the impressive skills and the lively creativity of the past can be preserved in today's world remains to be seen but the inherent talent will not be lost and the heirlooms are vivid reminders of the creative accomplishments and potential of the American Indian artist.

(1) Fraser, Douglas, *Primitive Art,* New York, Doubleday, 1962.

(2) Feder, Norman, *American Indian Art,* New York, Harry N. Abrams, Inc., 1971, p 23.

(3) Herskovits, Melvin J., *Man and His Works,* New York, Knopf, 1948, p 380.

(4) Powell, Peter J., *Sweet Medicine: The Continuing Role of the Sacred Arrows, the Sun Dance and the Sacred Buffalo Hat in Northern Cheyenne History,* Norman, University of Oklahoma Press, 1970, p xxv.

(5) Feder, Norman, *Two-Hundred Years of North American Indian Art,* New York, Praeger Publishers in Association with the Whitney Museum of American Art, 1971.

Andrew Hunter Whiteford is Director, Logan Museum of Anthropology, Beloit College, Beloit, Wisconsin and G. L. Collie Professor in the University's Department of Anthropology. With fellowships from the Social Science Research Council, The Wenner-Gren Foundation for Anthropological Research, the National Science Foundation, and the American Council of Learned Societies, Dr. Whiteford has researched archeology and social anthropology in the United States, Mexico, Colombia, Spain and Latin America. He has contributed numerous articles to professional journals and is the author of North American Indian Arts, *New York, Golden Press, 1970.*

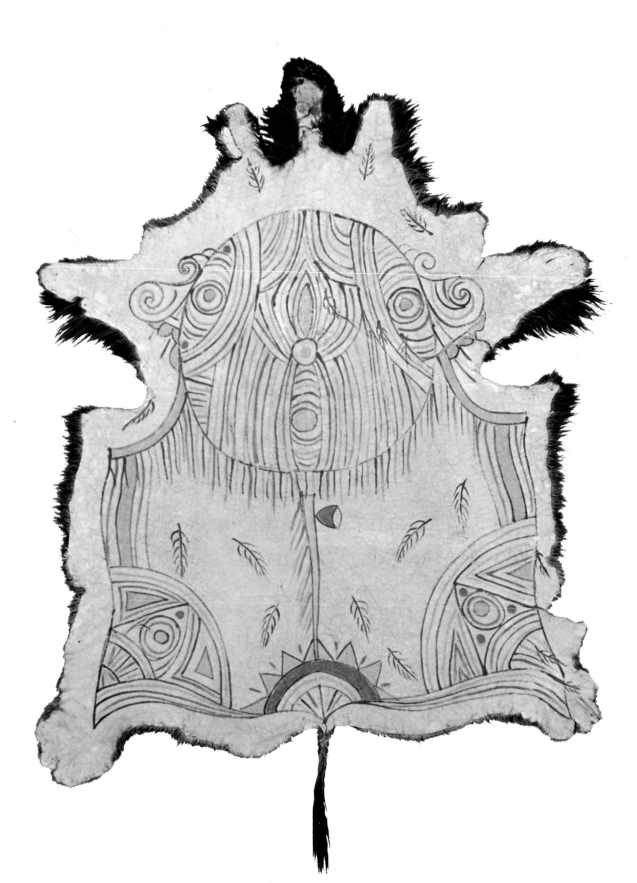

11 Ojibwa buffalo robe

cat no 460

Tribal People and the Poetic Image: Visions of Eyes and Hands

Gerald Vizenor

The poetic images of tribal family people are song pictures and thought rhythms of visions and dreams — timeless patterns of sacred forms of seeing and knowing the energy of life. Imagery in the songs of tribal people, Nellie Barnes wrote more than fifty years ago, is the product of " . . . cosmic feeling. The Indian's observation, esthetic sense, and vigor of thought shape the image to his need — a direct picture, a comparison or a contrast."[1]

> Now think of hands and eyes:
> ceremonial masks
> spider web charms
> the four directions
> winter count figures
> eagle feathers
> circles of the sun and heart
> bear claws
> hand prints on stones
> pictomyths of feeling
> eyes of woodland dolls
> wind in the trees
> rhythm

Now whistle on the wind and touch your eyes four times with your hands while you listen to these stories about seeing and knowing. Songs and stories have the power of words in the telling and the listening.

An old tribal holy man issued his eyes to the sacred cedar tree to see the prairie one spring morning. From the tree his eyes could see in the four directions.

> my eyes
> seeing across the prairie
> knowing summer
> in the spring [2]

A white man passed beneath the cedar tree. Looking up he saw the eyes of the holy man in the tree following him along the footpath.

"What are your eyes doing up there?" the white man asked.

"How can you send your eyes to see from a tree?"

"You are known as the trees see you with my eyes," the holy man answered while calling his eyes back from the trees.

"Show me how you do that trick."

"It is no trick," the holy man explained, "but a way of seeing and knowing the sacred way of the world."

The holy man taught the white man how to see with his eyes in the tree but warned him that he could not issue his eyes more than four times in one day. Eyes will not return after seeing more than four directions in one day.

The white man shook the hand of the holy man and was on his way thinking about his new trick. Next morning in the woodland he issued his eyes to the top of the highest trees four times in the four directions. He thought he could see the whole world. He thought he could own what he could see, but his eyes were nervous while the eagles and crows circled the trees.

In the excitement of seeing so much from the trees the white man had lost his way. Forgetting the warning of the holy man he issued his eyes the fifth time to find his way before dark.

When he called his eyes to return he could not see. His eyes looked down at him from the tree. The white man was blind from having seen too much in one day. He stumbled through the woodland while the crows and eagles plucked at his eyes hanging in the tree. (3)

Thundergods are sailing on the west winds of summer and the family people are dreaming of eagles and crows bringing the center of the world back to the heart.

> the crow
> I saw him when he flew down
> to the earth
> he has renewed our life
> he has taken pity on us (4)

Don Juan told Carlos Castaneda that a man of knowledge has special predilections. In his book *A Separate Reality* Castaneda asked his mystical teacher to explain predilections.

"My predilection is to *see*," he said . . . "Because only by *seeing* can a man of knowledge know."

"What kind of things do you *see?*"

"Everything."

"But I also see everything," said Castaneda.

"No. You don't *see*."

"I think I do."

"I tell you, you don't."

"What makes you say that, Don Juan?"

"You only look at the surface of things . . . *seeing* is not a matter of talk."

Don Juan told Castaneda that "once a man learns to *see* he finds himself alone in the world with nothing but folly." (5)

Manabozho, the compassionate culture hero and trickster of the *Anishinabe* people of the woodland, borrowed the eyes of the owl and the light of the firefly for his visit with the great evil gambler in the realms of darkness.

"I seek no one to come and gamble with me but those who would gamble their lives," the evil gambler told Manabozho. "All of these hands you see hanging around this wigwam are the hands of your people . . ."

The evil gambler was ready to play.

"Here are the four figures of the four ages of man, which I will shake in the dish four times, and if they assume a standing position each time, then I am the winner," said the evil gambler.

The four figures fell in the standing position three times. The destiny of the *Anishinabe* people depended upon the one remaining chance. Should the four ages of man remain in the standing position one more time then Manabozho would lose

12 Southern Cheyenne ledger drawing   cat no 745

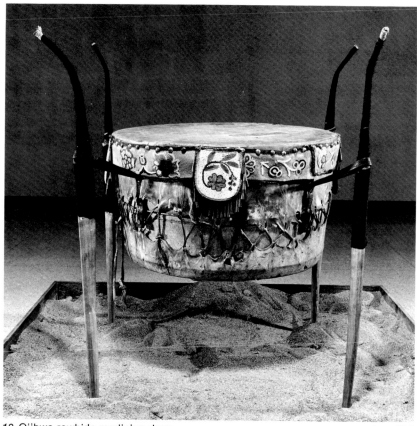

13 Ojibwa rawhide medicine drum   cat no 716

14 Ojibwa carved wood medicine dolls   cat no 389

and the spirit of the *Anishinabe* people would be consigned to the flesh eaters in the land of the darkness. The people would lose their hands and eyes.

When the evil gambler made the final shake of the game, Manabozho drew near and made a teasing whistle on the wind. The four ages of man were not standing. The evil gambler had lost.

"Now it is my turn, and should I win, you will lose your life," Manabozho told the evil gambler. [6]

The poetic images of the woodland are the rhythms of life: the drone of mosquitoes and thump of partridge, sprigs of white pine in the nests of eagles, ice cracks running the frozen lakes, the voices of bears, avian dreams of cranes and loons, eagles and crows, and visions of hands and eyes.

> in the sky, a moon
> on your face, a mouth
> in the sky, many stars
> on your face, only two eyes [7]

In *The Winged Serpent* Margot Astrov tells that "rhythm is the repetition of units that are either similar or contrasting." Rhythm may have a physiological basis which "corresponds to certain physiological processes, as for instance the contraction and expansion of the respiratory organs, the pulsating of the blood, the beating of the heart.

"But this drive that forces man to express himself in rhythmic patterns has its ultimate source in psychic need . . . the need of spiritual ingestion and proper organization of all the multiform perceptions and impressions rushing forever upon the individual from without and within." [8]

> the great sea
> has sent me adrift
> it moves me as the weed in a great river
> earth and the great weather
> move me
> have carried me away
> and move my inward parts with joy [9]

Eskimo people believe it is better for the world to sing songs that show the spirit of joy. "For the helping spirits," Margot Astrov wrote, " . . . avoid contact with human beings who dwell too long on sorrow, and evil prevails where laughter is unknown." [10]

> the lands around my dwelling
> are more beautiful
> from the day
> when it is given me to see
> faces I have never seen before
> all is more beautiful
> all is more beautiful
> and life is thankfulness
> these guests of mine
> make my house grand [11]
>
> I am as beautiful
> as the roses [12]

The people of the woodland did not have a written language. The words of the language are verbal images of family life — the colors and sounds of the lakes and animals and birds. Words had power and expressed the spiritual energy of woodland life — the people did not borrow words from the languages of other worlds to speak of their own. The past was a visual memory of dreams and stories retold in the present. Listeners bring the experiences of a story back to life again.

The great leaders of the people were masters of oratory — using contrasts and metaphors of consciousness and gestures of visual figures of speech.

"I desire you would open and clear your eyes . . . though you may hear birds singing on this side and that side, you must not take notice . . . but hear me when I speak to you, and lay it to heart, for you may always depend that what I say shall be true . . . at present I have no more to say, but when I hear any news you shall hear it, for your ear and mine are one." [13]

Teedyuscung, Delaware, 1760

"The white men are bad schoolmasters. They carry false looks and deal in false actions . . . The white men do not scalp the head, they do worse — they poison the heart. It is not pure with them . . ."

Black Hawk, Sauk, 1832

"My words are like the stars that never change . . . Day and night cannot dwell together. The red man has ever fled the approach of the white man, as the morning mist flees before the morning sun."

Suquamish, Seattle, 1853

"I want to tell you my heart . . . good words will not give my people good health and stop them from dying . . . I am tired of talk that comes to nothing.

"It makes my heart sick when I remember all the good words and all the broken promises. There has been too much talking by men who had no right to talk . . ."

Chief Joseph, Nez Perce, 1859

"The coming of the white man is no different for us than dissension, cruelty, or loneliness. It is a learning for us . . . I choose to stand by the Medicine Shields. I choose to be a Sun Dancer. I choose Peace."

Yellow Robe, People of the Shields

"My heart is filled with joy, when I see you here, as the brooks fill with water, when the snows melt in the spring, and I feel glad, as the ponies do when the fresh grass starts in the beginning of the year."

Ten Bears, Comanche, 1867

"I am a stone, broken and thrown away — one part thrown this way, and one part thrown that way . . . I am grieved at the ruin of my people; they will go back to the old road, and I must follow them; they will not let me live with the white people . . ."

Kicking Bird, Kiowa, 1867

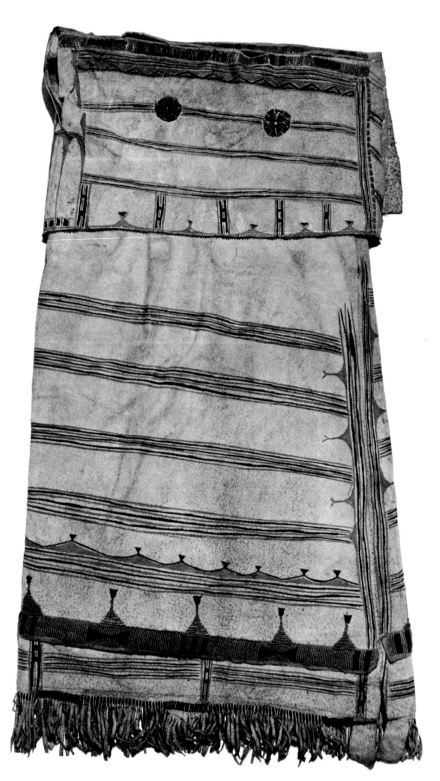

15 Cree painted and beaded buckskin dress

cat no 386

16 Winnebago beaded dance wand   cat no 235

The people danced to touch the sacred earth and sang with the winds and trees and thundergods to the rhythms of the heart.
A religious man could find the energy of himself in every form of life.

> with a large bird
> above me
> I am walking in the sky
>
> the clear sky
> loves to hear me sing
>
> I entrust myself
> to one wind [14]

The people were the color of creation and the earth — yellow and umber and red. The *Anishinabe* once believed that they were given life color from the sun reflecting on the sacred *migis* as the shell moved from the eastern sea along the inland waters to the woodland.

> it was the wind
> that gave them life
> it is the wind
> that comes out of our mouths now
> that gives us life
> when this ceases to blow
> we die
> in the skin at the tips of our fingers
> we see the trail of the wind
> it shows us where the wind blew
> when our ancestors were created [15]

> pleasant it looked
> this newly created world
> along the entire length and breadth
> of the earth our grandmother
> extended the green reflection
> of her covering
> and the escaping odors
> were pleasant to inhale [16]

The *Anishinabe* people measured time by the circles of the sun and moon and human heart. For the lunar months there were the moons of the spirits, moons of the crust of the snow, moons of red berries, wild rice and falling leaves.

The people were the living forms of the woodland. Alice Fletcher wrote that the songs of tribal people were "coextensive with the life of the people . . ." She pointed out that the songs of the people were a "medium of communication between man and the unseen. The invisible voice could reach the invisible power that permeates all nature, animating all natural forms." [17]

Charles Alexander Eastman believes that the religion and spiritual life of the people is the "last thing about him that the man of another race will ever understand . . .

"We believe that the spirit pervades all creation," Eastman wrote in his book *The Soul of The Indian.* "Every creature possesses soul in some degree, though not necessarily a soul conscious of itself . . .

"The *Indian* loved to come into sympathy and spiritual communion with his brothers of the animal kingdom, whose inarticulate souls had for him something of the sinless purity that we attribute to the innocent and irresponsible child." [18]

What the Informant said to Franz Boas:

long ago her mother
had to sing this song and so
she had to grind along with it
the corn people have a song too
it is very good
I refuse to tell it [19]

old woman was coming in
she was saying ditto ditto ditto [20]

"Poetry is valued primarily by the aboriginal for the reaction it produces within himself rather than for any effect he is able to produce on others by means of it," Mary Austin wrote in the introduction to *American Indian Poetry*. "By singing the soul of the singer is put in harmony with the essential essence of things." [21]

Now think about numbers:
one heart
two eyes seeing
four directions
five fingers touching
six directions and the self
four times seven equals
twenty eight lunar days
twenty eight buffalo ribs
twenty eight poles in the lodge

There were the four-legged and the two-legged, pairs of eyes and hands, seven orifices on the head, contrasts of day and night, man and woman, courage and fear, and the rhythms of circles of fires and hearts.

". . . it is not without reason that we humans are two-legged along with the wingeds; for you see the birds leave the earth with their wings, and we humans may also leave this world, not with wings, but in the spirit," Black Elk told Joseph Epes Brown in *The Sacred Pipe,* an account of the Seven Rites of the Oglala Sioux.

"We regard all created beings as sacred and important, for everything has a *wochangi* or influence which can be given to us, through which we may gain a little more understanding if we are attentive." [22]

The first human being in one of the creation myths of the *Anishinabe* people took four breaths of air and started life on the earth. The first four spiritual breaths were the four winds creating the four directions.

The north wind is the color of white and gives men wisdom.

The south wind is the color of green and brings life energy and a strong heart.

The west wind is the color of black and brings the power of the thundergods.

The east wind is the color of gold and gives a man the vision of morning eagles soaring over the woodland and prairie. [23]

Men of good spirits with the power to see the energy of life will know all the winds of the four directions. He will know himself and silence.

Joseph Epes Brown explains in *The Spiritual Legacy of the American Indian* that by adding the "vertical dimensions of sky and earth to the four horizontal ones of space, we have six dimensions, with the seventh as the point at the center where all the directions meet." [24]

The six directions include the layers of the sky and the earth upon which the people touch by dancing. The seventh direction is man reaching to the sky — the place where all six directions meet. The four winds times the seven directions is twenty eight lunar days.

The tribal singer had the eyes of the animals, the legs of the birds, the wings of the spirits, the heart of the bear and the breath of the wind. He was the breath and touch of the woodland and prairie and desert. His fingers were marked with patterns of the leaves and trees. He left the mark of his hands on the face of rocks and towered above the trees in his visions and dreams. In his songs he walked with the moon and soared with the eagles and crows.

my feathers
sailing
on the breeze

across the earth
everywhere
making my voice heard [25]

In the language of the *Anishinabe* there were many words for the spiritual power of breathing and flying and heart, water, wind, fire; and many words for night and snow, hands and eyes, bear, beaver, fish and the visual shapes of land and rocks along the waterways of the woodland. The songs of the people are the energy of life and the words are the sounds and pictures of spiritual power.

I will prove
alone
the power of my spirit [26]

There were very few songs of suffering and sorrow or self pity. The people sang to stay alive. Most songs were poetic images of animals and birds and sky and water.

Today we sing what we believe others have believed and trust the past for the future. Our songs of peace and timeless myths may bring all men together with a good energy to live.

In the language of the *Anishinabe* the word *wanaki* means to live somewhere in peace. [27]

Now sing *wanaki*.

(1) Barnes, Nellie, *American Indian Verse*. Humanistic Studies of the University of Kansas, vol 2, 1922.

17 Five California carved antler spoons   cat nos 678, 680, 682, 683, 685

(2) Vizenor, Gerald, *Anishinabe Nagamon*. Minneapolis, Nodin Press, 1970.

(3) A similar version of this story is included in *Tales of the North American Indians* by Stith Thompson. Bloomington, Indiana University Press, 1971.

(4) Bierhorst, John, ed., *In the Trail of the Wind*. New York, Farrar, Straus and Giroux, 1971. Translated from the Cheyenne by James Mooney and first published by the Bureau of American Ethnology.

(5) Castaneda, Carlos, *A Separate Reality*. New York, Simon and Schuster, 1971.

(6) A version of this tale of the compassionate trickster is told in *The Everlasting Sky* by Gerald Vizenor. New York, Macmillan, 1972.

(7) *In the Trail of the Wind*. Translated from the Otomi by Angel Garibay and first published in his *Historia de la Literatura Nahuatl. op. cit.*

(8) Astrov, Margot, *The Winged Serpent*. New York, John Day, 1946.

(9) *In the Trail of the Wind*. Translated from the Eskimo by Knud Rasmussen and first published in his *Intellectual Culture of the Iglulik Eskimos* — translated from Danish by W. E. Calvert. *op. cit.*

(10) *The Winged Serpent. op. cit.*

(11) *In the Trail of the Wind*. Translated by Rasmussen. *op. cit.*

(12) *Anishinabe Nagamon. op. cit.*

(13) All prose quotations from tribal leaders, with the exception of the quote from Yellow Robe, were published in *Indian Oratory,* compiled by W. C. Vanderweth. Norman, University of Oklahoma Press, 1971. The quotation from Yellow Robe was published in *Seven Arrows* by Hyemeyohsts Storm. New York, Harper & Row, 1972.

(14) *Anishinabe Nagamon. op. cit.*

(15) *In the Trail of the Wind*. Translated from the Navajo by Washington Matthews and first published in his *Navajo Legends. op. cit.*

(16) *In the Trail of the Wind*. Translated from the Winnebago by Paul Radin and first published in his *The Road of Life and Death. op. cit.*

(17) Fletcher, Alice, *Indian Story and Song*. Boston, Small Maynard, 1900.

(18) Eastman, Charles Alexander, *The Soul of the Indian*. Boston, Houghton Mifflin, 1911.

(19) Rothenberg, Jerome, ed., *Shaking the Pumpkin*. New York, Doubleday, 1972.

(20) *Shaking the Pumpkin. ibid.*

(21) Mary Austin in the introduction to *American Indian Poetry* edited by George Cronyn. New York, Liveright, 1934. Originally published under the title *The Path on the Rainbow*.

(22) Brown, Joseph Epes, recorder and ed., *The Sacred Pipe, Black Elk's Account of the Seven Rites of the Oglala Sioux*. Norman, University of Oklahoma Press, 1953.

(23) Storm, Hyemeyohsts, *Seven Arrows. op. cit.*

(24) Brown, Joseph Epes, *The Spiritual Legacy of the American Indian*. Lebanon, Pennsylvania, Pendle Hill Pamphlet, 1964.

(25) *Anishinabe Nagamon. op. cit.*

(26) *Anishinabe Nagamon. op. cit.*

(27) Baraga, Bishop, *A Dictionary of the Otchipwe Language*. Minneapolis, reprinted by Ross & Haines, 1966.

Gerald Vizenor is a teacher and writer of Anishinabe *heritage. He has been active in community programs for ten years and has published several books of poetry. His most recent book,* The Everlasting Sky: New Voices from the People Named the Chippewa, *was published this year. Mr. Vizenor is currently Director of the Department of Indian Studies, Bemidji State College, Bemidji, Minnesota.*

18 Kwakiutl killer whale mask   cat no 593

19 Tlingit carved and painted wood canoe ornament

cat no 223

Of Traditions and Esthetics

Martin Friedman

At last it's the Indians' turn! After 70 years of fascination with the powerful art of the far away cultures of black Africa and the South Pacific, today's art public has also become aware of the depth and expressiveness of the original Americans' esthetic legacy. Great collections of Indian masks, carved figures, pottery and weaving have, of course, long resided in museums, and scholarly documentation describes these evidences of material culture. Yet, the spiritual content of Indian objects eludes the white man, and the specialist's interest in them has been primarily historical and ethnographic; cued to respond to the aristocratic and monumental residue of past Western and Oriental cultures, the classically trained art historian has remained oblivious to American Indian art. African masks and figures, transmuted in the work of cubist and expressionist painters and sculptors, were crucial to the development of early 20th century European art, but no such direct parallel influence was exerted by Indian art on modern American painting and sculpture. (American architecture, however, was affected by the sober geometry of Indian structures. Frank Lloyd Wright's attachment to primal Meso-American forms is apparent in his early work; an updated, positive response to pueblo structures is evident in the stacked, prefabricated, cube-like apartments designed by the Israeli architect Moshe Safdie. And in the 1920s, Navajo, Zuni and Hopi geometric design motifs were freely adapted in the international Art Deco style.)

During the 19th century many American, Canadian and European artists roamed the West, documenting Indian life (fig. 21). George Catlin's early 19th century sketches and paintings of Indian chiefs, and Charles Russell's later spirited views of the Indian hunting and at war are irreplaceable chronicles. The factual styles of these peripatetic artists derived from European easel painting traditions, ranging from academic realism to the flamboyant romanticism of Delacroix. While many of these itinerant painters admired the form and design of objects made by the Indians, their work remained unaffected by these qualities. The white settler adopted some aspects of the costume and ornament of the Indian, whose spiritual art he considered primitive and idolatrous; masks and figures were looked upon as objects produced by a defeated, heathen people.

White attitudes about American Indian culture are obviously changing today. A belated awareness, coupled with remorse about the white man's earlier role in all but eradicating this culture, has in part brought about this metamorphosis, and a welcome consequence is a new admiration for Indian artistic achievement. Extensive exposure to the ideas and objects of contemporary American and European art has facilitated our receptivity to Indian expression. The inventiveness and psychological force of abstract art offers a basis for understanding the artistic sensibility of the Indian, but this is *only* a basis, because modern art and traditional Indian art are widely separated by time and usage. The white American has great difficulty resisting the application of his culture's artistic standards to Indian objects and the phrase "Indian art" is ours, not theirs. Some comparisons of current American and European attitudes with traditional Indian views about the relationship of art to society might help us to better understand Indian art on its own terms.

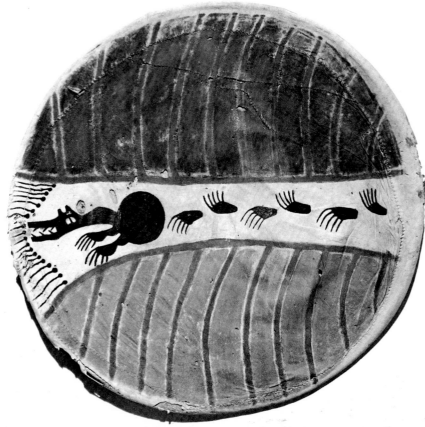

20 Crow painted hide shield   cat no 834

The dichotomies of ceremonial and utilitarian art, fine art and crafts, so prominent in our culture, are relatively meaningless in Indian life (fig. 17). The term "crafts" in our society connotes the fabrication and decoration by hand of "useful objects;" pottery, weaving and leatherwork are regarded as minor arts without the intellectual or symbolic overtones that presumably inform painting and sculpture. (This distinction is, of course, arguable.) Some of the strongest expression in Indian art occurs in tipis, buffalo hides, dance shirts and shields, and the quillwork and beading of Plains women are among the most dramatic manifestations of this vast region's art. In Indian culture, many seemingly commonplace objects such as bowls and pipes are invested with religious or legendary meaning and are made to be used on special occasions. Conversely, the meanings of many symbols appearing on pots, baskets and costumes have long since disappeared and most such designs persist only as decoration.

In settled Indian cultures, such as the Northwest Coast complex and the Eastern Woodlands groups, the artist's role was formalized and understood by society and considered essential to it. In current Western society the "pure" artist is a peripheral figure, admired by few, supported by fewer; he has difficulty finding a place in a culture overwhelmingly concerned with the production and consumption of goods. He may earn popular status if he romanticizes daily existence or produces objects of surpassing technical complexity, but his intuitive or lyrical qualities are not particularly esteemed by the majority.

The artist in Indian society is not confused about his role. He functions on a variety of levels and is wholly integrated into the culture, serving its physical, ritualistic and purely expressive needs. He is frequently involved with other activities: a sand painter might also be a medicine man. The making of art is often a hereditary and sometimes a sacred task, and many carvers of masks and figures learn their skills through long apprenticeship. In basically nomadic societies every man was his own artist and warriors frequently painted their own designs on shields and other objects. Art in white culture is predominantly personal expression, and the artist is heir to a history of individualism. No longer the servant of church or court, he has, particularly since the early 19th century, pursued his own course as an interpreter of reality, a social and technological revolutionary, a mystic, and on occasion even an outcast. By offering new forms he makes us regard the world in new ways, and his role in this culture has evolved into one of a challenger, not a preserver of the status quo.

In Indian art personal attitudes are subordinated to those of the group. The basic objects of Indian material culture are responses to physical and religious needs and, at their most elementary, pertain to food, shelter and the survival of the society. Indian art is concerned with continuity, and ceremonial objects, particularly, help preserve the culture. Masks used in dances and other rituals symbolize ubiquitous forces essential to the life cycle and, as in other aboriginal societies, were used during initiation ceremonies, or in relation to planting, harvesting and commemorative dramas dealing with the actual and mythical history of the group (fig. 18).

Basic object-types continued through successive generations; while such geographically dispersed objects as shields varied in detail in neighboring areas, the primary forms remained constant. The buffalo hide shield was carried by nomadic peoples to the Southwest Pueblos and to the Eastern Plains. Shields are identifiable as Santa Clara, Pawnee or Sioux by their painted iconography, which varies from one region to another and might include buffalo heads, eagles, bear claws or sun-disks. These shields are among the most powerful images in Indian art. Some of their emblematic designs derive from their owner's visions. These objects illustrate the Indian artist's ability to make a strong personal statement within a design convention. An excellent modern example of continuing formal tradition is the revitalization of Southwest Pueblo pottery that began in the mid-1930s, largely through the innovations of such admired artists as Maria Martinez at San Ildefonso Pueblo in New Mexico.

No overall view of the evolution of Indian art in North America exists except for those enduring objects related to the Meso-American cultures — mainly pottery, metal, mica and carved stone — and some important large-scale rock paintings and carvings, small ivories, fragments of textiles and basketry, wood, and shell work. Surviving examples of the past few hundred years indicate that Indian art was in constant change and susceptible to outside influences, but basic object-types persisted. Indeed, one strength of Indian art is its ability to incorporate forms of neighboring tribes as well as some designs and techniques introduced through contact with the white man. The motifs of the American flag, probably first borrowed from the white cavalry as a protective insignia, ornamented Sioux dresses, cradles and beaded pouches, and were even woven into Navajo blankets. Through sustained, often abrasive contacts with whites, the Indian was forced to adapt traditional techniques to new material; for example, many extraordinary drawings were made in lined paper books given to Indians imprisoned after the ill-fated Ghost Dance uprising in 1890. These detailed, schematicized views of Indians in battle continue the naturalistic hide painting tradition and the fact that they are on paper makes them no less Indian. Paintings on muslin, with similar figuration, were used as tipi-linings and later were done as commemorative and decorative objects.

Indian art and Euro-American art manifest entirely opposite attitudes about nature. From the Renaissance to the late 19th century, the theme of nature was domesticated in Western painting. The Impressionists shifted from an illusionistic consideration of the natural world to a quasi-scientific interpretation of light and color in the landscape. Although nature remained a theme for countless artists, Impressionism was the last great sustained sequence of pastoral painting, and modern art, a pluralistic phenomenon, has evolved within the context of urbanism. Early 20th century abstract painting, while frequently concerned with natural themes, was generated by the city, where vanguard artists lived and worked. The geometry of steel, concrete and glass afforded new themes, and nature represented the outside world, not the essential condition of reality.

The Indian artist has always been secure in his relationship to nature. This is implicit in his sensitive use of natural materials (wood, stone, skin, bone, leather, clay) and in the persistence of natural forms in his work — flowers, leaves, mountains and, particularly, animals. Such concern with elementary nature gradually disappeared from pre-urban Western culture and was supplanted by formalized religion, which produced hieratic art objects; but in Indian society, as in other aboriginal cultures, visual images assumed great significance in the absence of a complex written language.

Some animal imagery, as in Northwest Coast art, is totemistic, alluding to tribal ancestry; it is often descriptive of important events in the owner's life and in other instances, is purely decorative. The raven, bear, beaver and fish were basic ingredients of Kwakiutl and Haida heraldry, and the stylized forms of these animals were combined with human forms in carved poles, housefronts, blankets, boxes and bowls to create a harmonious, widespread expression. Albino deerskins trimmed with woodpecker feathers were worn by the Yurok in California, and buffalo and antelope head coverings are still featured in Pueblo ceremonials — the skins identifying the wearer with his animal brethren. In Pueblo mimetic dances of the hunting cycle, the costumed dancer imitates the animal, inducing it to give up its life, thereby insuring the successful kill. Strength, cunning, speed and other attributes of animals were invoked through objects and rituals: the painted hide shields of the Plains Indians carried animal insignia — indeed, actual bird carcasses were affixed to some and most were bordered by feathers.

Realistic and abstract themes coexisted in North American Indian painting and sculpture, often within the work of the same tribe. It is pointless to continue the tired arguments about which style preceded the other; no satisfactory explanation exists as to why these polarities are so closely juxtaposed. Nevertheless, some generalizations about degrees of abstraction are possible.

21 Catlin painting of Bull Dance, 1848

Sioux beadwork on vests and leggings, for example, is decidedly more geometric than similar work by Eastern Woodland artists such as the Ojibwa (the celebrated Ojibwa bandoleer bag is vividly embellished with flower and vine designs reminiscent of European folk art); within the generally naturalistic style of the Woodlands, Winnebago and Menomini bark fiber bags represent some of the most rarefied abstract designs of American Indian art.

The Indian's close association with nature, and his belief that the dream is as real as the waking state, provides him with an ambiguous concept of reality. His strong identification with the animal world, and with deities and forces resident in the natural environment, are basic to his artistic expression; what appears to our eyes as fantastic hybridizations of human, animal and demonic forms carved on a pole, or painted on a hide or dance wand, are objectifications of an all-inclusive reality. The actual, the dream and the spirit worlds are united in his art (fig. 20).

But the Indian artist could be highly descriptive as well as spiritual, and no better example of this exists than the buffalo robe paintings and painted muslins which celebrate the exploits of their warrior owners. In design these vary from stick figure pictographs to elegantly outlined profile views of warriors on horseback engaged in battle. The hero is shown in a sequence of dramatic situations; these might include his investiture as a warrior, his first battle (replete with scenes of killing and scalping), his capture and narrow escape, his elevation in rank. Groups of horsemen are indicated by layering generalized side views behind and slightly above one another, much in the manner of traditional Persian painting. No top or bottom exists in some of these glorified biographies which can be read from any position because the images race in a circle across the surface. Other hides are organized more conventionally and the tribe's travails and successes are presented almost cinematically from one event to another. These paintings, as well as muslins and ledger drawings, were important methods of recording great tribal events, and incidents in many historical battles, such as Little Big Horn, have been described in great detail on buffalo hides.

For all the inescapable differences between modern American art and traditional American Indian art, the two manifestations are related; their intuitive aspects and inventive forms, while proceeding from radically different premises, have something in common. Modern art has prepared us in some measure for the experience of Indian art because it has taught us to expand our definitions of reality. We have followed the artist as he explored the unconscious and the dream world. These are territories familiar to the traditional Indian artist whose vision of reality embraces the actual world and the dream.

Martin Friedman is Director of Walker Art Center, Minneapolis. He has organized and written catalogues for many exhibitions of contemporary painting and sculpture; a book on Charles Sheeler is in preparation. In 1967 Mr. Friedman brought a large part of the collection of Congo sculpture from the Museum of Central Africa, Tervuren, Belgium, to the United States and Canada for an exhibition entitled "Art of the Congo." This exhibition of American Indian art is an extension of the growing awareness of the relationships between traditional native American arts and contemporary expression.

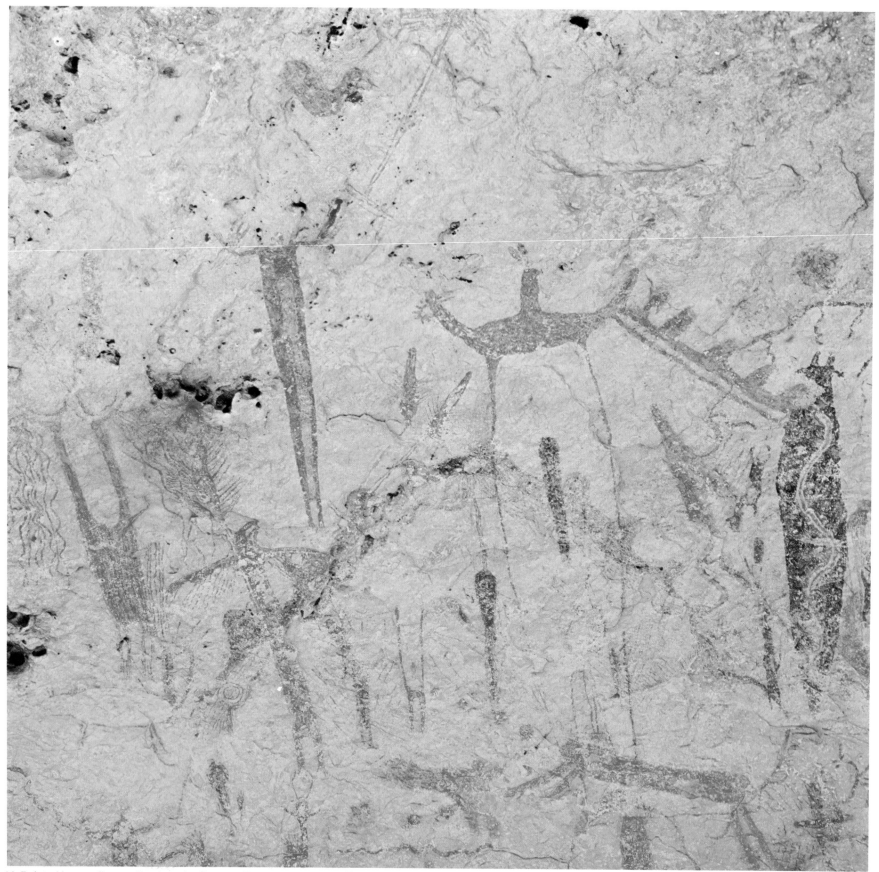

22 Painted human figures, Rattlesnake Canyon, Pecos area, western Texas, attributed to Pecos culture, date unknown

Rock Art

David Gebhard

The rock drawings of North America represent one of the few indigenous arts which have not been detached from their original surroundings. On an exposed rock on the shores of Maine, or tucked away in a small rock shelter in the coastal range of California, one can sense the relationship between art, its techniques, and the natural unaltered environment within which it was originally conceived. A visit to a rock art site is as far removed from the usual art experience as one can imagine. When an artifact — any artifact — is placed in an imposed setting, we are asked to respond to it as an art object. A rock painting still intact in its original site makes no such demand. It establishes its own world — a world which we today will never be able to penetrate fully.

North American rock art has attracted Western Europeans since the 17th century. In 1680, a New England clergyman, the Reverend Danforth, made the first copy of the famous rock drawing on Dighton Rock near the small Massachusetts town of Berkeley. Others followed in his footsteps making copies of the Dighton Rock drawings (Cotton Mather in 1712, Stephen Sewell in 1768, and James Winthrop in 1788) (fig. 23). Throughout the 19th century numerous travelers and settlers noted and in some cases made sketches of rock art sites from the Atlantic to the Pacific Coasts. As with any historic art, these sketches and what was written about them often reveal more about the views of the time than they do about the drawings themselves. Some writers in the 19th century thought rock art was evidence of early Phoenician settlements in the New World, or even earlier Egyptian exploration. Others, often with great passion, argued that they were concrete proof of the existence of the lost continents of Atlantis and Mu.

By the end of the century, the growing passion for science, and especially the acceptance of Darwinian theories of evolution, prompted many early anthropologists to see these rock drawings and paintings as "picture-writing" — as the first "barbaric"

23 Drawing of rock engraving, Dighton Rock, near Berkeley, Massachusetts

step on the upward and onward road to the alphabet and material high culture. With the development and codification of the new "science" of anthropology in the early years of the 20th century, examples of the rock art of North America continued to be noted, and in most cases very accurately recorded by means of measured drawings, squeezes and photographs. But the vast majority of professional North American archeologists were on the whole embarrassed by rock art. As scientists they were expected to feel uneasy about the subjective (irrational) world of art. Then there was what appeared to be the insurmountable difficulty of relating these drawings and paintings to the normal array of material artifacts which had painstakingly been excavated from stratified sites.

This confidence in the scientific method held sway until the mid-1960s. Since then there has been a dramatic loss of confidence in the traditional ideology and approach archeologists have taken in their reconstruction of North American prehistory. Partially as a result of this, and also because of the expanding concern for things "primitive," interest in North American rock art has recently increased appreciably. As a result there has been more information published on rock art in the past ten to fifteen years than was published in the previous 150 years.

Our ability to fully understand the rock art of North America will always remain limited; we will never be in a position to know what percentage of the total number of drawings and paintings have survived through the centuries. On the basis of what we know has disappeared, it is reasonable to surmise that the number of drawings still in existence is not only small, but may not even be representative.

Though drawings placed on protected rock surfaces can last several thousand years or more, many paintings on only partially protected or unprotected surfaces have completely disappeared from sight. Another serious limitation is the paucity of geographic areas within North America where all of the drawings in a geographic area have been fully recorded and documented.

One would normally assume that, with the existence of an extensive ethnological literature devoted to the North American Indian, we would possess a reasonable amount of information as to how rock drawings were made and what function they served within one or another of the historic Indian tribes — but this is simply not the case. We possess only the most meager information on the subject: the use of totemic figures and "wintercounts" of the Plains Indians and in the mountainous west; in the Southwest a limited number of drawings would appear to refer to specific historic events of the 19th century or to certain religious ceremonies. Among the Salishan tribes of the Plateau " . . . . adolescents of both sexes made records of remarkable dreams, pictures of what they desired or had seen, and events connected with their training. These records were made with red paint on boulders or cliffs, wherever the surface was suitable."[1]

There are only a few instances in North America where the style of rock drawings can be said to be the product of a known Indian group. In the Pacific Northwest, there are examples of rock drawings which are known to have been produced by the Haida, the Tlingit and others. In the Plains region there are sites which can be associated with the Crow, the Sioux, the Shoshoni and others. In Utah a convincing case has been made to attribute many drawings found in the central and eastern part of the state to the occupation of this area by the prehistoric Fremont people (ca 1150 A.D.) (fig. 24). In the Southwest there are a number of rock art sites which on the basis of style and other factors can be attributed to one or another of the prehistoric and historic groups which have lived in the region.

It has recently been suggested by several archeologists that certain rock art drawings in western North America depicting herds of mountain sheep and goats were a form of direct sympathetic hunting magic. Other rock drawings have been explained as elements of shamanism and fertility. Most rock drawings of North America involve the hunt, but a drawing which depicts a warrior spearing a deer or shooting a buffalo with a bow and arrow may not be a hunting scene in the usual sense of the term. The act of hunting can very easily stand as a symbol of an individual's power to manipulate a force in nature, or it can refer to a man's relation to a clan. Unless we possess direct ethnological evidence as to the symbolic content of the drawings, we can only say that a drawing depicts the "act" of the hunt, rather than the hunt itself.

On the basis of historic ethnological information, it is evident that almost all of the rock drawings of North America were viewed by their makers as a means to an end, not as an end in themselves. These drawings, then, were conceived of as a method of communication via images which would enable the individual and/or his group to control or to establish a rapport between the visible and the invisible world around them. It seems reasonable to suppose that, like Action Painting of the 1950s, the act of producing the images was often more significant than the completed drawing. A large percentage of the rock art of North America was an element within the context of a personal or group ritual, and as a material artifact it is in many instances the only fragment which has survived. One's reactions to rock drawings will be very close to the experience of seeing a classical, medieval or pre-Columbian ruin — we will respond to it in a visual as well as a contextual sense.

The physical terrain and localized weather conditions of North America affect the quantity and distribution of rock art sites. The geographic area east of the Mississippi River possesses only a few rock exposures which would have been suitable for drawings. This area also receives abundant rain and snow, which tend to severely weather exposed rock surfaces. The Plains area, west of the Mississippi Valley, presents even fewer exposed rock surfaces until one arrives at the foothills of the eastern slope of the Rocky Mountains. Both of these areas — the Woodland to the east of the Mississippi, and the Plains to the west, exhibit only a scattering of rock art sites. It is reasonable to suppose that throughout history the use of rock surfaces for drawings must always have been limited in both the Eastern Woodland area and in the Plains.

To the north, in the region of the Great Lakes and on into western Canada, the number of exposed rock surfaces increases as do the number of known drawings. But over 80 percent of the known drawings are found in the area from the eastern slopes of the Rocky Mountains to the Pacific; in this region the presence of exposed rock surfaces often forms the dominant physical feature, and the rock itself, usually sandstone, is soft enough so that it can easily be worked. The lack of moisture throughout much of the West has meant that even those drawings placed on more exposed surfaces have lasted for many years.

In the Eastern Woodland and Plains area drawings are generally found on large free-standing boulders or on exposed bed rock. In a few cases — particularly in the Midwest — the walls of small cave shelters were used. In the Great Lakes area and further north and west, low vertical cliff faces provided the needed surfaces, while in the mountainous West both vertical cliff faces and rock shelters were favored sites for drawings.

The techniques used to produce the rock drawings of North America are similar to those found elsewhere in the world. Some were engraved into the rock surface with a hard sharp instrument; others were pecked into the surface by a hard hammerstone or with a hammerstone and chisel; in other examples paint was used, alone or sometimes in conjunction with another technique. Regardless of technique, all of these rock drawings exhibit a wide range of technical proficiency: some were minutely and painstakingly drawn, with the artist exercising precise control over his instruments; others seem to be hastily drawn, showing little care in execution. Diversities like these may in some cases reflect differences in technical proficiency upon the part of individuals, while in other cases, the precision of workmanship or lack of it may well reflect general group values.

One widely held myth about North American Indian art should be dispelled: there is no evidence that the maker of rock art (or of Indian art in general) was concerned at all about such Western European values as "honesty" of materials or the expressive character of his final images. The North American Indian would often render exactly the same image via a three-dimensional carving, painted two-dimensionally on a skin, or incised into a rock surface. The value lay in the image, not in the technique employed in rendering it, nor the material of which it was made. In the case of historic Indian art, where we do possess examples on skin, bone, wood and stone, the images are modified as little as possible to accommodate to the different techniques and to the different characteristics of each material.

As is true of "primitive" art in general and specifically of North American Indian art, the styles found in the rock art of North America changed very slowly over the years. An exception, of course, is the late art of the Plains Indians which after European

24 Pecked and painted rock engraving, Dry Fork of Ashley Creek, northeastern Utah, attributed to the Fremont people, ca 1150

contact in the 18th century changed most radically. Most archeological and ethnological studies of North America have geographically sub-divided the continent into several areas — the Eastern Woodland, the Northern Woodland, the Arctic, the Great Plains, the Southwest, the Great Basin/Plateau, the Northwest Coast and California — while such an approach mirrors the differences between one environment and another, it does not mirror the complexity of the prehistory of the continent, nor does it reflect the major stylistic traditions of rock art which in many instances completely ignore the separateness of these environmental pigeon holes.

Instead of looking at the rock art of a geographic area, such as the Eastern Woodland, or attempting to analyze the drawings of a specific historic or prehistoric people, one should view this art (and North American Indian art in general) as the result of a limited number of basic traditions. The individual prehistoric and historic styles which have resulted from these traditions — the art of the Plains area, or the art of the lower Mississippi Valley — exhibits a particular mixing of these traditions, a mixture which has come about both in time and in place.

North America has experienced three major art traditions: (a) the Northern Residual; (b) the Meso-American; and (c) the Eastern Woodland. The style or styles which one encounters at a specific rock art site represent a modification and, in most cases, a mixture of these traditions. Many elements of each of these three traditions were originally diffused into North America from the outside: the Northern Residual tradition derived from Asia; Meso-American tradition from the materially more sophisticated and complex cultures of Mexico and Central America, and Eastern Woodland tradition came at various periods of time from Europe and the Mediterranean region.

The use of the term "diffused" in this context is not meant to imply that these traditions entered the continent as a single episode in time and place. Such would certainly not appear to be the case. Out of the Residual tradition, for example, developed at least two modes — the Pit and Groove aspect and the Linear-Connection aspect (figs. 23, 25). The Meso-American tradition was responsible for four aspects: the Non-representational Geometric (fig. 26); the Rectangular Human Figure aspect (figs. 24, 27, 28); the Linear "Figure" aspect (fig. 29); and the Shield Figure aspect (fig. 30). The Eastern Woodland tradition prompted a series of styles which were essentially representational (figs. 31, 32). These traditions entered North America over long periods of time. As far as rock art is concerned, the oldest of these aspects would be that of the early Residual tradition as seen in the Pit and Groove mode; the most recent would be the late Eastern Woodland tradition of rock drawings and paintings of the 19th century Plains Indians and of the nomadic groups of the American Southwest. These three traditions are seldom encountered in a pure state at any known rock art site. The closest one comes to the pure expression of a tradition (that of the Northern Residual) would be the Pit and Groove aspect, where in sites distributed from California to Georgia, the imagery of circles, dots, dots within circles, concentric circles and their accompanying straight lines are occasionally coupled with other linear non-representational connective motifs.

If this broad concept of tradition is taken into account, a new and more meaningful approach to rock art becomes possible. While the actual content of most rock drawings will never be known to us, it is possible to discover the process of diffusion and change which has come about in rock art, and it is possible

25 Rock engraving on Steatite Boulder, Jackson County, North Carolina, date unknown

26 Pecked rock engraving, Bernardo Gap, southern New Mexico, attributed to the Mogollen people, date unknown

to see how individual images or groups of images have been transformed from one style to another.

A fascinating example of the changes that can occur with a single image as it is diffused from one style to another is the Rectangular Human Figure mode of the Meso-American tradition. Though we cannot be positive as to the precise chronology and movement of this mode from one geographic area to the next, enough evidence has been collected so we can at least come up with a general picture of its pattern of diffusion and change. Examples of the Rectangular Human Figure mode are first encountered in the Pecos Style drawings (fig. 22) found in the spectacular, large cave shelters located in and around the confluence of the Pecos and Rio Grande Rivers in western Texas and adjoining sectors of northern Mexico. Here, the human figure is painted in one or more colors, rendered as an elongated trapezoid, accompanied by brief indication of a head, without features but occasionally with a headdress, with short stubby legs often indicated below it. From the Pecos area this conventionalized method of depicting the human image was diffused northward, occurring in the Barrier Canyon region of Utah, as an image in the early Southwest Basketmaker drawings and still further north as the dominant image of the spectacular Fremont drawings (fig. 24). At some point in this process of movement, the Rectangular Human Figure mode was taken up by the Chumash (fig. 28) and several other groups in central and southern California. This specific, conventionalized image also formed the dominant motif in the paintings situated in the cliff shelters of Baja California. Perhaps the last occurrences of this mode are the intricate interior line human figures concentrated in western Wyoming (fig. 27) and occasionally found at other sites throughout the West.

An equally intriguing transformation can be minutely followed in the 18th and 19th century rock art of the Plains region, where the earlier styles rapidly changed from a conventionalized naturalism that developed out of the Eastern and Northern Woodlands regions to naturalism which was the direct result of the encounter between the European and the Plains Indian (figs. 31, 32). The changes which came about in late Plains art from the 1750s through the 1870s was reflected not only in the approach the artist took to each individual image — whether a human figure or a horse — but also in the way he composed the figures. In the earliest known examples of Plains rock art, the human and animal figures appear in a closed composition; in the later drawings while a mounted horseman might be compositionally connected to another figure such as a buffalo, the overall composition has no boundaries other than that loosely conveyed by the contours and other features of the rock surface upon which the drawing was placed.

What are some of the consistent characteristics of each of the broad traditions? The Northern Residual tradition was committed to non-representational geometric images; only later, perhaps under the impact of new forms derived from the Eastern Woodland tradition, did it begin to incorporate a few animal and human representational images. The Eastern Woodland tradition was from the very beginning representational, with its major emphasis (until the late art of the Plains Indians) on animal images, rather than the human form. In the Meso-American tradition it was the human form, rather than the animal, which dominated rock art paintings and drawings.

There are also differences in technique, with the Meso-American tradition having a strong preference for paint, while both the Northern Residual tradition and the Eastern Woodland tradition

27 Pecked rock engravings of human figures, Dinwoody Lakes, western Wyoming, ca 1500

relied almost exclusively on engraving and pecking. There were differences between each of the traditions as to the physical size of the drawings. The Meso-American drawings were often of considerable size (in the Pecos area there are sites over 400 feet in length with human figures well over life size). By contrast, the styles which developed out of the Residual tradition and the Eastern Woodland tradition were almost always very small in scale (two to three feet in width, individual figures four to eight inches high).

From an analytical point of view the obligation of the professional archeologist and the art historian is to see that what remains of the rock art of North America is fully recorded, and then systematically and painstakingly studied. Except for those who are interested in the experience of art as an end in and of itself, the uniqueness of rock art is the relationship which still may be enjoyed between the drawings and their original setting.

(1) Teit, James, "Salishan Tribes of the Plateau," *The Annual Report of the Bureau of American Ethnology*, vol 45, 1930, Washington, D.C., p 283.

David Gebhard is Director of the Art Galleries, University of California, Santa Barbara. Since 1948 he has conducted field studies of the rock art of Wyoming, Utah, New Mexico and Texas under grants from the National Park Service and the Smithsonian Institution. The results of these studies have appeared as books, catalogues, articles and exhibitions of North American rock art, organized by Dr. Gebhard, at the University Art Galleries in Santa Barbara.

29 Linear style painting of human forms, Pressa Canyon, Pecos area, western Texas, date unknown (drawing from a photograph)

28 Painted human figure and other motifs, small shelter near Plate, southern California, attributed to the Chumash, date unknown

30 Pecked rock engraving of human shield figure, south of Santa Fe, New Mexico, attributed to Pueblo IV Period

31 Red painted deer, Carr Ranch, northeastern Wyoming, late 18th, early 19th century Plains Indian

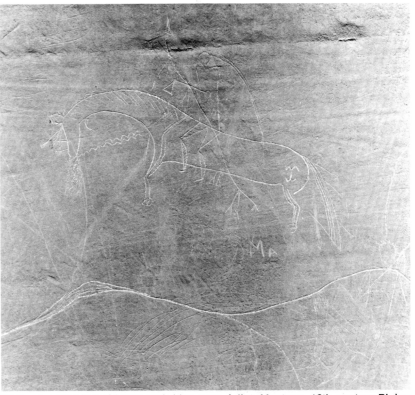

32 Rock engraving of horse and rider, near Joliet, Montana, 19th century Plains Indian

33 Tesuque Pueblo Corn Dance, Lake Peak beyond

Men and Nature in Pueblo Architecture

Vincent Scully

In an article so brief, it seems proper to touch only on the most important aspect of Pueblo architecture, which is the relationship between men and nature that it embodies and reveals. The environment inhabited by human beings is created partly by nature and partly by themselves. All human construction involves a relationship between the natural and the man-made. That relationship physically shapes the human cultural environment. In historical terms, the character of that relationship is a major indication of the character of a culture as a whole. It tells us how the people who made it thought of themselves in relation to the rest of creation. Are they, in their view, unique in the scheme of things, or have they no such conception? Do their buildings contrast with the forms of the earth or echo them? Primitive house types are normally too dominated by functional, structural, and internally symbolic preoccupations to be actively involved in evoking such relationships, though the actual congruence of shapes, deriving from purely practical considerations, may be startling. All this was generally true of the early Basketmaker villages of the Southwest, one feels sure. But the vast majority of early civilizations — Mesopotamian, Egyptian, Meso-American (fig. 34), and so on — fairly obviously set out to imitate natural forms in their monumental buildings and to geometricize them at landscape scale, so creating conscious images of mountain, sun's rays, river, swamp and cloud. Other references are to the heavens in patterns tied to the sun and the stars. Through all these links and images, human ritual borrows nature's forms and adjusts them magically to human measure and human ends.

The Greek revolts from this calculated symbiosis. As the landscape is sacred it embodies divinity separate from man, who places in it a house, a *naos,* as a shelter for his own image of the god of that place. Then he surrounds it with columns, like images of standing men, and later in his history he describes them verbally in such terms. But for the exterior body of the peripteral temple as a whole he seems to have had only two special imagistic words: *aëtos,* eagle, for what the Romans were later to call the pediment; and *ptera,* wings, for the peripteral colonnades. So, while the triangle of the *aëtos* may seem to echo mountain shapes a little, that is apparently not how the Greek primarily saw it. His temples embody not the natural but the man-conceived divinity. They are heroic; they confront and balance the earth shapes but are not of them. They are the eagles of Zeus, wingspreading, through whom mankind bursts free.[1]

Western civilization has lived with that fundamental concept of freedom from nature ever since. Right now it is clearly abusing it according to a frame of reference which, whether Liberal or Marxist, has been largely shaped by 19th century materialist thought. The industrial and scientific revolution was primarily directed against nature's boundaries, and it has pushed them back step by step. In the process, it has tended to poison and ruin the natural world for the gratification of mass human desires. What nature's counterattack may eventually consist of is not our concern here.

Our problem is: how can we perceive the architecture of the American Indian, who has such an entirely different view of men and nature than the one we hold? We have even lost the Greek's constant awareness that nature indubitably exists. We ignore it; we confront it no longer. To the Greek the relationship was tragic; to us it is trivial. Since this is so, how can we hope to penetrate even deeper to that landscape of the consciousness where we and the mountain are the same? In the Indian world, no conception whatever of any difference between men and nature can exist, since there is in fact no discrimination between nature and man as such, but only an ineradicable instinct that all living things are one. And all *are* living: snake, mountain, cloud, eagles, and men.

The Pueblo architecture of the Southwest can best help us toward some understanding of this state of being. It is, first of all, much the most permanent of all North American Indian architectures, and is, therefore, always related to specific sites with their special sacred or, at least, religiously functioning landscape forms. It also has a complex ritual connected with it — a ritual still wholly alive and hence illustrative of how its architectural frame was originally conceived. That architecture is also described by a verbal language, by which its visual language can be supplemented and clarified for our restless eyes — eyes not yet blind but progressively disconnected in most instances from the intellectual centers of our being.

Here even the apparent deficiencies of language serve our turn. Whorf tells us, for example, that the Hopi have no special names for special building types or building shapes or rooms except *yé-mokvi,* meaning equally "inner room" and "cavern;" and *te-wi,* meaning alike "setback," as in a building, and "ledge," as on a mountainside.[2] And in that meaning, so Mindeleff and Stephen told us long ago, *te-wi* is also used for the bench around

the sides of a kiva's interior.[3] (Even for kiva there was no word, since it is a foreigner's corruption of *ki'he,* which means a building of any kind.) From all this, no less than from the forms of Hopi architecture itself, it would seem apparent that buildings and mountains are all one for the Hopi (fig. 35). Man-made structures are works of nature, too, no different in that from the homes of the bees. Looking like natural rock outcrops on the crowns of their mesas, Hopi towns are not exactly engaged in "fitting in" with nature, as so many Western romantic buildings have tried to do. They *are* nature, pure and simple, but their resemblance to the shapes of the earth is not accidental. It is to the Hopi, I think, at once an act of reverence and a natural congruence between two natural things.

The Hopi employ, of course, many other architectural terms. Putting those words together can indeed do much to resolve the question which troubled Whorf concerning the Hopi's lack of space — and shape — descriptive terminology; because the words which the Hopi do possess unmistakably lay out for us the major cultural function of Hopi architecture, which is to use buildings to frame a plaza in which ritual dances can be performed and from which they can be watched (fig. 36). Using Whorf's list we find that all the words are there: *ki-coki,* "village;" *ki-sonvi,* "plaza;" *te-wi,* "ledge" or "setback," here along the house front, so that spectators can lean back against the *tekᵂni,* or "wall." Above, just about exactly defining what turns out to be the height of a file of high-masked *hemis* dancers in the plaza, is the *kigálmo,* the "eaves" or "cornice." Above it is the roof, *ki'ami,* upon which the watchers stand, a frieze of men at the size of the dancers. And there is a word for "on the roof" to place them there, whence they can see the landscape as well. The human

34 Teotihuacan Temple of the Sun from the "Citadel"

35 Hopi Second Mesa, Mishongnovi, foreground, Shipanlovi beyond

scale is precise, so that the buildings become an exact frame for ritual. Even a conscious sense of the plaza itself as a spatial volume may not be lacking, since the word, *tekʷwánmène,* "encircling wall," exists to describe such a condition.

There is another important word: *kiska,* for a covered way between buildings leading into the plaza. Such passages can best be seen at Walpi and Shongopovi: at the former very deep, a good thirteen lintels long; at the latter arranged in a splendid sequence of tunnels from plaza to plaza, with wooden boards spanning shallow trenches in the passages, which thus reverberate like thunder underfoot. In these passages a direct reference is retained to the time when the village as a whole was all one house, where the inhabitants went from room to room *ensuite,* bending under the pine or cedar lintels that supported the many stories of wall above them. Scores of prehistoric ruins show that organization: many in Chaco Canyon, for example, which the Hopi claim as one of their earlier homes.[4] At Pueblo Bonito, as in the other vast structures there, the word *yé-mokvi,* or some equivalent, must have functioned appropriately: almost all the rooms are deeply "inner," and "cavernous." *Te-wi* would have applied, too, as the rooms are set back in elevation to form sunny external ledges within the embracing "D" of the great house's outer wall (fig. 37). Across the Canyon from Pueblo Bonito, the cliff opens in a cross canyon, and that cleft must have caught the eye from the terraces, but all the major relationships seem inward. The house is not really turned outward to focus on any natural feature external to itself — except, of course, upon the regal sun. It is an internal world, a hive, a dizzying constellation of cellular units (fig. 38). The cylindrical kivas, packed round with earth to retain their original

subterranean character, supplement the dwelling and storage cubicles and intensify the effect of internal geometric order. In the kivas, stepped altars, mountain and cloud at once, would probably have been found, and their own *te-wi* circled the walls of this ultimate cave. Yet in the floor the symbolic hole of the *sipapu* gave spiritual access to still another world deeper below.

The largest kivas at Pueblo Bonito and elsewhere are of the so-called Great Kiva type (fig. 38). They were probably intended to serve a larger social unit, perhaps a moiety, than the smaller ones, which were probably for the clans.[5] The Great Kivas also seem to have been the vehicle of two major developments in Pueblo architecture. These were: first, an opening out of ritual focus beyond the building to external natural features with, later, a concomitant loosening up of the massing of the Great House itself; and, second, the transition of the Great Kiva into the plaza of the modern town. In my opinion it is likely that progressive desiccation led to a more intensive attempt to draw more of the earth and the sky, as well as more of the larger human community, into the web of ritual. As Chaco's stream cut its arroyo and the water table fell, and as the scanty rain failed and the run-off from the side canyons was carefully husbanded, and canals — if that is what some of those channels really are — were built to bring water from considerable distances, so the Great Kivas began to be built out in space on their own.[6] The ritual on their roofs thus began to call out to vast distances. Casa Rinconada, rising as a squat cylinder out of the earth, is placed on its own swell of ground across from Pueblo Bonito, and it commands a sweeping view up and down the Canyon. Kin Nahasbas, perhaps the first Great Kiva built to serve more

36 Hopi First Mesa, Hemis (Home) Dance, 1911

than one Pueblo, is set near the top of a distinctive natural cone, and it is inflected toward the startling Fajada Butte, which focuses the view eastward from it, while the drying stream runs snake-like far below (fig. 39). There is also a kiva — though technically not a Great Kiva — topping a cone at the Mesa Verde, while elsewhere, as below Shabik'eshchee at Chaco and at Nutria near Zuni, Great Kivas built in clusters near the mouths of canyons as if to tap the water seeping through underneath.

The steps by which the prehistoric Great Kiva underwent its metamorphosis into the plaza of historic times are not all known. Kinishba, in the White Mountains of Arizona, a compact, single-building village with a tightly enclosed court, is often cited as a transitional example.[7] The tiny, deeply engulfed, but clearly main plaza at Zuni has always seemed to me another. Finally we arrive at the fully organized ki'sonvi of the Hopi villages, which we discussed before. In them, too, is a board-covered sipapu, along with other relics of kiva furniture, such as the te-wi as bench, now exterior (fig. 36). But the pattern can probably be seen at its most fully evolved in the large plazas of the towns of the upper Rio Grande. Ortiz has shown how the plaza of Tewa San Juan makes use of all the major elements of the old Great Kiva, including the outward-reaching landscape focus of its developed phase. Now the plaza takes cognizance of four sacred mountains in the four directions, with four sacred hills standing before them along the same axes.[8] Conspicuous from San Juan are the horned Truchas Peaks, which the Tewa call "rock horn mountain,"[9] and which Ortiz identifies as San Juan's sacred mountain of the east, upon which the long axis of its larger plaza is exactly

oriented. When the long files of dancers fill that space the architectural pattern is complete; the natural and the man-made together frame and encourage the human ritual act. All is one. The photograph from Tewa Tesuque, slightly to the south, shows it well (fig. 33). The ridge line of Lake Peak, Tesuque's sacred mountain of the east, is redrawn close at hand by the profile of the building, while the ranks of corn-dancers complete the unison of natural, man-constructed, and human lines.[10] The same is true at San Ildefonso, another Tewa town, where the outlines and masses of the buildings trace those of the Jemez range, culminated in this view by Tsi-como, cloud-gatherer, sacred mountain of the west (fig. 40). Here the kiva in the plaza lifts up like the old Casa Rinconada, but now with a stairway like a gentle memory of Mexico far off. It is framed in those stepped profiles which, like the altar within, are apparently intended to invoke both mountain and sky.

But Taos, as always, seems most dramatically to embody the ancient intentions, like a place of special power, a great Teotihuacan of the North. Its splendid, sweeping plaza is as imperial a container of pickups and trailers today as it was of horses and nomad booths in the past.[11] It grandly receives the full force of looming Taos Mountain, cleft and terraced, with its sacred Blue Lake cupped within its peaks (fig. 41). The plaza taps the mountain's water, and the buildings to the north and south open outward as if dancing to celebrate its flow, which rushes undying between them in a lively stream. The north building demonstrates what the "inner room" unit and its concomitant "set-back" massing can do when they are released from the old Chaco-like containment and when the

37 Pueblo Bonito from above; Casa Rinconada is across the arroyo under the canyon wall in the right distance

sensitivities of a virtuoso community reign.[12] Together they organize an articulated mass which echoes the mountain and abstracts it to the measure of human units, picks up its beat in fact, exactly as the dancers do who move in file stamping up and down before its face (fig. 42). Between it and the mountain, the kivas are sunk deep into the earth. They are edged about with wooden palings like medieval *chevaux-de-frise,* and their ladder poles, heroic in scale, ride extravagantly high. Across the stream the southern building masses up into its own perfectly obvious pyramid, and it exactly mirrors and fits into the green or blood-red glowing foothills of the Sangre de Cristo beyond it to the east (fig. 41). Southward, beyond a long, low range of buildings, the horns of the Truchas loom far off, while westward behind the church all structures fall away to the high Rio Grande plain. Only the church, its form European in origin, stands up flat against the mountain, but here, as always

the Pueblos subdue and adjust their towered massing to the mountain's ridge line.

A comparison with Meso-America should be made here. It is true that a little influence from Toltec Tula, Chalchihuites, and La Quemada may perhaps be felt in some details of pier and massing at Chetro Ketl and elsewhere in Chaco Canyon. But on the whole, the valley of Mexico — unless, as some have believed, it inspired the masked dances — seems to have affected Pueblo culture only slightly, providing sacred parrots perhaps, and silver bells.[13] In architecture the cultural impact was clearly much less than that which inspired the Mound Builders along the Mississippi to raise their Mexican-like temple bases to the skies. The deserts of Chihuahua were a formidable barrier, not a highway like the Gulf, and even when they were crossed by Mexican traders and settlers, the Pueblos seem to have retained their own special ways. At Casas Grandes, in Chihuahua, the

38 Pueblo Bonito from above showing Great Kivas in plaza

39 Chaco Canyon and the Great Kiva "Kin Nahasbas" in the foreground with Fajada Butte in the center distance

two cultures can be seen juxtaposed, hardly overlapping but complementing each other, so that the Pueblo apartment house is placed to enjoy a view of the more or less Toltec-style temple platforms framed by the hills behind them.

Mexico monumentalizes, compacts, and abstracts. The set-back organization of its temple bases tends toward the purely pyramidal. Its "inner room," if any, is only a tomb chamber far below, though its ancient hut type is lifted in masonry to the heavens. Religious specialization has otherwise gone far. Teotihuacan shows the archetype: compressed and compacted man-made mountains repeat and abstract the real mountains beyond them (fig. 42). The same is true at Monte Alban, and indeed everywhere that mountains shape the world. Where they do not, as in much of the Petén and in northern Yucatan, the

Mayan temples ride above the trees like clouds and, indeed, breathe out a chill rain breath from their cool corbel-vaulted interiors. Their bases are springs to lift them there.

The Pueblo builder settled in the end for something less specialized, gentler, and more off-hand. His largest building, that most at the scale of the mountains, remained his communal dwelling, and his room units built to a looser massing than that of Mexico, no less pyramidal in fundamental intention, perhaps even more evocative of nature's shapes, but curiously reticent, deceptively casual in profile. His Great Houses have thus been able to pass themselves off through all the centuries of bondage as simple accidents of conglomeration, not the passionate human contributions to natural divinity they really are. When, today, the priests of Taos stand wrapped in their

40 San Ildefonso Pueblo showing kiva with Pojarito Plateau

41 Taos Pueblo showing north building on the left and south building on the right with Taos Mountain in the right distance

40

blanket-cloaks at the apex of their two buildings — and call to each other with strange bird-like voices and observe the sun — they are surely carrying on a rite not unknown in ancient Mexico, and they are doing so from the same kind of place. Man-made, their platform is yet a cavernous mountain, so that the mountain, too, is theirs.

(1) I explore some of the concepts mentioned above in *The Earth, the Temple, and the Gods: Greek Sacred Architecture,* New Haven, 1962; new ed., New York, 1969. The present article forms the basis for Chapter 1 of, *Pueblo: Mountain, Village, Dance,* to be published by Viking Press, 1973.

(2) These and all ensuing references to Whorf are to his "Linguistic Factors in the Terminology of Hopi Architecture," *Int. J. Amer. Linguistics, 19* (1953), pp 141-145; reprinted in *Language, Thought, and Reality: Selected Writings of Benjamin Lee Whorf,* ed. with an introduction by John B. Carroll, Cambridge, M.I.T. Press, 1956.

(3) Mindeleff, Victor, "A Study of Pueblo Architecture: Tusayan and Cibola," in the *Eighth Annual Report of the American Bureau of Ethnology, 1886-87,* Washington, 1891, pp 3-228. Report on Hopi nomenclature by A. M. Stephen, pp 220-223. There are a few differences between Stephen's and Whorf's transcriptions and interpretations but no critical discrepancies.

(4) For Chaco in general: Hewett, Edgar L., *The Chaco Canyon and its Monuments,* Albuquerque, 1936. There have since been some excellent specialized publications, but Hewett's brilliant study, with many plans and restoration drawings, remains the best general account.

(5) For the Great Kivas and their development, with bibliography: Vivian, Gordon, and Reiter, Paul, *The Great Kivas of Chaco Canyon and Their Relationships* (monograph 22 of the School of American Research), Santa Fe, 1960.

(6) On these questions see especially, Vivian, R. Gwinn, "An Inquiry into Prehistoric Social Organization in Chaco Canyon, New Mexico," in Longacre, William A., ed., *Reconstructing Prehistoric Pueblo Societies,* Albuquerque, 1970, pp 59-83. Some of the channeled tracks identified as canals may in fact have been narrow ceremonial roadways stretching out across the mesa top.

(7) Vivian and Reiter, *op. cit.,* pp 106-7; for relevant publications by Haury, Emil W., *ibid.,* p 109.

(8) Ortiz, Alfonso, *The Tewa World. Space, Time, Being, and Becoming in a Pueblo Society,* Chicago, 1969, esp. pp 139-142.

(9) Harrington, John Peabody, "The Ethnogeography of the Tewa Indians," in the *Seventy-ninth Annual Report of the American Bureau of Ethnology, 1907-08,* Washington, 1916, pp 29-636. The reference to the Truchas Peaks: p 340. Harrington, p 44, identified Lake Peak above Tesuque as the sacred mountain of the east for all the Tewa, but Ortiz, noted above, now identifies the Truchas Peaks as at least San Juan's eastern mountain, to which the actual topographical relationships lend credence.

(10) Horgan, Paul, *Great River: The Rio Grande in American History,* New York, 1954, writes sensitively of the Indian relation to nature and notes that the pueblos "looked like mesas" (1968 ed., pp 29-30). Even without the corroborative linguistic material cited earlier, the intrinsic and essential relationship of modern pueblo and mountain is obvious enough. In the absence of such evidence, therefore, the art historian must have the confidence to explore meaning and intention through his analysis of the physical forms alone. They are, after all, the material in which he is presumed to have special competence and through which he is required to make his own special contribution to human perception.

(11) For an aerial view and plan of Taos (as of all other pueblos except Hopi Bacavi and Hotevilla): Stubbs, Stanley A., *Bird's-Eye View of the Pueblos,* Norman, 1950, pp 24-28. The School of American Research is now preparing a new set of photographs and plans to bring this essential work up to date.

(12) Jackson, J. B., "Pueblo Architecture and Our Own," *Landscape 3* (Winter, 1953-54), p 11 ff., stresses the room unit and posits a "sacred room" which the proliferation of other units is symbolically intended to protect. The legend of the deeply buried secret room is persistent; it is heard from Zuni to Taos, though there seems to be no clear physical evidence for it in prehistoric or (even more difficult to explore) contemporary pueblos.

(13) Here the main archeological work has been done by Charles Di Peso, Director of the Amerind Foundation, Dragoon, Arizona. cf. his "Cultural Development in Northern Mexico," in *Aboriginal Cultural Development in Latin America: An Interpretative Review,* Meggers, B. J. and Evans, C., eds., Smithsonian Miscellaneous Collections, 146 (1963), pp 1-16. Di Peso's monumental report of the Foundation's excavations at Casas Grandes is now close to publication.

Vincent Scully is Professor of Art History at Yale University. Dr. Scully has received several fellowships for extensive travel and research in Europe and has written on many aspects of art and architecture including such recent materials as Pueblo Architecture of the Southwest, *Fort Worth, Amon Carter Museum of Western Art, 1971 and "The Puberty Rites of the Mescalero," Art in America, vol 60 no 4 July-Aug. 1972. He is currently finishing a new book that includes as its first chapter the above essay.*

42 Taos's Geronimo Day showing north building and Taos Mountain in the distance, early 20th century

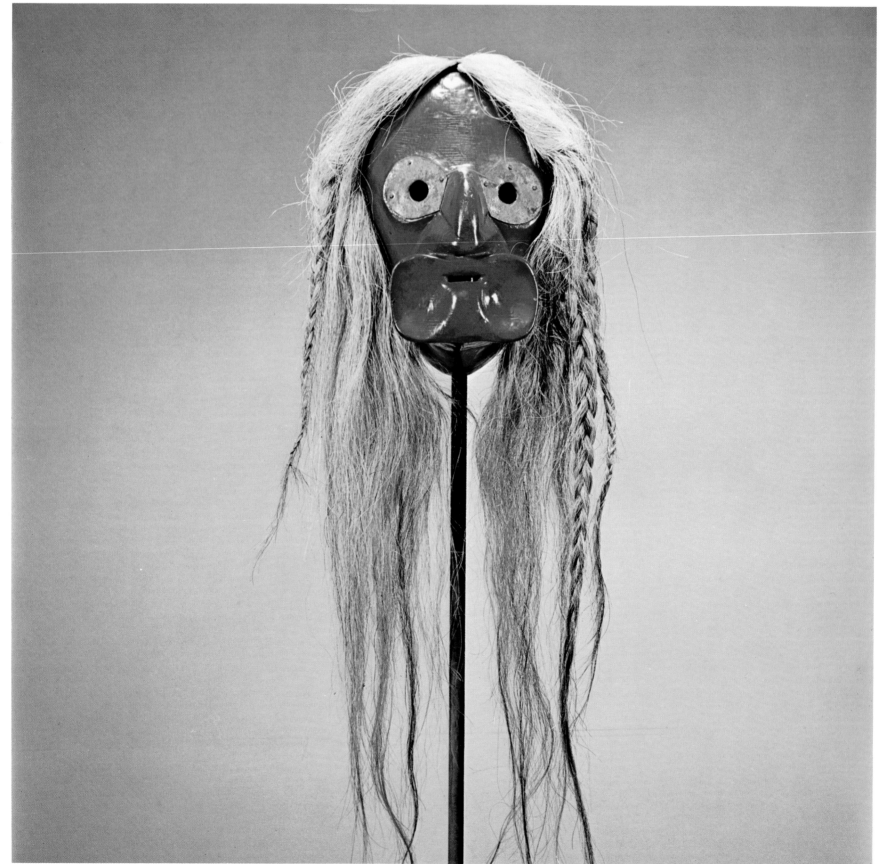

43 Iroquois (Seneca) false face mask

cat no 549

Iroquois Masks: A Living Tradition in the Northeast

William N. Fenton

Wooden masks, or false faces, from the Iroquois are prominently featured in contemporary shows of American Indian art both because they are compelling in and of themselves and because a generation of museum visitors, which includes discerning collectors of primitive art and even school children, know Iroquois masks and expect to see them. What few people realize is that they belong to a living tradition: they are sacred objects of an ongoing American Indian religion. Carvers are still making them for their own use as well as for collectors because the masks have a continuing role in the annual round of ceremonies that are still being fulfilled in Iroquois communities in upstate New York and in neighboring Ontario. As religious objects they are entitled to respect; as art objects they represent several styles; and as cultural objects they relate to a whole genre of carving in the round and to techniques of working in other media to make domestic tools and implements.

The Iroquois produced a wide range of beautiful artifacts including carved wooden bowls, spoons, clubs, pottery vessels and elm bark utilitarian objects, but I shall limit my remarks here to wooden masks as an art form and as performing religious objects.

In a search for Iroquois ethnological collections in the museums of the world, I have found false faces as far east as Leningrad, notable examples in Stuttgart, Frankfurt, Copenhagen and Stockholm, and as far west as Los Angeles; but the great Iroquois collections repose in the museums of eastern Canada and the northeastern United States.[1] The great period of collecting was at the turn of the century when Iroquois buffs Harriet Maxwell Converse, David Boyle, Joseph Keppler, and George Heye were active, and their efforts stimulated M. R. Harrington and Arthur C. Parker, pioneer anthropologists, to collect for museums. Du Simitière's Philadelphia museum was the first to show masks collected by Sullivan's Army during the American Revolution. A few extant Iroquois masks have been attributed to the late 18th century on shaky documentation; but the first false face collected and documented in the field, now the type specimen for the genre, and a notable piece of carving, is the mask Lewis H. Morgan obtained on the Grand River in 1849 for the New York Cabinet of Antiquities, illustrated in his classic *The League of the Ho-de-no-sau-nee* (1851), and described in his *Report to the Regents of the University* the same year. It is now in the New York State Museum.

Each of us — whether museum visitor, collector, anthropologist, or Iroquois — views these masks with different eyes, for we see only what we are prepared to see. Superficially, they are of two kinds — those made of corn husk, and those of wood, most of which are painted red or black. The wooden masks, or false faces, have deep-set eyes encircled by reflectors of tin or brass, the noses are frequently bent, and the mouths distorted. The brows are arched, deeply wrinkled, and sometimes divided above the nose by a crease or comb of spines, like those on a snapping turtle's tail. The mouth, however, is the most important and variable feature because its shape determines the composition of the face and its range of contortions impart mood and suggest its role in the ceremonies as sanctioned by myth. In fact one can classify the masks by this attribute alone and reach a valid typology that the Iroquois recognize and partly accept because they tend to name masks for the mouth shape. Since I have discussed this classification elsewhere,[2] I shall mention only its most conspicuous features.

There is a group with mouth corners upturned in a smile, or grimace, showing teeth (fig. 44); another series of mouths are distended ovally, sometimes with protruding tongue; or they are puckered, as if whistling; or the tongue is conventionalized and the cheeks sucked in to form spoon-like disks, which sometimes resemble two funnels, again for blowing ashes; other mouths are straight with distended lips, sometimes twisted up at one corner and down at the other in conformity with a bent nose; and finally, both corners may be turned down in an expression of utmost pain. Some Grand River masks have a prominent chin, which helps the masker adjust the mask to his face. Generally a false face is framed by a long wig of horsetails which fall on either side from a part in the middle of the forehead — a hair style that no longer strikes me as outlandish, but modish, when I look out on a lecture hall of undergraduates.

The back of an Iroquois mask often reveals its history. If used it will show patina and wear; if one knows wood he will see that it is of basswood, pine, or maple; and visible marks of the crooked knife, chisel, gouge, howel, or brace and bit tell that it was made after these tools reached the Iroquois. Recent examples have three holes for attaching head bands, like a catcher's mask. If five or seven holes are burned through the rim, for tying on the hair and head throw with thongs of twisted woodchuck hide, it belongs to an earlier period. One or more bags of sacred tobacco tied at the crown indicate that the mask has seen use in ceremonies, for these are tokens of gratitude for services rendered. These criteria are helpful when there is no documentation, the usual circumstance in older collections. None of the masks that I have seen is older than the early 19th century.

Carving styles are localized and tend to follow a tradition long established in a community. Recognizing this fact is more important than trying to attribute the masks to a particular nation of the Iroquois Confederacy. Masks are Seneca because they were made at Allegany, Buffalo Creek, Cattaraugus, or Tonawanda in western New York (fig. 45); they can be Cayuga, Onondaga, or even Mohawk when from the Six Nations Reserve on the Grand River, Ontario; and of course, Onondaga from Onondaga, New York, near Syracuse. From study of collections, interviewing carvers and showing them pictures of older masks, and observing carvers at work, I discern a few main styles. Often the work of a single artist stands out. A ridge of spines above the nose bridge occurs frequently on masks from Allegany and Cattaraugus, both Seneca communities, and this feature is often combined with bi-funnelate lips, or exaggerated labial protrusion. Treatment of the face is generally smooth. The spoon-mouth is predominantly from Cattaraugus and is seen in the work of such artists as James Crow, Kelly Lay, and Jesse Cornplanter. Massive carving, large faces, heavy supplementary wrinkles and lines which emphasize the distortion of nose and mouth, indeed of the whole face, as in partial paralysis, are characteristic traits of the Grand River style. With it belong the chin and protruding tongue, which also occur at Onondaga, New York. Certain older Onondaga masks have a marked negroid appearance, and it may be relevant that the Black

Prince, one of the great Onondaga chiefs at the mid-18th century, was a mulatto. Thus the distinctive character and quality of local styles affect the carver's art and afford an interesting illustration of the relationship between mental stereotypes and overt behavior. This relationship, moreover, comes out clearly in the interaction of myth and ritual.

Although local tradition tends to dominate style, it does not prevent innovation. The masks illustrate a rather consistent attempt of the Iroquois to caricature themselves and the peoples who became their neighbors. If we divide the masks into periods of 50 years going back to 1800, we may see a gradual evolution and note some trends in style. Masks from Buffalo Creek at the turn of the 19th century are the least grotesque, and the narrow facial types portrayed resemble remarkably skulls from Seneca graves a century earlier. Protruding lips and teeth (alveolar prognathism) in some early masks scarcely exaggerates surviving Cayuga and Seneca physical types. This tradition of portraiture, or social commentary, persists among the Senecas who have commemorated American folk heroes from Charlie Chaplin, Popeye, the Hula girls of the South Pacific, to Sumu the Japanese wrestler, in the class of beggar masks which is most plastic. At Onondaga and at Grand River the trend has run to massive carving and in recent years toward fine lines. The art has changed too with better carving tools.

Over the years, Iroquois carvers have portrayed the primordial shaman of the World Rim in crooked mouth masks and the spirits of the bush in the common faces. They have also revealed themselves and their anxieties as manifest in dreams, sometimes representing specific disease symptoms and pathological states that the false faces are believed to cure. The Society of Faces may be called in to perform the blowing ashes rite in cases of hemorrhage of the nose, facial and body paralysis, mouth drawn to one side, dream persecution by false face spirits, hearing the songs, and annoyance by frights in the bush; also swelling of the face, toothache, sore eyes and earache. Some older masks suggest measles or smallpox, and the false faces are supposed to have rid the Buffalo Creek settlement of a cholera epidemic in the 1830s. I see a parallel between the crawling, hip-sliding gait that the maskers affect when they first enter a house — the humped back, the distorted faces, and the moaning querulous speech, a kind of regressive infantile behavior — and some classic types of paralysis known to modern medicine. Old people recall cases of hysterical possession among people watching maskers: persons who fell into spasms, imitated a cry, suffered momentary or prolonged facial paralysis, and plunged into the hot ashes. These catatonic states are reported most often among women at the approach of the maskers on their rounds during the midwinter ceremonies. The maskers are invariably men who sometimes take advantage of the situation to "feel up" the women when ostensibly blowing ashes, much to the amusement of the crowd.

The myths which purport to tell the origin of the false faces, prescribe the behavior of the maskers (and provide the rationale for identifying the supernaturals whom the maskers impersonate and the masks portray) are the intellectual property of only a few old people who have participated in all stages of the rites. They naturally feed their own experience back into the telling. As boys

44 Iroquois (Cayuga) carved and painted wood mask   cat no 546

they first joined a band of beggars at midwinter to go around to the houses and to the longhouse begging food and tobacco and dancing in competition. Next they joined a more serious troop that in spring and fall purges the settlement of disease. Either role may suddenly demand that one perform cures by blowing ashes on some householder. They have now graduated to the status of "common faces" and have acquired their rite. But the role of doorkeeper, in the rite of "lifting and bumping feet" *(Diyenˀsiˀdaˀdi has),* is reserved for two more experienced participants. So are the two husk face messengers who race through the community ahead of the wooden maskers (fig. 46). The Society of Faces is run by two women representing each half of the tribe; each appoints a man to lead the procession, burn tobacco to the spirits, sing, and perhaps recite one of the legends or myths about the false faces. Thus by listening and taking part the Iroquois learn.

In the 1930s when I first lived among the Seneca my purpose was to study and learn their ways, to observe the ceremonies and not to collect religious paraphernalia for a museum. My host, Jonas Snow, was a carver, and I sought out the learned men and women who knew "stories" of the false faces and the "bushy heads" or husk faces. The tales they told by the fireside are of two types: human adventures and myths. Both involve encounters with supernaturals — humans with forest spirits, and the culture hero with the Great World Rim Dweller, a shaman.

An incident in the Iroquois cosmology relates to the creator meeting a shaman who controlled the game, high winds and disease. The Senecas call him *Sagodyowéhgo: wa hodjáˀdothaˀ,* "our great defender, the doctor;" to the Onondagas and Cayugas he is *Hadúˀiˀgò: nah,* "the great humpbacked one" or simply *Hadúˀiˀ.* Once given to roaming the earth and following the path of the sun, he was afterward confined to the margin of the earth so as not to be harmful to men. Of giant stature, he is said to carry a staff made of a tall pine or a shagbark hickory tree, its limbs lopped off to the top, and like the dancers who imitate him, he shakes the earth as he walks. He stops at noon to rest and regain his strength by rubbing the huge turtle rattle which he carries on the giant elm or pine which stands in the center of the earth. It is from this diurnal journey that they say his face is red in the morning as he comes from the east (the sun is always ahead of him), divided red and black at noon, and black in the afternoon as he looks back or returns from the sunset. They visualize his face as resembling the masks which represent him in the doorkeeper role, as red, black, divided with the broken nose and twisted mouth that he suffered when he contended with the creator at moving a mountain, when he anxiously looked over his shoulder as the creator was making medicine and the mountain struck his face. Because he had such power *Hadúˀiˀ* was allowed to stay out there so as to answer the call of the people to avert disasters.

From these two types of tales arise the two main classes of masks. The latter are really the ranking class, while the common faces of the forest are ill-defined and miscellaneous. There is a tendency for masks to jump grades as the owner moves up through the ceremonies or the mask passes into the second or third generation of the family. Although there is more to this subject, there are four kinds: 1) representatives of the Great World Rim Being,

2) common faces of the forest, 3) beggars of infinite variety, and 4) husk faces.

The husk faces are really a race apart because they represent folk who inhabit a remote valley on the other side of the earth where the seasons are reversed and they grow prodigious crops between the stumps. They come at midwinter to help the people and to encourage them that summer will return. They dramatize the introduction of agriculture to the Iroquois.

While most of the Iroquois masks in collections are the work of unknown artists, I am aware from watching carvers that each has an individual style, which is recognizable to Iroquois who know their work, and in a sense there is a local "school of art" exemplified by the work of particular carvers. Jonas Snow, Clarence White, and Chauncey Johnny John, from whom my father collected masks in the 1920s at Allegany, were noted for smoothness of line in their work. Later when Chauncey Johnny John replicated for me the whole prescribed procedure of burning tobacco and carving a mask on a living basswood tree, imploring the basswood to impart its curative powers to the wearer, he pointed out that no sensible carver did this any longer, and asked me to procure an old seasoned barn beam that would not check. At Cattaraugus, James Crow and others of the "Newton School" specialized in fierce faces which made me wonder whether some of the "meanness" was transferred from their reputation for "dirty lacrosse" and bitter hatred of the whites after the loss of the Buffalo Reservation. The masks that were produced for me at Grand River were all of one genre, and I observed that Tom Harris worked rapidly, carving in broad and sure strokes to produce in a few hours a classic crooked face, deeply lined in the local style. Today Jake Thomas, perhaps the most gifted and prolific carver, turns out masks of the same kind.

Mask making, once ritualized and undertaken in response to a social demand, responded to the contact situation when steel tools enabled artists to work rapidly by elaborating a few simple concepts into more complicated designs. The craft is now sustained by the competing interests of collectors and the artists are getting more money for their works. Over the years the finest old masks went to museums and were lost to the ceremonies; today the quality pieces are destined for the market.

The entire mask complex, from myth to the ritual of carving, to the songs, dance and shamanism, is loaded with symbolism. Having once inhabited small villages scattered in the forests of New York state, the Iroquois developed a deep and abiding awareness of the dichotomy of clearing and forest. Clearing was the small patch of cleared land, or a natural opening in the forest, which contained a palisaded village surrounded by fields of maize. Beyond was the endless woods or bush. Only hardy hunters and brave warriors ventured on the forest trails for fear of marauding war parties or the danger of meeting cannibal monsters and unfriendly spirits. With certain of these, like the false faces, man had a contract, but others were beyond prediction. They were propitiated and avoided. Encounters were to be reported and interpreted by the elders and a ritual solution prescribed. Protocol demanded that embassies of other nations stop at the woods edge until greeted and ushered into the village to the house of a chief.

45 Iroquois (Seneca) false face mask

cat no 551

46 Iroquois corn husk mask   cat no 540

The tree motif pervades Iroquois political and religious philosophy. In the shade of a tall dark pine, the symbol of peace, sits the Council of the Iroquois Confederacy, and the evergrowing tree, its roots extending to the cardinal directions, protects the people. The American elm is important economically, but it is also the source of the Great Defender's power. His staff and the folded bark rattles which beggars carry derive from the hickory. The snapping turtle which provides the shaman with his magic rattle also supports the earth on his back, and the therapeutic basswood is the traditional source of masks.

Every member of the Society of Faces keeps his mask and rattle bundled in a cloth or bag, out of sight of little children lest they be frightened or injured by its magic power. Occasionally it requires a tobacco offering and is "fed" with sunflower oil. If it is sold or transferred to a new owner, it must be told where it is going and why. An unfed mask is cause for anxiety.

Finally, as medicine men the false faces are "grandfathers" of the people and are entitled to the respect granted to old people. Though capable of clowning they are at once awesome and funny and they evoke mixed reactions. One may smile in approval at their antics while doing the formal things required to placate them. When worn by actors performing their rites before an appreciative audience of members of their own society the masks then constitute an entity that vanishes when they are kept in a museum or simply regarded as art objects.

(1) The more important collections of Iroquois masks, some numbering upward of 100 specimens,* are found in the following museums:
American Museum of Natural History, New York City
Denver Art Museum, Denver, Colorado
Ethnographical Museum, Stockholm, Sweden
Field Museum of Natural History, Chicago
Landes Museum, Stuttgart, West Germany
Milwaukee Public Museum,* Milwaukee, Wisconsin
Museum of the American Indian, Heye Foundation,* New York City
National Museum, Copenhagen, Denmark
National Museum of Man, Ottawa
New York State Museum,* Albany, New York
Rochester Museum and Science Center,* Rochester, New York
Royal Ontario Museum, Toronto
University Museum, University of Pennsylvania, Philadelphia
Other museums and collections numbering but few choice specimens are not listed.

(2) Fenton, William N., "Some Questions of Classification, Typology and Style Raised by Iroquois Masks," *Transactions of the New York Academy of Sciences, Series II,* No. 18. New York, 1956, pp 347-357.

William N. Fenton is Research Professor of Anthropology, State University of New York, Albany. He was formerly Assistant Commissioner for the New York State Museum and Science Service and Senior Ethnologist, Bureau of American Ethnology, Smithsonian Institution. A life-long student of the Iroquois, he has written numerous articles and books on their ethnology and history. (See Bibliography, this catalogue.) His English edition of J. F. Lafitau's Moeurs des Sauvages Ameriquains, *1724, is in press. He was awarded the Cornplanter Medal for Iroquois Research in 1968.*

47 Potawatomi beaded moccasins

cat no 286

Woodland Indian Art

Robert E. Ritzenthaler

The Woodland culture area, made up of about 33 almost exclusively Algonkian-speaking tribes, extends from the Mississippi River to the Atlantic Coast and from the Mason-Dixon line well into Canada. The relatively flat land is dominated by forests (with some prairie to the south) generously sprinkled with lakes and streams. We shall be concerned with the western portion of this area, the tribes of the present states of Minnesota, Wisconsin and Michigan, particularly the Chippewa (Ojibwa), Menomini, Potawatomi and Winnebago. All are Algonkian-speaking except for the Winnebago, a Siouan remnant which was left behind (although not far) in the gentle surge of the Indians westward over a period of at least 10 centuries.

Immediately west of the Mississippi River was a shatterbelt of tribes with mixed Woodland and Plains culture. Beyond was the Great Northern Plains with nomadic, buffalo-hunting tribes and classic Plains culture. Here were the Sioux, Blackfeet, and Crow, all of whom utilized the buffalo as a major resource for food, clothing and shelter. That this "Plaininization" was a rapid process is illustrated by the fact that the Cheyenne, who left a Woodland way of life in the western Great Lakes area around 1700 to move onto the Plains, had become by 1830 a classic nomadic Plains culture, although they retained their Algonkian language, among other vestiges of their past.

Nearly all of their graphic art was done on buffalo (and other) hide. Their finest art comes in the form of hide painting: tipi-covers and liners, buffalo robes, and winter counts (pictographs of important episodes) which were done by men in a representational style. The geometric designs painted by women on parfleche bags or executed in beads and quills were less exciting, but usually of high quality. Their extreme mobility placed limits on their art products in terms of size (small to tiny) and materials. Pottery, for example, is highly impractical for any nomadic people and the Plains Indians ignored it, although the Blackfeet did utilize some.

In contrast to Plains culture the Forest tribes developed a less specialized way of life involving a variety of economic pursuits: hunting, fishing, gathering wild foods, and gardening. Although they were less mobile, their food quest still demanded a certain amount of movement and was within a smaller area of exploration. Their seasonal cycle consisted of a move to the sugarbush in spring to collect the sap and convert it to maple sugar; a return to the summer camp for gardening, berrying and fishing; a trip to the wild rice fields in autumn; then to the hunting grounds in winter. Such movement also placed limitations on the size and media of their art and craft products. They could, and did, get by with pottery, rather crude grit-tempered and cord-marked, but it was readily abandoned in favor of the metal pots of the European trader. All Woodland art consists of small, even tiny, products. The resources were there for carving monumental wood sculptures, such as the totem poles and life-sized figures of the Northwest Coast tribes, but their semi-nomadic way of life discouraged this. A Woodland wood carving over a foot in length is a rarity.

Wood The forests supplied rich and varied materials for Woodland Indian material culture. Wood was the favorite and certainly the most accessible material. Almost all of the wood carving consisted of utilitarian objects: bowls, ladles, spoons, bows and arrows, cradleboards, snowshoes, flutes, lacrosse sticks, snow snakes, canoe parts, and objects with magical and ritual purposes. A profusion of bowls and ladles were carved from the burled sections of such hardwoods as maple and birch, and many of these articles possess a simple beauty of form that causes some connoisseurs to rank them as the acme of Woodland art. Some were embellished with simple, decorative forms like the bird heads on Winnebago ladles and the effigy flute stops. Fish lures, carved in the forms of minnows and frogs, were dangled through a hole in the ice to attract fish to the spear. The intent here was realism, as with all Woodland sculpture, and some were quite beautifully executed. The wood sculpture in the form of birds, animals or humans, carved for magical and religious purposes, most closely approaches the Western world's idea of "pure" sculpture as opposed to the decorative elements found on utilitarian products. Besides carving in the round there were engravings on wood panels — mostly outlines of zoomorphic forms functioning as mnemonic devices for songs intended to aid the hunter in a magical way. Simple, outline engravings of the totemic animal of deceased persons were carved on grave markers (upside down to denote death). Only the men practiced woodworking — primarily using their favorite tool, the crooked knife.

Birchbark   A distinctive aspect of this culture was its use of birchbark: bark of the paper birch was the "skin" of the birchbark canoe for which these tribes, especially the Ojibwa, have been famous. It was a fine product technically, and of a graceful shape. Panels of birchbark sewn together covered the upper portion of the wigwams, the cone-shaped winter houses.

In lieu of basketry, which occurred but was unimportant, they made containers of birchbark — for carrying, storing and even cooking. The bark was peeled from the tree in late spring, heated over a fire or steamed to make it pliable, bent into the desired shape and sewn with basswood bark or spruce roots. Perhaps the most attractive of these are the storage vessels for wild rice and maple sugar called *makuks,* shaped like truncated pyramids. Bark was also the medium of a unique art form, the dental pictographs done by women for pure enjoyment. Designs were bitten onto a thin sheet of folded birchbark which, when opened, revealed a geometric mirror pattern. These pictographs also represent a Woodland Indian rarity — "art for art's sake."

Weaving   Mats, used as floor coverings and house partitions, were woven from bulrushes gathered in early summer. These were bleached, dried and dyed a variety of colors with vegetable dyes, and the ends of the rushes were braided to form an even edge, then hung from a crossbar between two posts set in the ground. A basswood cord weft was passed from left to right with rushes twined around it; the weft rows were about a half an inch apart, and the weaving progressed from top to bottom. A braided edge finished it off. Most of the designs were geometric, but zoomorphic motifs, particularly the thunderbird, appeared on smaller mats that served as wrappers for war bundles. The inner bark of the red cedar was used for making mats in a checkerwork technique, in two colors, with a simple design.

Weaving was also done in soft materials: basswood bark sometimes incorporated with buffalo or nettle and, later, commercial yarn. The primary product was a rectangular bag used especially for storing medicines and the sacred objects employed in the Medicine Dance. The warp strands were suspended between two sticks set in the ground and the finger weaving progressed downward. On the older bags zoomorphic designs of thunderbirds, panthers, and humans were interspersed with bands of geometric motifs. On more recent bags the designs were limited to bands of floral and geometric motifs. The designs, especially on the older bags, were different on each side.

48 Ojibwa medicine doll, Milwaukee Public Museum

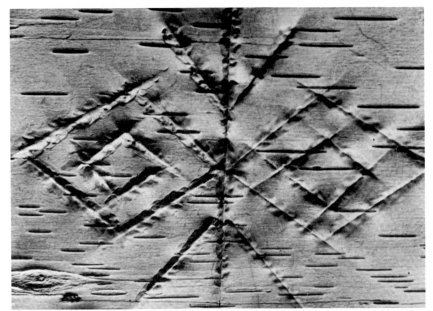
49 Ojibwa dental pictograph, Milwaukee Public Museum

50 Ojibwa cord and yarn twined bag   cat no 13

Sashes and garters were woven of commercial yarn in three or more colors. The technique was finger weaving, although netting or braiding was used occasionally. Floral and geometric motifs were the mode. Women wore the sashes around the waist as a decorative belt to secure the dress and men wore them for decorative purposes at the waist, over a shoulder, or as a turban. Garters were worn by both men and women just below the knee to support the leggings.

In 1921 Alanson Skinner wrote, "It is truly astonishing that the ability of the Woodland tribes in the matter of textile arts has been so little recognized by students." The old bags of native materials with zoomorphic designs are particularly prized by museums and this writer feels that this medium and the quillwork are the highest artistic expressions of the Woodland Indians.

Quillwork   Articles of buckskin clothing, birchbark boxes, pipe stems, knife sheaths, and medicine bags were often decorated with dyed porcupine quills. The women moistened them in their mouths, then pulled them out between their teeth to flatten them; special bone flatteners also were used. The quills were embroidered onto clothing, woven on looms, then inserted into awl-holes in birchbark boxes, and both floral and geometric designs were employed. The Western Cree did some of the most delicate and beautiful loom quillwork to be found. Quillwork is a very old art form, not found outside of North America, and is now almost a lost art among the Woodland Indians — the only product now made is the quill-decorated birchbark box and this by just a few tribes.

Beadwork   Women transferred their skill from quillwork to work with glass beads brought in by Europeans. Both loom and embroidery methods were employed. Although geometric designs were used, floral designs are most characteristic of the Woodland tribes. Their forest environment would seem a natural source for such motifs, though some scholars feel the French introduced floral designs. It is acknowledged that French Catholic sisters introduced a type of floral work to the Iroquois, but even if we accept the probability that the French introduced *some flower patterns* to the other Woodland Indians, it would seem that the use of floral design is old and traditional. It is difficult to believe that these people could have ignored the designs in nature which so completely surrounded them. It should be emphasized that the term "floral" is used in its widest context and includes, in addition to flowers, any plant, and a count of Woodland motifs would show the use of more leaves than flowers.

Silk Appliqué   It is likely that silk appliqué, or "ribbonwork," came into use by the Woodland Indians about the middle of the 18th century. It is still practiced, but to a very limited extent. Another art form of the women, it consists of cutting designs from one color of silk and sewing them onto a panel of silk of another color; the panel is then sewn onto a broadcloth garment to form a decorative border. Silk appliqué was used primarily on women's garments, but it was also found on men's leggings, cradleboard wrappers, and buckskin moccasins. The designs were floral and geometric; the early work was done with silk ribbon, later with bolt silk, nylon, and rayon.

Silk appliqué was concentrated in the Western Woodlands. Most skillful were the Prairie Potawatomi, Miami, Kickapoo, Sauk and

Fox. Close behind were the Winnebago, Forest Potawatomi and Menomini.

Leather While rawhide and tanned leather were not used as extensively as they were among the Plains tribes, leather was an important material to the Woodland Indians. Rawhide was used mainly for drum heads and snowshoe lacings; tanned buckskin for clothing, dolls, quivers, thongs, *midé* drum heads, and tobacco bags.

Clothing Tanned buckskin was the primary material for both men's and women's clothing until cloth was introduced by the Europeans. The men wore breechcloths, leggings, and moccasins. The flap of the breechcloth was often decorated with quillwork, later with beads, and then ribbonwork on cloth. Leggings also were decorated with beaded embroidery or ribbon appliqué and on dress occasions, loom-beaded bands or garters were fastened below the knees.

Woodland moccasin soles were soft, not like the rawhide sole of the Plains moccasin. In many cases, both the sole and sides were formed from a single piece of buckskin with a seam up the back. Sometimes the front was finished with an elliptical piece, serving as a vamp, and another piece was added to the back half to serve as a cuff. Only the vamps and cuffs had quillwork or beadwork decoration. The second basic style also was made from one piece of buckskin, but with a central puckered seam running down the upper front. This was the fundamental Woodland style, although the moccasins of the Prairie groups had cuffs which flared diagonally outward at the front. The Indians called these flaps, and they were added as two separate pieces, each piece having different designs of either beadwork or ribbonwork on a single moccasin. Both sexes wore the same tribal style, although Winnebago women had a type with a square front flap.

In cold weather buckskin robes were worn and men wore turbans of colorful yarn sashes, often with feathers. On ceremonial occasions, otter hide turbans were worn, sometimes with beaded decorations, ribbons and eagle plumes. In time of war, the men wore a roach, a crest of animal hair set on top of the head. In these, the short tail hair of the deer, dyed red, was combined with rows of longer white hair of the porcupine. (Moose hair could be used, and in the Prairie area, turkey beards were substituted for porcupine hair.) The entire roach gave a brush-like effect and a single eagle feather hung at the rear, swiveling on a bone socket attached to the center of the roach. The Sauk warrior had his hair plucked except at the top center, where a scalp lock was left to help secure the roach to the head. In more recent times the roach was held by a headband mount of strap leather and sometimes hung down to the shoulders. The roach itself was constructed on a bow loom and when it was not worn, it was folded carefully and wrapped over a cylindrical stick.

Women wore a sleeveless dress of two buckskins fastened at the shoulders over a shirt of woven nettle fiber; buckskin leggings, fastened below the knee with a thong and moccasins completed the costume. The long fringed dresses were a relatively recent innovation and later, of course, broadcloth was substituted for the skins. The hair was worn in a single braid down the back and, in historic times, ribbons were intertwined in the braid. For dress

51 Ojibwa beaded cloth bandoleer bag   cat no 10

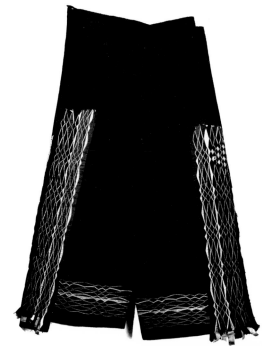

52 Miami leggings   cat no 323

occasions the braid was doubled up into a "club" and decorated with quillwork or beadwork.

Stonework   In prehistoric times Woodland peoples had a rather extensive stone tool kit. This, along with pottery, was rapidly abandoned in favor of more efficient, lighter metal tools and implements introduced by the European traders. During the historic period, however, they did fashion stone pipe bowls of a style and of materials not previously employed, and some of those in effigy form exhibited skillful sculpturing. The favored material was catlinite, obtained from the famous Pipestone quarry of southwestern Minnesota, and "blackstone," a shale, was used to some extent. When freshly quarried, catlinite is quite soft and can be worked readily with a saw, drill and file. A block was roughed into shape with hacksaw and rasp; holes for the bowl and stem were drilled and the final shaping was done with a file. The surface was smoothed with sandstone or sandpaper and rubbed with deer tallow to give it polish. Sometimes stone pipes were decorated (or repaired) with lead inlay. Channels, up to a quarter of an inch in depth, were cut into the stone and molten lead poured in. When this had cooled, it was filed flush with the surface of the stone. While all of the extant pipes ascribed to the historic Woodland tribes were probably made with metal tools, catlinite disk pipes of the prehistoric Oneota people (800 to 1600 A.D.) attest to the fact that beautiful carving could also be done with a stone tool kit.

Silverwork   Silver jewelry and ornaments were prized possessions of the Woodland Indians. Women, especially, but also children, wore such items as rings, earrings, bracelets, hair ornaments and brooches. The most popular (and most numerous) were the German silver brooches women wore in profusion on their blouses. The men made some use of arm bands, gorgets, medals, earrings and nose pendants. These products, made mostly in London, were introduced to the Eastern Woodland Indians by European traders around 1740 and almost immediately became popular, important trade items. By the early 1800s silversmithing shops had been established in the New World with important centers in Montreal, Philadelphia and New York.

In the very early 1800s the Iroquois and some of their neighbors began doing their own silversmithing, an art which spread ultimately to nearly every Woodland tribe. Most of the earliest work was in the form of brooches hammered from silver coins and decorated with perforated and engraved designs. The later work retained the techniques and to a limited extent the use of silver coinage, but it was done primarily in German silver, an alloy of nickel, copper and zinc (no silver) purchased in sheet form by the Indians. To make a brooch, the form was cut with a chisel and hammer, usually with a pattern; the perforated designs were put in with punch and chisel, and engraved designs were added by means of a number of implements: dividers for arcs and circles, a toothed wheel for rouletting, a chisel for other designs. While some designs give the impression of having been stamped, stamps were not used.

The forms and designs on both trade and native silverwork were nearly all European derived and were purely ornamental. There are some instances in which they functioned otherwise, such as the Menomini bracelet, reported by Skinner ". . . on which had been etched a rattlesnake as a fetish against disease and witches,"[1] but these are uncommon. The heart-shaped Luckenbooth brooch of Scotland, which functioned as a love token, carried no such significance among the Indians. Even the crucifix and the cross of brass or copper, imported by French missionaries during the 17th and early 18th centuries, were treated later as ornaments, especially the cross which, in German silver, became an item of some commercial importance. The Masonic brooch, so popular with the Iroquois, and made up of compasses, squares and distortions of other Masonic emblems, was worn upside down — an indication of its function as sheer decoration.

Except for wood, stoneworking, and silversmithing, Woodland arts and crafts lay in the hands of the women. It was my good fortune to meet several of these old-timers, women who were knowledgable and skillful, and who reflected the flavor of traditional Woodland culture. Hardworking and versatile, they were responsible for the decorative arts for which these groups are famous. It is sad to recognize that the production of Woodland Indian arts and crafts has been reduced to almost nothing.

(1) Skinner, Alanson, "Material Culture of the Menomini," *Indian Notes and Monographs,* vol 20, New York, Museum of the American Indian, Heye Foundation, 1921, p 128.

Robert Ritzenthaler was a member of the Anthropology Department, Milwaukee Public Museum for 34 years and retired as Curator Emeritus in March, 1972. Dr. Ritzenthaler has participated in archeological excavations in America, Guatemala, Micronesia, Africa and Mexico. He has done extensive field work among the Woodland Indians of Wisconsin, and has written many articles and books relating to this area, including The Woodland Indians, *New York, Natural History Press, 1970.*

53 Eastern Sioux pipe bowl   cat no 765

54 Crow painted shield

Plains Indian Art

Ted J. Brasser

From the mountainous backbone of the North American continent, the Plains extend eastward to the Mississippi Valley and from Texas north into Canada. This near-treeless grassland was a country of immense herds of bison, nomadic hunters and riverine gardeners. The Plains Indian, in colorful costume on horseback, his feather headdress streaming in the wind, has captured the imagination of the entire world. Yet, it is a curious fact that this Plains Indian emerged only after, if not due to, the coming of Europeans to America.

Prior to the late 17th century, the ancestors of most Plains Indians lived around the fringes of this area. Small bands of hunters occupied the foothills of the Rockies and the northern parklands where natural resources were more abundant. From there they made hunting forays into the Plains. Their material possessions were few because of their nomadic existence. They lived in small tipis; hunted with bows and arrows; painted and engraved intriguing pictures on rocks and bone tools, on round shields, skin tipi-covers and skin clothing. They made pottery and rawhide containers decorated with incised designs. Their only domesticated animals were the dogs they used as pack animals.

Coming from the Southeast, gardeners settled in earthlodge-villages on the eastern prairies, and after A.D. 1000 they spread along the rivers into the Plains as far as Alberta in the Northwest. They tilled their gardens in the valleys and occasionally went hunting on the Plains; they made basketry as well as pottery. Their small sculpture reveals the Hopewellian[1] origin of their cultures and they played an important role in the dissemination of Southeastern religious ideas.

Although the ecological pattern of the area developed before the dawn of history, these agrarian people did not have anything resembling the glamour and wealth of the later Plains Indians.

Long before Europeans appeared on the scene, their influences reached deep into the interior and caused native societies to change. During the 17th century Indians on the Southern Plains became acquainted with Spanish horses, and by barter and theft horses slowly spread northward. In 1739 the first horses arrived among the Mandan, just after the first European tradegoods had reached them from the East. The Mandan were gardeners on the Missouri River and at their head village, nomadic hunters traded their products against those of the agrarian villagers. Through native middlemen, far-off Europeans now entered this market with their tradegoods, including firearms. For more than a century the furtrade was the sole medium of contact between Euro-American society and the Plains Indians, and it had a profound effect upon the latter.

As soon as horses and the furtrade had reached the Plains, native groups began to drift in from all sides and quickly adapted to an economy based on bison-hunting. Nomadic hunters became ascendant over the gardeners, many of whom abandoned their villages to become nomadic hunters themselves.

The new Plains Indian world sprang from different cultural traditions, originating from the Southeastern Woodlands, Boreal Forest, and western mountains. At least five language-families were represented by the newcomers. Starting in this early chaotic period, intertribal wars and intertribal alliances became salient features of Plains culture. Public ceremonials, based on reinterpreted ancient religious elements, clearly functioned in the socio-political reintegration of new tribes. By about 1800 the gross cultural differences had disappeared and the Indians rapidly became dependent on the furtrade. The result was a way of life which would have been impossible without the furtrader, yet it was distinctly Indian in character.

With the exception of an eastern fringe of agrarian groups, most tribes consisted of loosely organized independent bands. Tribal cohesion was achieved by ceremonial and military societies, each with their own special regalia. Warfare served the same purpose and also provided social prestige for men.

Fundamental to Plains Indian religion was the belief that animals and other natural phenomena possessed supernatural power that could, under proper circumstances, be manipulated to one's own, or to the group's advantage (fig. 55). The person seeking this power went to a lonely spot where he fasted and prayed until he met a spiritual guardian in a dream. Such experiences gave rise to individual rituals which either disappeared when the recipients died, or became increasingly popular. The Sun Dance, one of the most renowned of these rituals, is an annual ceremony for many tribes.

The buffalo and other game animals were the staff of life and the main source of raw materials. In addition to skin and bone, cloth and metal tools provided by white traders were used. Since it was necessary to follow the buffalo herds, people lived in tipis and possessions were portable. Pottery making was given up in favor of imported kettles.

Artistic expression among the Plains Indians was of a utilitarian nature and was manifest in many things they made, each tribe according to its own standards of beauty. It covered the whole range from skin tattoos, clothing, rawhide containers, wooden bowls (fig. 56), horn spoons, stone pipes, metal jewelry, feather bonnets, horsegear, tipi-covers, to impressive boulder monuments laid out on the ground.

Art is found not only in the decoration of the objects but in their actual form. Ceremonial items, as well as tools related to hunting and warfare, were often made with great attention to detail. Prestige was acquired by the wearing — and giving away — of richly decorated clothing. A newborn child was honored by relatives competing with one another to present the most handsome cradleboard. Women boasted about the quality and quantity of their quillwork and beadwork.

Decorated items figured in intertribal trade. Teton-Sioux painted robes were popular among the Crow, who traded their own decorated clothing to the Hidatsa and Mandan. Mandan-Hidatsa quillworked costumes were highly prized by Cree and Assiniboin, and Assiniboin beaded moccasins found eager customers among Blackfeet women. Richly decorated clothing was made in great quantities by the Red River Métis for trade with all tribes on the Northern and Central Plains. Exotic raw materials were eagerly sought for their prestige value. As a rule, however, the Indian artist used whatever material was most readily available; his aim was good craftsmanship.

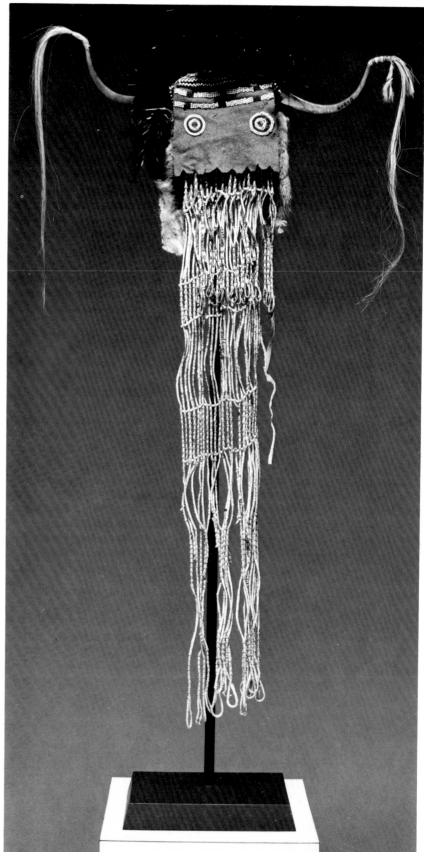

55 Hidatsa or Mandan men's society headdress

cat no 415

As with most tribal peoples, there was a definite division of craftwork by sex. Women prepared skins and made clothing, tipi-covers and rawhide containers. They carried out all quillwork and beadwork, silk embroidery and conventional geometric painting. Men, on the other hand, produced equipment for the hunt, war and ceremonial activities. They carved wooden bowls, horn spoons and stone pipes, they painted realistic and symbolic pictures on tipi-covers, tipi-linings (fig. 57), robes and shields. While each family could produce almost everything necessary for its survival, certain individuals were known for their exceptional ability in a specific craft. Even for them, however, artistic production was not a permanent or exclusive occupation. The Southern Cheyenne had a women's society for outstanding beadworkers.

Before the introduction of cloth by the furtrader, Indians relied on animal skins for their clothing. After 1850, cloth became as common as skins. The dressing of skins required considerable skill; they were prepared either natural white, smoked brown or dyed black. Shields were made of heavy, raw bison skin and protected by a painted buckskin cover.

Etching probably antedated painting on rawhide containers among the Blackfeet, Crow and Santee-Sioux. This art was very similar to etching on birchbark containers in the Boreal Forest, from which it may have originated. Skin-etching apparently was given up in favor of painting at an early date.

"Paint-gatherers" were people who specialized in the procuring and preparing of mineral and other pigments for painting. Many localities derived their native name from some color obtained

56 Sioux carved wood bowl   cat no 144

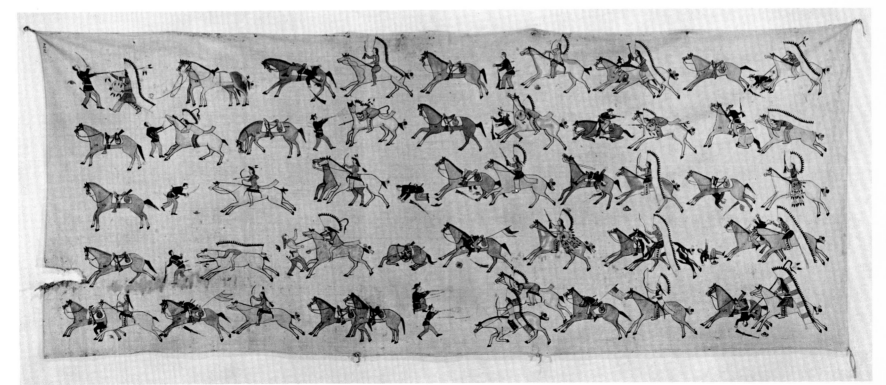

57 Crow muslin pictograph   cat no 746

there from rocks or vegetation. Commercial colors, however, were imported by the furtrader as early as the 1770s. Mixed with hot water or glue, paints were applied with pieces of porous bone. Willow sticks were used as rulers in outlining geometric designs, which were pressed in the skin with sharply pointed bone pencils. Colorless glue sizing, showing up as white after some time, was only used in geometric patterns. The hide to be decorated was staked out on the ground, the artist crouched over it, sometimes helped by an assistant. During the early reservation period Indians frequently used canvas and European notebooks, commercial inks and pencils for pictographic paintings.

Occasionally a design, normally painted, was executed in porcupine quillwork on buckskin. Quillwork is unique to North American Indians; nowhere else has this art form been recorded. Originating probably in the Northeastern Woodlands, the craft was popular all over the Northern and Central Plains. Tribes living outside the range of the porcupine obtained quills in trade, although sometimes substitutes were used, such as split birdquills and vegetable fibers. Native vegetable dyes, as well as imported dyes, were used to color the quills. Sometimes quills were colored by boiling them together with pieces of red or blue woolen cloth. They were stored in bladderbags together with bone or metal awls and sinew thread. Quills were used in four principal techniques: wrapping, sewing, plaiting and weaving, but the latter technique was confined to the northeastern margins of the Plains (fig. 58).

In the early part of the 19th century white traders introduced glass beads. The early ''pony-beads'' were fairly large and usually white, blue, and black. About 1830 the smaller ''seed-beads'' came into use in a great variety of colors, after which beadwork gradually replaced the time consuming quillwork (fig. 59). Old quill sewing techniques were adapted to the new media, but new techniques were developed,too. In the North the ''overlay'' stitch was most popular, whereas the ''lazy'' stitch was typical in the Central Plains. Woven beadwork was practiced in the Northeast and the ''gourd'' or ''peyote'' stitch was popular on the Southern Plains. Distinct tribal variations occurred within these general techniques (fig. 60).

A limited amount of carving in wood and stone was done by Plains Indians, in relief as well as in the round. Red catlinite pipe bowls from the Central Plains, and wooden bowls and war clubs from the eastern areas are well known carving types. Occasionally this work reflects some ancient stylistic idea from the Southeast. Other minor crafts were metalwork, some basketry and the making of yarn bags and sashes; feathers were used extensively (fig. 61).

The art of the Plains ranged from realistic to extremely abstract, from symbolic to purely decorative (fig. 62). Very little is known about stylistic developments before 1800. However, art analysis corroborates the general culture history of the Plains; i.e. most Plains Indian art shows close relationships with old traditions in other areas, from which it probably originated. Both through population movements and through intertribal trade these extraneous associations were continually reinforced. However, the Plains Indian artist was not an imitator; new ideas were stimulating, but acquired a distinct Plains flavor in the process

58 Sioux quilled deerskin vest   cat no 361

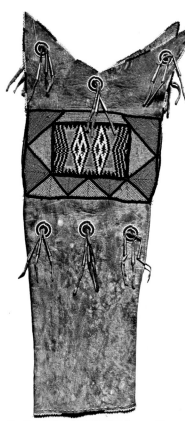

59 Fox (Mesquaki) pipe bag with seed beads   cat no 38
60 Sioux beaded hide pipe bag (right)   cat no 40

61 Mandan war calumet

cat no 758

of creation. In this connection the controlling power of a traditional style is noticeable. Even though many Indian artists claimed to have received their designs in dreams — that is, subconsciously remembered and reinterpreted — the result usually was another individual variety of the regional or tribal art style.

Representational painting was either of a symbolic nature or pictographic. The former, mainly executed on shields and tipi-covers, originated from religious experiences and represents the extremes of imagination allowed in traditional art. Substantial information, however, shows distinct tribal styles. Underlying these styles and exclusively used in symbolic paintings are certain ancient features that may have derived from prehistoric animal representations on the Eurasiatic steppes; i.e. the frequent drawing of the so-called life-line, kidneys and joint-marks in animal and human figures.

Pictographic painting, reserved mainly for war exploits, was done on skin robes, tipi-covers and tipi-linings. Human figures and horses predominate, perspective is absent and the paintings usually consist of a number of separate scenes. The early phase of this style shows the human figures in the frontal position with outlined or solid long bodies, angular shoulders; legs and arms are thin bent lines, the arms raised upwards, and round heads, frequently showing a specific tribal hair style. In an early Pawnee example, the bodies of many warriors disappear completely behind round shields, a style reminiscent of regional prehistoric rock paintings. Animals were pictured from the side; hooves and paws were frequently pictured as if seen from underneath. To emphasize the hunter's interest in foot prints, and add a suggestion of animation, tracks of hooves were marked behind the animal.

A more naturalistic phase developed on the Central Plains in the 1830s, as a result of the meeting of talented Indian painters and visiting white artists. Increasing attention was given to proportion, body-movement, detail and color. This development acquired a baroque quality in the early reservation period when the old way of life was gone, and the white man appeared in his role as collector of curios.

Abstract designs consisted mainly of straight lines, rectangles, triangles and diamonds in a great variety of combinations. Often these designs were bilaterally symmetrical and filled the entire space, as on the side of a bag. Also in abstract art we discern a range from symbolic to decorative designs though in many cases the distinction had become vague during the 19th century. Geometric designs painted on robes belong to the symbolic group. Most of them are versions of one or another of five basic patterns, called Border-and-Box, Border-and-Hourglass, Feathered-Circle, Horizontal-Striped and Bilaterally-Symmetrical. In contrast to these robe patterns, the decorative paintings on rawhide containers divided the surfaces into several small portions filled with geometric units.

Most geometric designs executed in quillwork and beadwork were purely decorative. Although one might expect a smaller range of designs here than in painting, due to technical limitations, the reverse is actually true. Elaboration, however, developed only

59

with the availability of large quantities of small beads in the 1860s. Traditionally decorated portions of clothing also became larger in this period. Short narrow decorative strips, covering the seams of shirts and leggings, were replaced by long wide bands of beadwork.

In the same period an increasing number of Plains tribes started to produce floral designs. This does not mean that such designs were unknown on the Plains before that time; Red River Métis had made and traded this work far and wide since the 1830s. This source, however, rapidly decreased after the crushing of Métis nationalism, causing the Indian women to develop distinct tribal varieties. Plains Indian floral work shows two major styles: delicate naturalistic style in the northern areas, clearly derived from the Ojibwa-Métis tradition; and a highly conventionalized style in the Southeast, adapted from similar work observed among displaced tribes from the Midwest and further east. The ultimate origin of all these floral designs goes back to French-Canadian and other Euro-American folk-art traditions. However, the double curve motif, prevalent in Indian adaptations, appears to be a floral interpretation of bilateral symmetry which is basic to Indian art of the Woodlands and the Plains.

Apart from the widespread features mentioned above, sub-areal differences evolved, although exact borderlines are hard to define and open to discussion. Most of these sub-areas were not confined to the Plains, but extended into the surrounding regions.

Northwestern Plains   Symbolic paintings on Blackfeet, Sarsi and occasionally Gros-Ventre tipi-covers were executed by specialists in a very distinct style. Animal pictures were usually placed between geometric designs, covering the top and the bottom of the tipi. In pictographic painting the old schematic figures without internal detail persisted until recently. Geometrically painted robes were mainly of the Horizontal-Striped type, consisting of a number of narrow parallel bands made up of smaller design units in different colors.

Most popular in geometric quill and beadwork were simple bars and trapezoidal designs, consisting of many small squares. These designs covered only a small portion of a usually blue background, which was frequently surrounded by a frame of short diagonal lines. Large rosettes, centrally placed on the front and back of men's shirts, appear to have been a fashion introduced by the Assiniboin. Simple floral designs, particularly on moccasins, became popular after the 1870s.

Western Mountain Region   Crow fame for their decorative art dates back to their annual trading expeditions to the Hidatsa in the 1830s. They strongly influenced the Shoshoni, Ute and Jicarilla to the south, as well as a large number of Plateau groups across the Rocky Mountains. Decorative paintings on rawhide containers frequently show an hourglass, diamond or rectangle in the center, flanked by triangles. Solidly colored rectangles were placed in the four corners of the field, which was surrounded by a frame of two parallel lines.

Whereas beadwork from other areas shows the influence of earlier quillwork, Crow beadwork designs appear to find their origin in rawhide painting. The colorful designs were outlined in white

beads; red trade cloth was extensively employed as background material. Floral designs were made only after the 1890s.

Central Plains   Representations of the thunderbird were frequently used in symbolic paintings as well as in other media, particularly among the Teton-Sioux and Cheyenne. The naturalistic development in pictographic painting in this sub-area has been mentioned before. Of the geometrically painted robe patterns, the Feathered-Circle and Border-and-Box were very popular, whereas the Cheyenne appear to have specialized in the Bilaterally-Symmetrical type. A composition of many small units in geometric painting on rawhide containers was typical here.

Decorative designs in early quillwork and beadwork were simple and consisted of lines, rectangles, triangles and diamonds. They show a surprising resemblance to decorative skin paintings in the Boreal Forest. Another association with the Northeast is noticeable in the decorative patterns divided over a number of quillwrapped strips at the bottom of Sioux pipebags. A limited use of color was typical and a white background for red and blue designs prevailed. By the 1870s tribal styles slowly developed in beadwork, in which the Teton-Sioux appear to have exerted influence on all of their neighbors. Triangles and lines predominated in new elaborate compositions which may have been influenced by the designs on Caucasus rugs, brought into

62 Northern Cheyenne dress

cat no 305

the country by an increasing number of white settlers. Whereas the Sioux tribes also developed a floral style inspired by Ojibwa-Métis work, the Cheyenne added to their geometric repertoire realistic designs, based on pictographic paintings.

Northeastern Plains Continuous change in population groups and the early settlement of whites in this area resulted in a complex development of art styles, the history of which is as yet not completely clear. However, a growing amount of information points to the Ojibwa-Métis group as a very productive center of decorative art. In contrast to this group, the Santee proper were rapidly giving up any artistic production whatsoever as early as the 1830s. Starting in the same period the Ojibwa-Métis appear to have produced a large number of skin coats, pouches, and moccasins, decorated with loomed geometric and sewn floral quillwork until late in the 1840s, when bead and silk embroidery became prevalent. By trading this colorful work, the Métis stimulated the adoption of this style by other tribes, particularly the Cree. On the other hand, the Cree and their Assiniboin allies adopted a variety of art expressions from the Central and Northwestern Plains.

Eastern Prairie This is a collective term for several distinct art traditions, which show strong relationships with their eastern neighbors in the Woodlands. Early ethnographic specimens are rare but include twined bags of buffalo hair, fingerwoven sashes, sculpture in stone and wood, and perhaps some painted robes, now in European collections.

Ribbon appliqué and highly stylized floral designs in beadwork became popular in the second half of the 19th century.

Southern Plains In the early days, artistic expression in this sub-area appears to have been largely confined to painting. Symbolic painting on tipi-covers and shields is well documented, particularly for the Kiowa and Comanche. Geometric paintings on robes were of the Border-and-Hourglass type. We know that the Kiowa, at least, painted war scenes in the pictographic style. During the early reservation period hunting scenes, ceremonials and other memories of the past became popular themes and the style became increasingly naturalistic, including notions of perspective. This style executed on hides was transferred to paper as well. Encouraged by white teachers and artists, some of these Indians played a role in the development of a modern school of Indian art.

Skin garments were painted in a monochrome, yellow being the most common color. Since quillwork was absent, embroidery techniques developed only when beads were introduced. Simple geometric designs were executed in narrow beadwork strips. The "peyote" stitch was originally used to cover large surfaces with beadwork; later this technique was used in the decoration of paraphernalia of the Native American Church. As part of a Pan-Indian configuration, the floral style of the Eastern Prairie spread all over the Southern Plains after 1920.

Some Plains Indian art had symbolic meaning, particularly where it related to religion. Symbolic art was usually executed in traditional techniques and materials, i.e. skinpainting, sculpture and quillwork. In some areas even these old techniques were considered sacred, a phenomenon already noticed in relation to garments and tools of an archaic character. Painted designs on shields and tipi-covers referred either to the owner's war exploits or to his religious visions. Magical protection and supernatural power were usually derived from such vision-paintings. The Border-and-Box robe pattern represented the organic anatomy of the buffalo and may have symbolized the earth and fertility. Such robes were worn by women, whereas men used the Feathered-Circle pattern on their robes. The Feathered-Circle represented the sun and the feather headdress; both referred to war honors. The symbolic meaning of the other robe patterns is less clear as they had lost such meaning by the time ethnologists arrived to record traditional culture.

Symbolic meaning in quillwork and beadwork depended largely upon the fancy of the maker; most of this work was purely decorative. Sacred beadwork of the Cheyenne was one of the exceptions. Designs on the hoods of Cheyenne cradleboards symbolized the desire for a long, good life for the baby. Bearpaw designs embroidered on Sioux moccasins referred to supernatural power and protection which the owner owed to a bear spirit. Colors often had symbolic meanings although these were not the same for all tribes. Human and animal effigies carved on pipe bowls, particularly when facing the smoker, may have represented spiritual helpers.

Contact with elements of Euro-American society sparked the florescence of Plains Indian culture as suddenly as the full impact of white civilization disrupted the Indian world by the end of the 19th century; yet Plains Indian culture did not vanish together with the buffalo herds. There are still many Indian craftsmen active on the Plains, creating a range of objects for their own use as well as for trade or sale. Their art has never been self-conscious; it is woven into the fabric of daily life. Over the years the Plains Indian has bridged cultural gaps and changed his traditional art forms as he has encountered new materials and new groups of people.

(1) Hopewellian refers to a prehistoric culture that flourished around the first millenium A.D., named for its type site, Hopewell, Ohio.

Ted J. Brasser joined the National Museum of Man in Ottawa, Canada, after several years at the Dutch National Museum of Ethnology. He has researched Indian tribes of the Plains, Midwest, and Atlantic Coast, as well as the Lapps of northern Scandinavia. One of his recent articles on the Coastal Algonkians appears in North American Indians in Historical Perspective, *New York, Random House, 1971.*

63 Pueblo (Hopi) politaka (cloud) kachina

cat no 502

Indian Art in the Southwest

Frederick J. Dockstader

The commonly accepted stereotype of the American Southwest is that of a hot, desert region, with cactus, sand and rock in abundance. While there is truth in this, of course, it is not the whole story: the northern portions of Arizona and New Mexico are mountainous plateau areas, with great pine forests, fertile valleys and cool, clear streams; the central areas are well covered by grassland, some tree cover, heavy brush, rivers, lakes, and a relatively fruitful land base; the desert sections, with the sand, rock and cactus are in the south and these extend from Texas in the east to California on the west.

The Indian cultures which developed in the Southwest are equally diverse. The early migrants into the region found a natural environment with an astonishing variety of resources, which they incorporated extensively into their art forms. These early migratory peoples developed cultures which can be divided into four major subdivisions. The first, and oldest, is the Basketmaker-Cliffdweller-Pueblo group, centering in northern Arizona and along the Rio Grande Valley of New Mexico. The second, to the south, were the Hohokám-Mogollón, ancestors of the Pima and Papago. The third were the nomadic Athapascan[1] peoples, who came south from the far Northwest, raiding as they traveled, coming to rest in much the same area, but also ranging farther south to eventually form the present day Apache and Navajo. Finally, there were many small enclaves of varied origin who today comprise the Yuma, Mohave, Ute, Paiute, Havasupai, Huálapai, Chemehuevi and related groups. These settled in peripheral regions of the Southwest, yet each became responsible for an individual esthetic expression — often of remarkably high quality.

Prehistorically, one of the unique features of the Southwest is that it provides one of our greatest sources of reliable data on early man, for it is only in this region that scholars have been able to accumulate a truly sizeable body of information. The dry caves and cliff houses have protected thousands of examples of perishable materials — basketry, worked wood, pottery, even textiles; and the development of tree-ring dating made possible the establishment of an accurate dating sequence. Although the tree-ring calendar has not been pushed back much beyond 250 B.C., as compared to the ca 7000 B.C. date suggested by radiocarbon dating, it is far more precise. Thus, only in the Southwest can we ascribe specific dates to various cultural activities, establish definite relationships between tribal inhabitants, and achieve at least some understanding of the cultural relativism of the early peoples and their descendants who still live in the region.

A greater variety of art expression occurred here than in many parts of North America. Coming from widely separated areas, each group settling here put into action the combined psychological, philosophical and esthetic qualities which made them individually identifiable; and their culture reflects these many factors.

Architecture is perhaps the single most important distinguishing art form of this region, for the monumental stone "cliff houses" remain as eloquent testimony to the superb construction skills of the ancient Southwesterner. After progressing from simple, below-grade pit houses through surface level ground dwellings to the cliffdwelling stage, the ancient people moved onto the plateau regions and built remarkable multi-level stone structures, some of which were true apartment houses; the largest of these, Pueblo Bonito in New Mexico, had well over 400 rooms on four floor levels.

While these buildings changed somewhat in time, the concept was never wholly lost, and today the visitor to the Southwest can see the same architectural designs in use among the Pueblo villages of Arizona and New Mexico, affected only slightly by European influences. While these structures seem picturesque, they were, above all, efficient and well designed for their purpose. Developed over centuries, these buildings survived the heat, dryness and other problems of the environment, and in their design allowed for the physical necessities of everyday living and social relationships. Such esthetic considerations as the massing of these complexes of living units were not neglected in the development of this great architectural form. The cultures which produced such effective housing were distinguished for artistic expression in other areas as well. These

people, masters of the applied arts, were able to embellish simple forms with an astonishing variety of designs. Painting was perhaps the predominant art form, followed by pottery, much of which was extensively painted. Then came basketry, and the textile arts, in which the basic weavings were frequently embellished with appliquéd designs or embroidery. Most Southwestern art served utilitarian purposes, but one must not fall into the common error of regarding all Indian art as purely "functional;" while far less common, design applied to objects to make them visually attractive was not entirely unknown. The older, rich ceremonial art has largely been lost; some was buried and some deliberately destroyed. Fragile masks, costumes and ritual paraphernalia either no longer exist or are found only in unidentifiable fragments.

The tendency to decorate utilitarian objects is best exemplified by the large quantity of pottery objects which have survived. Many of these clay forms were modeled with only average facility, yet their crisp black-on-white designs remove them at once from the commonplace. And this same vital expression

64 Apache (Western) coiled basket

cat no 63

65 Navajo first phase chief blanket   cat no 120

extends to the weaving of intricate colorful designs on the soles of fiber sandals — seen only when the wearer turned up his toes! This weaving practice was later adopted by the Plains tribes.

Southwestern prehistoric art is essentially linear, with little of the realistic decoration one might expect from such an advanced civilization. Only a few early sculptures are of stone. Some stone images — or fetishes — have been found, but early Southwest artists apparently preferred to carve in wood and few examples survive. Early pottery and basketry were sparsely decorated; later black-on-white wares were more decorative, and the embellishments on textiles seem to have kept pace with this elaboration. During the flowering of the Pueblo "Golden Age," about 1050-1400, major efforts were exerted towards designing for specific purposes. At this time the great religious arts, in which symbolism and ceremonial figure portrayal were so prevalent, began to develop as did the cities of the early historic period — Awátovi, Pottery Mound, Kuaua, Pueblo Bonito and others. Recently excavated murals at these sites reveal a previously unsuspected wealth of mural paintings depicting the ceremonial life of the period.

The relationship of the Southwestern Indian to his later descendants shows striking parallels in cultural development. If we interpret correctly, Pueblo art today is a definite continuum of earlier techniques and forms, affected more by the introduction of new tools than by new ideas. It should not be assumed that there was only one common art form throughout the Southwest. Even in such a relatively compact area, there were different concepts and skills. The work of the Hohokám people, forerunners of the contemporary Pima and Papago, is marked by more fanciful designs than the conventionalized geometric forms of the Anasazi peoples further north. The early Mimbres people who lived slightly to the east produced unique linear patterns attesting to the isolation and perfection of a single artistic form — or perhaps the work of an individual master. One is tempted to regard the examples of Mimbreño ware excavated thus far as the expression of, at most, a handful of potters; it is not impossible that the entire production emerged from a "stable" or studio of clayworkers. Basic Mimbres ware is poor in form, due primarily to the lack of high quality clay; but the delicately drawn designs in black on a white ground are astonishingly lively genre forms, replete with drama, humor and sharp observation.

The early Pueblo peoples developed a strongly conventionalized art, rigid in form, apparently with none of the imaginative, free-flowing artistic concepts more commonly found farther east. The Southwesterner seems to have been more concerned with expressing his life and art along established patterns which found acceptance over a long period of time. He also made use of a vocabulary of symbols unequalled elsewhere, except perhaps in the art of the Plains Indians. Certainly symbolism seems to have reached its peak in the Southwest. At its best, this region's art is characterized by extreme technical competence and firm control of line and form, but it shows little tendency towards experimentation, and rarely ventures beyond accepted set patterns, which were applied and reapplied in many intricate combinations. These Indians were masters of involved design concepts, and could play endless variations upon a theme.

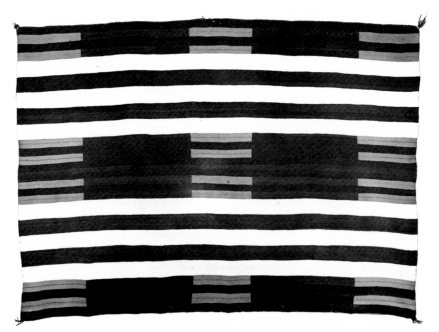

66 Navajo second phase chief blanket   cat no 121

The Athapascan invasion, ca 1000 A.D., introduced a few new concepts, but by and large was an interesting example of cultural adaptation — these people seem to have received more than they brought with them. We lack sufficient evidence for conclusive evaluation of Athapascan art. They appear to have practiced a rudimentary form of weaving using grasses and fibers to make belts and matting; however, their contact with the Pueblo loom and cotton resulted in an immediate explosion of proficiency in making textiles. Athapascan women did the weaving, whereas the sedentary Pueblo men were the textile artists; the Navajo descendants of these two earlier peoples came to dominate the field of North American textiles. Why this same artistic stimulation did not take place among the cognate Apache — who came at the same time — is still a question.

Such neighboring tribes as the Yuma, Mohave and Ute developed a distinctive combination of forms, designs and identifiable styles. They made their major contributions in pottery and basketry, which were usually ornamented with linear designs. Few artists have been as adept at applying designs to various materials and surfaces as the people of the Southwest; and an extremely rich variety of art forms characterizes this region (fig. 64).

From prehistoric times to the present, the Southwestern Indians were active traders, using ancient routes extending from the Pacific Ocean to the hinterlands of the Great Plains, and from Taos to the Gulf Coast. Shells were exchanged for turquoise, weaving for buckskin, and feathers for foodstuffs. In traveling the lengthy distances traders absorbed other ideas about form and design and exchanged concepts as well as materials; these foreign ideas were frequently improved upon by ingenious local craftsmen. Adaptation is particularly evident in sand painting, another unique Southwestern art form: the Navajo not only borrowed Pueblo weaving techniques but adapted the sand painting techniques of the Pueblos; they mastered the form and in time expanded it into an incredibly complex art form. Today, sand painting has disappeared from the Diegueño and is far less commonly practiced among the Hopi and Zuni, but remains a major category of Navajo religious ceremony.

It is fascinating to speculate as to why one group replaced another in the manufacture of a given craft. One cause may have been the fact that Pueblo weavers had worked primarily for home — or neighboring — consumption, whereas the Navajos, who also supplied domestic needs, seem to have been far more interested in trade. As soon as the white man came into the Navajo world, he became a prime consumer of Indian produced goods. He taught the Indian the fine art of merchandising, and encouraged him to adapt design to non-Indian needs. With such encouragement, at one period, perhaps three-fourths of all Navajo women were weaving for commercial outlets at least part of the time (figs. 65, 66).

Silversmithing also increased in importance. Its origins have been traced to a few Navajo men who learned the rudiments of metalworking from Mexican ironsmiths in 1853, and brass and copper (some from the newly-introduced telegraph lines!) provided the first raw materials, followed quickly by Mexican silver coins. Later, traders introduced U.S. coins, then slug or

67 Pueblo (Zuni) kachina

cat no 532

68 Pueblo (Zuni) pawik (duck) kachina   cat no 518

sheet silver. Although other tribes, particularly the Hopi and Zuni, produce silver objects, the public automatically associates silversmithing with the Navajo, and in truth, the bulk of silver jewelry in the Southwest is created by that tribe. Rich mineral deposits and geological resources provide natural pigments especially evident in Navajo and Hopi sand painting. These minerals were also widely used in Southwestern jewelry.

Southwest sculpture was primarily made of wood, and there are few known examples in either stone or metal. One of the best-known objects is the Zuni *Ahayuta,* or War God effigy, a powerful form that has been created for centuries. But the Pueblo kachina doll, now a prized item for collectors, is much better known: in these the woodworking ability of the artist is most effectively combined with color and feather elaboration. In earlier times, kachinas were relatively simple stick-form figures without extensive ornamentation; the emphasis was upon the mask, and the body was of secondary importance. As the art developed, the body form was strengthened, and with the increased interest of non-Indian collectors, and the greater appreciation of this carving style, the forms became more realistic and detailed. In time the kachina came to imitate the physical form and stance of the dancer, and some Hopi carvers now employ extreme realism in their art. The actual purpose of these small figures is the representation, in miniature form, of a male performer wearing a painted leather mask and a beautifully decorated costume. While familiar to all Pueblo peoples, this art form has been most highly developed by the Hopi and Zuni. Painted and costumed in a traditionally prescribed pattern, each masked figure represents one of the more than 350 kachina beings — supernaturals responsible for a wide variety of religious and social activities in the Pueblo world. There are few duplications among these many designs and the people have developed a tremendous range of types in order to distinguish and identify their supernatural personages (figs. 67, 68).

At one time, each man provided his own objects for everyday use, and for his religious or ceremonial activities. He might occasionally apply to an exceptionally skilled neighbor for a particular object, but by and large, tended to make whatever he needed. As economic activities in the arts increased, the individual found it more profitable to specialize in one product or craft which he could perfect to a point where his skill was sought out by others (fig. 69).

This specialization is manifested in the finely detailed, intricate inlay work of coral, turquoise, shell and jet produced by the Zuni and neighboring Pueblos; in the heavier, cast silver jewelry and strongly designed textiles of the Navajo; and in the lighter weight, more delicate ceremonial robes, dance sashes and belting of the Hopi weavers. The other Rio Grande Pueblos have almost entirely ceased making textiles, and depend upon trade for their needs. Basketry is also an almost lost art in the neighboring Pueblos, with only the Hopi producing any quantity.

Pottery has likewise suffered serious change. While many Pueblos still create clay objects, few maintain the great pottery traditions of earlier times (fig. 70). Much of the pottery made today is for the tourist market, and designs and styles have been adapted to that demand. Surface decoration predominates and is skillfully applied, but the vessel's basic function is no longer that of a container; it has become primarily an *objet d'art* for the display shelf.

Painting has become an end in itself, particularly with the increased interest in Indian art. Earlier painting occurred in *al fresco* murals, or was done on wood or clay. Contemporary graphic expression is found in watercolor, tempera and acrylic paintings on paper or, occasionally, in oil on canvas. As the number of potters, basketweavers and textile artists has declined, the number of painters has proportionately increased, but in this instance, the market is completely non-Indian — motifs, compositions and themes are often dictated by the patron, rather than the artist.

This should not be regarded as an overall condemnation of commercialism; while in some instances the results have been unfortunate, in many others the discerning artist and patron have had the wisdom to maintain high standards, and have reaped resulting benefits. Some artists have employed new techniques and concepts to great advantage.

Mere age does not bestow a *cachet* of quality and many contemporary art works are as fine — or finer — than earlier examples. A case in point is contemporary Navajo weaving, which at its best equals, or often exceeds, much of the earlier work in technique, design and quality.

The pressures of today's economic system, combined with political demands for social conformity, leave little room for the individual differences which are so much a part of a healthy balance. The Indian is now caught up in this situation, like everyone else. As he tries to fit into new cultural patterns, he has to abandon much of his traditional life style, and often, art is a part of that abandoned tradition. It is this very matter of trying to select from both cultures which so tragically frustrates today's younger Indian people.

At one time, almost every Hopi man wove, every Hopi woman made pottery; not too long ago, most Navajo men practiced silversmithing, and the women were active weavers. Today, less than one-tenth of these people work as artists, and this proportion is declining, even though technical achievement has increased. There has been almost no inclusion of this magnificent esthetic expression in our national consciousness — a loss of the only truly indigenous heritage this nation possesses. It is certainly not too late to preserve these early art forms and their contemporary manifestations.

(1) Athapascan is an alternate spelling for Athabascan. Many Indian names have several accepted spellings and we have attempted to be consistent in this catalogue.

As Director of the Museum of the American Indian, Heye Foundation, New York City, Frederick J. Dockstader is a recognized authority on the American Indian. He has served as Chairman of the Indian Arts and Crafts Board of the United States Department of the Interior and is a strong advocate of the increased recognition and appreciation of American Indian art. Dr. Dockstader is the author of numerous publications on Indian art including: The Kachina and the White Man, *Cranbrook Institute of Science, 1954 and* Indian Art in America, *New York Graphic Society, 1961.*

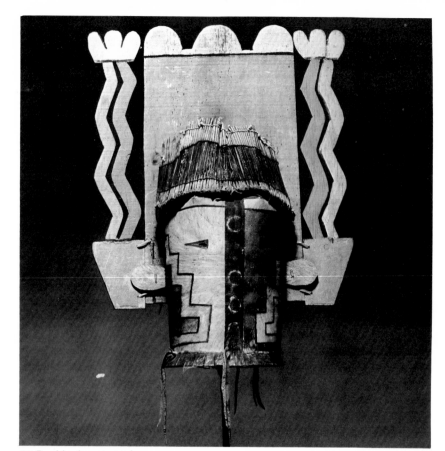

69 Pueblo dance mask   cat no 564

70 Pueblo (Zuni) painted pot with terraced rim   cat no 819

71 Pima baby carrier with beadwork, feathers

cat no 669

72 Klikitat coiled imbricated basket

cat no 77

Indian Arts of the Intermontane Region

Richard Conn

The area between the Rockies and the Cascades was the last part of the continental United States to be occupied and settled by the white man. Even today, portions of this area show few traces of the 20th century and the culture of Indian people of this region is relatively unknown. Spectacular artifacts of the Northwest Coast tribes and other Indian groups have caught popular fancy while the Intermontane peoples have gone unappreciated.

Intermontane implies a region lying between major mountain ranges, in this case the Rockies to the east and the Cascades and Northern Sierras to the west. On its other axis, the area runs from southern British Columbia to southern Nevada and Utah.
The people of this region were the last to be studied, and today there are still no complete accounts of some of the native tribes. For some time, the whole Intermontane zone was treated as a uniform area and described by default — that is, by citing the cultural traits the Intermontane people did not share with ultramontane groups. Further study[1] showed a distinct Intermontane way of life that existed in two important variants called the Plateau and Basin after their specific areas of occupation.

The Basin comprises the southern portion of the Intermontane region. It includes all of Nevada and Utah, Colorado west of the Continental Divide, the southeastern quarter of Oregon, and a triangular slice of Idaho lying below Boise. The Basin tends to be arid, with little rainfall and sparse to moderate vegetation that limited the food resources and consequently human occupation. Today the problem of little water has been overcome somewhat by irrigation, but the native people had to deal with the sparse environment on its own terms.

Nature's limitations shaped Basin culture. Having no agriculture, these Indians gathered a wide assortment of native vegetable foods, hunted, and occasionally fished. The constant food search required the Basin people to disperse in small isolated family units to avoid overtaxing the meager food supply. Little communication existed between groups and an elaborate social life was impossible. Only in good times, when there was a reserve of food, could any number of people gather for a few days of visiting.

The Plateau lies directly north of the Basin and includes: Montana and Wyoming west of the Rockies, Washington and Oregon east of the Cascades, interior British Columbia about as far north as Wells Grey Park, and all but the southwestern tip of Idaho. The area tends to be dry in terms of rainfall and humidity, but abounds in lakes and rivers. Most important are the two great river systems, the Columbia and Fraser, that rise in Canada and drain the entire Plateau. Each spring, these rivers are filled with salmon and other fish. This magnificent food resource determined the character of Plateau life — a cycle of food-gathering correlated to seasonal abundance. As salmon runs began, people moved to river-side fishing camps and men tended the traps, while women cleaned and dried the catch for winter food. Later in summer, some people moved upland to pick berries which were also dried for winter use. When the fish runs ended late in summer, men began to hunt. The meat was usually eaten fresh, but the surplus could be dried and preserved. In early spring the cycle continued when several important native root foods — camass and bitterroot, for example — were dug. It is evident the

Plateau people were well off, and any diligent family could gather all necessary food. Because effective fishing with traps and weirs required many hands, the Plateau people tended to live in multi-family camps. Further, their reserve stores made possible large social gatherings and allowed the development of organized religious cults and simple tribal governments, along with indulgence in some favorite Plateau diversions: gambling, horseracing and dancing.

Both the Basin and Plateau were protected and isolated from other Indian peoples by the mountains and deserts that surrounded the region. Consequently, Intermontane life was conservative and changed very little of its own volition. Important forces of innovation came to this region from the outside, and the nature of these influences will be evident as we examine the arts of this region. We will first consider some arts and crafts forms known to be ancient in the Intermontane, and then examine two great formal impulses that affected subsequent artistic production.

Basketry   The relative dryness in the Intermontane has helped preserve old artifacts of perishable materials. Some very early Basin and Plateau sites have yielded pieces of basketry and matting that are remarkably like those made in the 19th century. Coiled baskets were prevalent, although they have since declined in the eastern Plateau. Regional variations exist in materials, forms and techniques. Basin coiled baskets tend to be small, structurally simple and well made. One seldom sees a Basin coiled basket over ten inches high and evidently these masterpieces were reserved for holding small, precious objects. The Basin women coiled with multi-rod foundation bundles and used few variations in the basic process. Decoration was usually accomplished by varying the color of the stitching material, if the Basin weaver had little time or inclination to invent variations. She did take pride in precise workmanship and quality compensated for the lack of variety (fig. 73). Basin coiled basketry usually exhibits careful fine sewing, careful centering of design, and control of difficult shapes. To illustrate this last point, most coiled baskets were rounded bowl forms with incurved rims. To develop these forms, the weaver had to expand or reduce her foundation coil with exactness. It is not surprising that a Basin woman became the best-known Indian basketmaker. Luisa Kayser, or Datsolalee, lived in Nevada in the early 20th century and her work, prized by museums and collectors, ranks with the finest basketry made anywhere.

Plateau coiled basketry, on the other hand, has more structural variety and tends to be large. While some groups used a multi-rod coil foundation, several Canadian tribes used a wide, flat splint. Most Plateau basketmakers added decorative rims to their work. Basket shape varied considerably: Canadian Plateau baskets often had rectangular bases and flat, spreading sides; those from northeastern Washington had ovoid bases and unevenly curved sides. The Klikitat women were renowned for their fine, pail-shaped basketry, while other Sahaptian weavers made cylinders. Although Plateau women made small coiled drinking cups and berry baskets, most of their work was medium-sized to large; tribes along the Fraser River even made huge, trunk-like storage baskets. Most large Plateau coiled baskets were functional utensils; some held dried food or clothing, many were woven

73 Washo coiled willow basket

cat no 96

74 Nez Perce twine and corn husk wallet

cat no 79

75 Klamath effigy of Pock-San-E (Place in Meadow)   cat no 197

very tightly to hold water and were used as pails or kettles. Food could be boiled in some tightly woven baskets by heating the water with red-hot rocks.

The unique Plateau quality of a coiled basket is its decoration. Unlike their southern neighbors, Plateau basketmakers decorated their work with added elements. One process, imbrication, was unique to the Northwest and may have been developed in the Plateau.

Plateau women made coiled work baskets, but Basin weavers twined theirs. In this technique they produced large conical forms for gathering food, globular storage baskets, and even cradles. Like their coiled basketry, the twined pieces were well-made and care and control are evident, but decoration is limited.

Plateau twined basketry, while simple in technique, has a decorative character. The weavers sometimes used "false embroidery" to make full or partial designs on twined bags and baskets. Women's caps and soft bags are the best known Plateau twined forms. The caps, about the size and shape of a Shriner's fez, are often fully covered with false embroidery in wool yarn or split corn husk. Flat soft bags, often called "Nez Perce bags," were woven in one piece with closed bottoms and sides. Large flat bags made to hold dried food were embroidered with bold, open figures in beargrass over the natural cocoa-brown foundation fiber. Today, flat bags are generally made as women's handbags and embroidered in yarn and corn husk with complex geometric designs. Several Plateau groups made soft bags with round bottoms, the best known being the "Sally Bags" made around the Dalles region of the Columbia River. These are decorated in brown and beige self-patterns with remarkable designs of stylized human and animal figures, including deer, bird forms and elongated skeletal humans.

Carving   The Intermontane people have been carving in various forms and materials for centuries. Pictographs, or incisions on natural rock surfaces, are a well known form found from Canada through Nevada. They were made so long ago that living Indians are unsure of their meaning. The pictographs include simple representations of life forms as well as pure geometric figures such as circles, groups of dots, lines, etc. The Basin pictographs tend to be fluid and individualistic, if not as skillfully carved as those of the Plateau. Moreover, the Plateau carvers worked out a vocabulary of distinct designs, such as mountain sheep with spiral horns, pairs of humans holding hands, and an unusual bird form locally called the Spedus owl, a design which also appears on Sally Bags as well as on other carvings.

Besides pictographs, the Intermontane carvers made rudimentary utensils in stone, wood and horn. Generally these are undecorated, but the Dalles region produced some fine, attractive carved utensils and figurines (fig. 75) ornamented with the same figures used on the Sally Bags and in pictographs: skeletal humans, the Spedus owl and geometric patterns — evidently the early inhabitants of the Dalles region had worked out a design style applicable to many materials.

Influences on Horseback   The first series of changes in Intermontane life entered on four feet. By the late 17th century, the Spanish garrisons in Santa Fe and San Antonio had sizeable horse herds. Local Indians quickly began to acquire animals — first by barter, later by "appropriation" and soon horses were being traded on to tribes far from the Spanish settlements. By the early 18th century, horses were known in Washington and British Columbia, and an intertribal trading route had been established along the western slope of the Rockies. Horses made hunting and travel easy and promoted a subtler, but important change — increased intertribal contact. Indians also acquired Spanish riding gear and then made their own after the Spanish models. Today, Plateau girls riding in parades still use saddles and trappings that may be traced back to medieval Spain. But, it may also be possible that the Indian who never saw a Spaniard got some ideas from the Apache or Comanche who sold him his first horse. As an example, the Basin people had worn basketry sandals in prehistoric times; as the horse days began, they switched to moccasins with rawhide soles like those the Apaches wore. The change may have been a result of contact with new people who had come to sell horses.

The horse continued to cause changes in the Basin/Plateau area. The Basin people could travel farther in search of food, and the hunters could carry game back to camp with ease (fig. 76). In the Plateau these benefits were extended to include longer trips over the Rockies where it was possible to hunt buffalo on the Plains. In time, the eastern hunting trip became an annual fall event after the summer's food had been dried and packed away. Some Eastern Basin groups such as the Ute also began to go Buffalo hunting, and encountered Plains Indians with whom they fought and traded. The Plains people were also new in the saddle, and their spectacular equestrian society was beginning to develop. Their influence on the Plateau and Basin societies was important. From the Plains, the Intermontane societies adopted the tipi, the portable leather house so perfect for nomadic existence, and by 1800 the Tipi was in use throughout most of the Plateau and Eastern Basin. Other useful new ideas included parfleche (buckskin and rawhide carrying and storage cases), catlinite pipes and the craft of porcupine quill embroidery. There is some question as to the origin of the distinctive skin clothing worn by Plains and Plateau people. The traditional view has been that the Plateau copied everything from the Plains, but journals of early traders and visitors to both areas indicate that these garments may have been worn a little earlier west of the mountains. The question needs further study.

Most borrowing by Intermontane people from the Plains peoples concerned material things (fig. 77). Only those tribes living closest to the Plains Indians seem to have adopted any of the intangible elements of Plains culture. One Plateau tribe, the Kootenai, developed their own version of the Sun Dance, the great Plains religious festival. This group, among others, also developed a taste for that good, old Plains game — war. Flatheads, Nez Perces, Utes, and Shoshonis began to cross the mountains to steal Plains horses and take a few scalps, but didn't adopt the formalized concepts that surrounded war on the Plains such as the honors system or the military societies.

In time, trade goods from the East began to appear on the Plains. Those intended for decorative use — beads, cloth, and paint — were taken by the nationalistic Plains groups to develop tribal decorative styles. The Plateau tribes saw these new forms and copied them. We may, in fact, point out three specific cases in which a Plains tribal decorative style was adopted by one or more Intermontane group.

The first and most obvious of these borrowings runs from the Crow to the Nez Perce and their Sahaptian-speaking neighbors. The Crow had devised a decorative style rendered in beadwork and in painting on rawhide, distinguished by the use of many colors, the frequency of long isosceles triangles, and the practice of edging major elements of a composition with an outline of varying width. The Nez Perce, Umatilla, and others copied this style so perfectly that it is sometimes difficult to distinguish their work. But as a rule, Nez Perce beadwork is less complex and contains fewer colors than that of the Crow.

The second example of borrowing runs from the Blackfeet to the Flathead and their Salish-speaking neighbors to the west. Blackfeet design is rendered in quillwork and beadwork and its hallmark is a combination of certain bead and quill techniques with designs composed of many small squares or rectangles. The Blackfeet also had distinct color preferences — they were among the few Plains tribes to use black. All these traits, showing unmistakable Blackfeet influence, are seen in the work of the Flathead, Spokane, Kalispel, and adjacent groups. But in this case the Plateau borrowers have been less faithful to their model. For example, Spokane beadworkers tended to make designs bolder and simpler than the Blackfeet equivalents and the Plateau people changed the Blackfeet colors considerably.

The final case of borrowing is the least apparent. It runs from the Cheyenne and Arapaho to the Ute. These former styles were rendered in beadwork and involved a combination of lazy-stitch technique, limited colors and combinations, and a number of specific design elements, including tall stepped triangles and horizontal stripes. The Ute borrowed the beadwork method and some designs and colors, but added other designs and colors and worked out an amalgam related to, but distinct from, the Central Plains original. Two examples may show what the Ute did. Cheyenne and Arapaho beadwork generally has dark-colored figures on a white background. If there are internal colors in the dark figures, they are chosen with a sensitivity to value relationships. The Ute took a freer approach: backgrounds and figures were often of neighboring values, and the classic Cheyenne idea of dark-on-light was seldom observed. A second example concerns the figures themselves. Cheyenne design is marked by strong, well proportioned figures; if a main figure is elaborated, the other colors are placed so as to contribute to this strength. The figures in Ute beadwork are less specific, varying in proportion as in color, and are often so confused with distracting internal elements that their effectiveness is destroyed.

Influences by Canoe   In the very early 19th century, European traders arrived in the Plateau; they had come across Canada via the network of waterways that carried them from Montreal over the prairies and down the Columbia, and their arrival set in motion new influences in Plateau life. The traders brought all sorts of wonderful new things that the Plateau people had heretofore seen only on the Plains: firearms, cloth, beads and metal. The Plateau and Basin peoples had seen their first European trade goods in the hands of other Indians and tended to use them as the latter did.

76 Yakima saddle bag   cat no 53

77 Shoshoni man's beaded buckskin leggings   cat no 332

But another facet of this European arrival was to have equally significant consequences. The Canadian and American traders brought Eastern Indians with them as boatmen and laborers. The Plateau people got to know these displaced peoples, many of whom married Plateau women and stayed on as their terms of service expired. Eastern Indians brought with them an introduction to Christianity and a warning that the white men might in time overrun the West. The first idea was accepted by some, the second ignored until too late.

The Easterners also introduced floral beadwork designs that were copied by Plateau women. As on the Plains, floral beading gained slow popularity on the Plateau but by 1900 it had almost supplanted the older geometric styles. This new idea of using flowers, leaves, and other semi-natural forms in beadwork slowly spread south into the northern portion of the Basin, until today most Bannock and Northern Ute beadwork is floral.

The floral beadwork introduced into the Plateau between 1810 and 1860 probably exhibited certain common features: small, stylized designs, symmetry, and frequent use of the "double curve." This last is a design arranged around a pair of similar but opposed curves joined at a common center. The double curve was distributed across Canada from Labrador to Lake of the Woods, and the Eastern Indians carried it farther west.

The earliest examples of Plateau floral art show elementary versions of the above features. The Plateau women simplified the compositions and omitted many fine details that add so much charm to Eastern beading. In time, they and the Basin people would introduce still other modifications, and by the late 19th century, Intermontane floral beading had taken on a character of its own. The double curve motif and symmetry had almost vanished. Instead, the Westerners were making asymmetrical compositions of naturalistic flowers and animals, a trend that continues today.

Except for the introduction of Christianity to parts of the Plateau, the Eastern Indian migrants made few changes in the social or ceremonial life of the region. Like the Plains Indians before them, they influenced the arts and crafts and the material culture of the Intermontane region most, and the basic cultures of both the Plateau and Basin continued largely unchanged until the imposition of reservations.

In both regions, many of the arts and crafts discussed here are still being produced in quantity. Visitors to the Intermontane province in summer still see people dressed in their finery enjoying annual encampments, dancing, and gambling. The Basin and Plateau have been overlooked by many people who profess an interest in American Indian arts, but a consideration of their works will reward anyone who undertakes it.

(1) Kroeber, A. L., "Cultural and Natural Areas of Native North America," *University of California Publications in American Archaeology and Ethnology,* XXXVIII (1939).

Richard Conn has worked in a number of museums including: Eastern Washington State Museum, Spokane; Manitoba Museum, Winnipeg; The Heard Museum, Phoenix, and is presently Curator of Native Arts, Denver Art Museum. In addition to the essay above, Mr. Conn has written notes and supplied pertinent data on many of the works for the Catalogue of the Exhibition.

78 Kwakiutl multiple-headed mask

cat no 581

Heraldic Carving Styles of the Northwest Coast

Bill Holm

Diagram by Bill Holm

Several centuries have passed since the first European vessels made their way to the waters of the North American Northwest Coast. Impressions of the land and its people have come down to us in journals kept by men aboard these ships. They were for the most part practical navigators and businesslike traders with little interest in the artistic products of the Indians they encountered, except as curios of strange lands. Nevertheless, sensitive descriptions of native Northwest Coast culture appear in the journals, and enough of those "curios" have been preserved from the early voyages to give us a fairly clear notion of the character of art in the Northwest Coast at the time of first European contact.

From this evidence, and as a result of new developments in archeology, we know that the several art traditions of the Northwest Coast recognizable at the close of the 19th century were present and highly developed at the time of first historic contact. Certainly the arts continued to evolve during the intervening centuries, but their basic structures were solid and well rooted in time.

Though many scholars over the years have stressed the diversity of art and material culture within this area, we still hear of an all-inclusive "Northwest Coast" Indian art, a term which generally refers to that of the 19th century Haida, Tlingit and Tsimshian. If the production of other periods or areas of the Coast are given any attention at all, they are lumped with that of the northern area, or seen as unsophisticated offshoots of the northern tradition. Classic northern art, with its characteristic fine craftsmanship, elaborate detailing and perfection of form is apparently more easily appreciated by people raised in the Western European tradition than are the less elegant and complex styles of other areas and other times.

The geographical limits of the Northwest Coast culture area are not as easily defined as might be assumed given the natural boundaries of the sea to the west and the nearly continuous range of mountains to the east. The southern limit is particularly nebulous and is often placed as far south as northern California. In terms of the area's art, the Columbia River Valley seems a more logical boundary, and techniques and materials seem increasingly more Californian south of that boundary. Eastward and northward, up the major rivers penetrating the mountain barrier, fingers of Coastal culture merge with those of the interior. Some of these influences go back to ancient times when the Salish migrated from the interior in the south, and the Haida, Tsimshian and Tlingit moved out to occupy the inlets and islands to the north. Salish art produced on the Coast perhaps can better be seen as a development of a general Salish art tradition than as an interior-influenced Northwest Coast art.

The Nootka and Kwakiutl of the southern and central British Columbia coast may be descendants of very early coastal dwellers who shared culture features with their then Eskimo neighbors and who developed a powerful, straightforward, freely sculptural art style, termed "old Wakashan" by Wilson Duff. This style is best exemplified in historic times by Nootkan sculpture, and less perfectly by early Kwakiutl work before it was influenced by the intellectualized northern art spreading down the Coast in the 19th century. Nootka specimens collected on Captain James Cook's third expedition in 1778 show this naturalistic, ingenuous style. They differ little from pieces collected a century later by James G. Swan, or from the treasures just now being unearthed at the Nootkan Ozette site on the Washington coast, which predate Cook by some three hundred years. The Ozette material, miraculously preserved over the centuries by engulfing mud slides, will certainly expand our knowledge and understanding of old Wakashan culture and the early development of Northwest Coast art and culture in general.

Apparently this early style was at one time much more widely practiced throughout the Coast and may have been the basis upon which classic northern sculpture was developed. Some major concepts and design details characteristic of 19th century northern art are to be found in very early Salish material as well. We do not know which of many possible factors combined to direct the Haida, Tsimshian and Tlingit artists to perfect their sophisticated art from its humble beginnings; perhaps heredity or pre-coastal cultural experience played a part. Interestingly, the three major stylistic divisions of the Northwest Coast paralleled linguistic divisions. Influence from China seems less preposterous today when archeologists are steadily pushing the beginnings of Northwest Coast art back toward contemporaneity with superficially similar Chinese works. We may be able to test these similarities (and resemblances to other circum-Pacific arts) as more scholars interest themselves in analyzing the basic structures of these arts, and meaningful comparisons become possible. (See "Asiatic Sources of Northwest Coast Art," p 85 of this catalogue.)

Environmental factors cannot be discounted. The old saw that an easy life with abundant food leads to development of the arts only partially holds true for the Northwest Coast. Certainly people who spend nearly all their waking hours in the struggle for survival must give a low priority to time spent in purely cultural pursuits. The relative abundance of food on the Coast made this time available, but the most spectacular art production occurred in the least hospitable region and the bountiful Salish area nurtured the least imposing arts. It has been suggested that the more locally concentrated resources in the north influenced the development of the concept of rank and privilege, which in the last analysis is the direct motivation for much northern heraldic art.

Although we might well protest the casual lumping together of the art traditions of the long Coast, they share certain concepts and forms. The artists of the whole Coast enjoyed a rather homogeneous environment (at least in relation to neighboring areas) which gave them similar resources and techniques. The importance of wood in Northwest Coast technology is well known: the western red cedar, which furnished so much of the raw material for the culture, grew in all parts of the region except the northernmost; alder, maple, spruce, Alaskan cedar, yew and a dozen other woods, each of which had its special uses according to its qualities, were found over much of the area. Other materials which went into the arts, such as animal bone and dressed skin, were universally obtainable, while certain others — sea mammal ivory, whale bone, mountain sheep, goat horn and opercula — were available only locally and in some cases became regular articles of trade. Wood-working tools of stone, shell, bone and

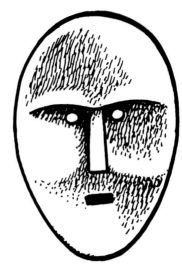

79 Drawing of Coast Salish mask type, by Bill Holm

80 Nootka human face mask

cat no 600

81 Kwakiutl sea urchin mask   cat no 594

82 Bella Coola carved and painted wood mask   cat no 571

teeth, and their later steel counterparts, varied only slightly in form and use from one end of the Coast to the other. It is not surprising that artists from widely separated areas produced works related in their basic structures.

The human figure, a subject common to all Northwest Coast art, furnishes examples of these shared characteristics. In sculpture it generally appears in a somewhat static, frontally oriented pose. The knees are slightly bent or drawn up against the chest and the knee caps are frequently flattened. Scant attention is given the feet, which may merge with a solid base. In contrast, the hands and fingers are usually carefully delineated. The arms are often down alongside the torso, the hands on hips or thighs, although elbows bent and forearms crossing the torso are not uncommon. The head is typically very large in proportion to the body, often equaling the shoulders in width. Such figures occur in all media and in every scale, from tiny amulets and shaman's figures to monumental wood sculptures.

We can look to other features to differentiate the work of artists of the various sub-cultural areas. Since the human face (or perhaps better, humanoid, since many non-human faces are similarly handled) is a subject common to sculpture throughout the Coast, it can serve as a basis for some general comparisons.

Sculptured faces in the entire Salish area from the middle Columbia to southern British Columbia are characterized by their flatness and frontality (fig. 79). The principal form — the three-dimensional unit within which the face is constructed — is a flat oval. In a fully three-dimensional figure such as a Quinault shaman's power figure or a Puget Sound spirit canoe figure, the back of the head is deep and rounded, while many amulets and small bone and wood carvings like those of the middle Columbia are essentially two-dimensional. In both, however, the face itself is composed of two or three flattened planes stepped back under the brow and sometimes at the cheek line. The nose is a narrow ridge projecting downward from the forehead plane and the eyes are small and round, close set under the projecting brow on the cheek plane, without any distinct orb. The mouth is small and flat with little or no projection. Even on Vancouver Island where figures become more fully sculptural and the influence of Kwakiutl art is felt, the frontal, planar face structure prevails. A curious exception is seen in some small, prehistoric stone figures from the area, which are strikingly similar in structure to more northern work.

Masks and large carved figures have a much greater role in the art of the Nootkan tribes of Vancouver Island's west coast. The flat oval of the Salish sculptured face gives way here to a prism-like structure formed of two planes intersecting on the median of the face, and some Nootka animal masks are actually constructed of separate flat pieces joined at the nose. A typical humanoid face on a mask or carved figure is deep from front to back (fig. 80). The profile is rather straight and the forehead is seldom rounded, but slopes straight from the eyebrows which are narrow, without pronounced curve. The most characteristic feature, shared with Salish sculpture, is the placement of the eye on the upper cheek plane, with little or no orb, under a projecting and sloping underbrow. Unlike Salish examples, the eyes tend to be large with a circular inner ovoid and long, open eyelid lines. The nose is long and narrow and merges with the backswept cheek planes. The nostrils are narrow and upthrust and the lips are thin and drawn back along the principal prismatic form. A deep prismatic face with long sloping underbrow and large eyes on the cheek plane will almost invariably prove to be Nootka.

At the line of demarcation between Nootka and Kwakiutl we can see a major change in sculptural style (fig. 81). The humanoid face illustrates this change most graphically in the structure of the brow-eyesocket-cheek complex: to the south the eye is invariably defined by carving or painting on the plane of the upper cheek; to the north the eye is constructed on a bulge or orb more or less sharply defined. In many Kwakiutl masks this orb is large and rounded, sometimes in the form of a truncated cone, and frequently intersects sharply with the upper cheek and underbrow. These planes are usually well defined. The principal form is rounded, almost a half cylinder. The forehead rounds back over medium to heavy curved brows and the nostrils are large, wide and sharply defined. The pronounced mouth projection forms a distinct cheek line with the forecheek plane. The lips are drawn back and usually form a continuous band from upper to side to lower lip. Taken on its sculptural form alone a typical Kwakiutl humanoid face is characterized by strongly defined planes in the eyesocket and mouth area, with eyes on a pronounced orb. The many representations of animals, birds and fish in Kwakiutl art follow these same principles in typical examples.

Bella Coola sculpture resembles that of the Kwakiutl in boldness of conception and in its strongly defined intersecting planes (fig. 82). Some transitional carvings are difficult to identify, but a typical Bella Coola piece is unmistakable: the middle of the face often projects boldly and the forehead and chin slope back, the principal form suggests a hemisphere; the brows are very heavy and projecting, bending sharply over each eye and sloping down over the temples. The sharply defined underbrow extends downward over an upper cheek bulge at the outer corner of the orb, one of the most distinct Bella Coola characteristics. The orb itself is very pronounced in the shape of a truncated cone with round, flat eye, often without carved eyelid lines. The nose sometimes features a flat front plane and the nostrils, clearly defined by a continuation of the forecheek plane, are rounded and flaring. In keeping with the general bulbous character, the mouth projection is strong and conical. The lips are open and flat, drawn back along the cone. The upper and lower lips are not continuous, but are separated by the mouth line to their ends. Some Bella Coola masks are more subtly modeled, but the eye and cheek structure and lip and nostril form are unique and almost always recognizable.

Adjoining the Bella Coola country to the west and north are several groups whose language relates them to the Kwakiutl, but whose social organization and art link them to their Haida and Tsimshian neighbors. They have been called collectively Bella Bella, after the modern name of one of their villages. The sculpture of these people resembles that of the adjoining tribes and is very difficult to identify. Although by no means a universal characteristic, a distinctive eye socket form does occur with some frequency (fig. 83). In an otherwise Bella Coola or Tsimshian-like face a large, somewhat flattened and nearly circular orb is defined

83 Bella Bella carved wood mask   cat no 568

84 Tsimshian poles at Kitwankool, British Columbia, 1910

by narrow upper cheek and underbrow planes. In more naturalistic masks this may be subtly modeled, whereas in more stylized faces its angularity and boldness approaches the Bella Coola form, but the Bella Coola cheek bulge seldom occurs.

The Tsimshian speaking tribes, especially those of the upriver Gitksan and Nishga groups, developed the northern sculptural style to subtle perfection (fig. 84). Human faces on some of their dancing headdress frontlets are marvels of sensitive, expressive modeling. The same underlying structure, with bold exaggeration of the features, is found in large face masks and colossal figures on totem poles. Unlike the typical Kwakiutl and Bella Coola humanoid face, the planes, although distinct, intersect in rounded transition, with the effect of smooth, taut skin over an underlying strong skeletal structure. The forehead slopes back from narrow arched brows, with front and side planes apparent. The eye socket area is large and open, with a rounded orb deeply set at the bottom, suggesting a large, spherical eye behind smoothly stretched lids lacking the painted or carved line along their edges. There is a smooth dip at the juncture of the brow with a somewhat aquiline nose, and the mouth is wide, with narrow lips; the chin is prominent, although often vertically short. The most distinct feature is a cheek pyramid formed by the intersection of the upper cheek, forecheek and cheek planes (fig. 85).

85 Drawing of Tsimshian pole type, by Bill Holm

86 Haida poles on Anthony Island, British Columbia, 1901

In the design of totem poles, Tsimshian artists tended to compose their subjects within the half-cylindrical limit of the split log, without excessively deep carving or the addition of projecting parts (fig. 84). In this, the Tsimshian and their Haida contemporaries differed from the artists of the Kwakiutl, who felt perfectly free to cut deeply or even through the log and to add projecting beaks, wings or arms to achieve their sculptural ends. The limits of the log cylinder and the monumentality of the figures led the artists to exaggerate some of the features on Tsimshian totem poles: the eyes tend to be very large, round and bulging under broad arched brows; the nose, flattened by the influence of the log cylinder, is often very broad; the very short chin accentuates the wideness of the mouth.

Very realistic masks of the Haida and their northern neighbors are often difficult to differentiate, primarily because of their realism. The more stylized a sculptured object becomes, the more easily is it seen to belong to one or another style. Naturalistic Haida face masks and carvings resemble those of the Tsimshian, with a less pronounced cheek pyramid and usually with sharply defined eyelid lines. As they approach the stylization of totem pole faces they show more distinct Haida characteristics.

Many examples of Haida sculpture illustrate the great compulsion of the artist to preserve the basic form of the sculptured material. Totem poles are the clearest example, but horn spoon handles, speaker's staffs and other objects illustrate the principle. In these pieces the great influence wielded by the northern style of painting on flat surfaces is apparent. This highly developed, intellectualized system of space organization and form, overlaid and molded certain Haida sculpture to the extent that it appears to be two-dimensionally organized relief carving arranged on a cylindrical surface. On large totem poles, where the half-cylindrical form is closely retained (fig. 86), this effect is particularly strong. The forehead slopes back only slightly and the front and side planes are discernible. The eyebrows are very broad, with the semi-angularity of the formline system of two-dimensional design. As always, it is in the eyes and eyesocket area that we find the clearest indication of tribal origin. On a stylized Haida face, the eyesocket is a clearly defined hollowed ovoid enclosing a moderate orb, usually more deeply set at the bottom. The iris of the eye very often has the semi-angular ovoid form and is bounded by eyelids with a distinct carved and painted edge. The nose is usually bent sharply down at the bridge to conform to the basic cylinder, and the nostrils are large and moderately flaring. A sharp cheekline borders the forecheek and defines the nostrils and the ends of the broad lips. The carving is only moderately deep and in general the effect of the two-dimensional design system is very apparent.

The Tlingit, northernmost of the Coastal people, produced sculpture which conforms to the northern conventions but retains individual characteristics: a typical Tlingit humanoid face has rounded contours; the forehead is rounded back from moderately wide, curved brows (fig. 87). The eyesocket area is open and indistinctly defined, with a pronounced, smooth orb deep set at the bottom. The iris is large and round, bounded by carved wide-open eyelids, often with a painted edge line. The nose tends to be small and rounded, with slightly flared nostrils and the upper cheek area forms a long slanting plane from below the orb to the projecting lip. The mouth projection is not usually drawn far back along the sides so that the lips, forming a broad, continuous band, project forward from the cheek. The mouth is usually open and often furnished with teeth, either carved into the wood or inlaid with abalone shell or opercula. Copper lips, eyebrows or nostrils, and human hair inset along the upper rim are fairly common on Tlingit masks. The features of totem pole figures are similar, or suggest a combination of these and Haida features.

Painting and the closely related shallow relief carving cannot be separated from sculpture in Northwest Coast Indian art. The important part it played in the development of classic northern sculpture, both in its influence on sculptural form and its function as surface detail, is easily seen. A sequence of development for this superlative painting style has not been established, but it appears to have evolved from concepts and design elements which made up an ancient pan-coastal design vocabulary. Examples are the "Northwest Coast eye," the eye-like joint and certain other individual elements such as T-shaped and crescentic figures which were conceived as being slits or negative spaces between positive design elements.

Two-dimensional surface decoration in the Salish area was geometric in character; concentric circles, parallel lines, chevrons and crescents, rows of dots and triangles and the above mentioned Ts are found in painting and relief carving from the Columbia River to the Gulf of Georgia. Simple semi-naturalistic silhouettes of land and sea mammals, fish and birds also occur, sometimes with anatomical details rendered with combinations of the geometric design elements. Art often portrayed the supernatural so that interpretation from our foreign, time-removed viewpoint is uncertain or impossible.

Nootka artists shared the use of many of these geometric elements in their painting and detail carving. They combined large rectangular areas of solid color with lines, rows of dots and other geometric figures to decorate the representational paintings of animals, mythical and natural, which make up much of Nootka painted art. These same free geometric forms were used to detail masks, and again much of the specific symbolism is unknown to us. Black and red were the usual colors, as throughout the Coast, with the frequent addition of white and blue, and later yellow, orange and green. Sometime in the early 19th century the northern formline system began to gain a foothold among the Nootkan painters and although it had no profound effect on their art its influence was felt and certain Nootka paintings include formline-like elements and combinations of design units similar to those of the north.

The Kwakiutl, on the other hand, were strongly influenced by northern painting in the 19th century. Artists of the northern Vancouver Island region eagerly incorporated the superficial trappings of the sophisticated northern system, but without ever completely bowing to its exacting rule. The work of some artists followed the northern spirit so closely that it appears on first view to conform to the northern rules. This resemblance results from the use of formlines and eye and U forms in arrangements suggesting formal northern compositions, but their painting remained exuberant and free. On sculptured faces this bold and flamboyant painting style is often so strong as to overshadow even the vigorous Kwakiutl carving.

The Bella Coola assimilated the northern formline style of painting and developed a modification of it for mask painting so distinctive that it served as a primary means of identification. Broad areas of a medium blue paint, separated into U-shaped lobes, contrast with the natural wood background, the black eyebrows and vermilion lips, nostrils and detailing. Dotting, often roughly applied, recalls the Salish ancestry of the Bella Coola.

The two-dimensional painting and relief carving art of the northern tribes was applied to every manner of object and exerted a powerful influence on the form of sculpture in the area. On sculptured faces it takes several forms: the stylized faces on Haida poles and related objects are painted like their flat counterparts, black eyebrow, eye and eyelid, red nostrils and lips and blue eyesockets; on some more realistic faces the same arrangement prevails with added painted detail on the cheeks and forehead; on very naturalistic masks large and bold abstract designs with scant suggestion of formline origin, or smaller detailed designs in the formline system, are often seen. Tlingit paintings often make much use of a blue paint, somewhat paler and greener than that used by the Bella Coola.

The number of objects from the central and northern coast is staggering, and the total was no doubt much greater than we know. The bulk of this material was produced by relatively few prolific professionals whose work was in demand by chiefs

motivated by the extreme emphasis on rank and lavish crest display. We tend to simplify the number of different beings represented in the art to a few obvious crest animals: eagle, raven, wolf, grizzly, hawk and so on. But in 1909 Swanton published a list of 62 Haida crests, including such unlikely creatures as rainbow, cirrous cloud, drying frame and cedar limbs.[1] Boas, in 1916, listed 99 Tsimshian crests including victorious arrow, burning ground, sliding people and food of copper beaver.[2] All these could be represented in the art, often in a form which could easily be misinterpreted as some very ordinary bird or animal.

The peculiar historical circumstances of the late 18th and 19th centuries also played their part in the burgeoning of the arts. European contact and the furtrade brought steel tools in abundance which increased the artists' volume of production, and introduced new materials which were assimilated into the already mature art. The economic boom that resulted from trade influenced the form and frequency of potlatching, consequently putting more demands on the artists. The foreigners also created a market, not only for the obvious commercial arts of argillite carving and silverwork, but for all kinds of "curios" including masks, rattles and other ceremonial goods. Although many of these were used objects purchased from the Indian owners, the artists very early began to produce these same articles for sale to visiting whites, and in the late years of the 19th century anthropologists and museum collectors began to commission Indian artists to produce specimens for study collections.

Carving and painting continue today on the Northwest Coast and in the last decade production has increased and quality has improved. A sizeable portion of this production is for traditional Indian use, but most of it is for sale to whites, and today it is possible to obtain an original piece of traditional Northwest Coast art by a living, working Indian artist, of a quality comparable to the best of a century ago.

(1) Swanton, John R., "Contributions to the Ethnology of the Haida," *Memoirs of the American Museum of Natural History,* Vol. 8, New York, 1909, pp 114, 115.

(2) Boas, Franz, "Tsimshian Mythology," *Bureau of American Ethnology Annual Report,* No. 31, Washington, D. C., 1916, pp 503-6.

Bill Holm is presently Curator of Northwest Coast Indian Art, Thomas Burke Memorial Washington State Museum, University of Washington, Seattle, and a lecturer in Art History and Anthropology at the University of Washington. He has written many articles and books on Northwest Coast Indian art including: Northwest Coast Indian Art: An Analysis of Form, *Seattle, 1965;* Crooked Beak of Heaven, *Seattle, 1972. An article on "The Art of Willie Seaweed, a Kwakiutl Master" is in preparation.*

87 Tlingit or Haida sea bear mask   cat no 614

88 Haida button blanket

cat no 133

Asiatic Sources of Northwest Coast Art

Ralph T. Coe

Critically speaking, Northwest Coast Indian art was allowed to be "art" long before Plains art came of age. It is still held to be more sophisticated than the arts of the Southwestern Indians. Considering this verdict it is surprising that more study has not been given the Asiatic quality of this most "oriental" North American Indian art. It feels or looks oriental in its bilateralism and in its animal designs of restrained ferocious power, which call to mind the ancient *T'ao-t'ieh* mask. As Geldern, Covarrubias and Schuster pointed out about a quarter of a century ago, the widespread use of the hocker device (anatomical joints articulated by decorative devices), as well as a particular regard for *horror vacui* in Northwest Coast art, recalls Bronze Age China.[1] Boas also felt that Northwest Coast songs had affinities with Mongolian music. However, so much observation of Northwest Coast style has been confused with accounts of ceremonialism, society, and material, as well as oral phases of the culture, that its visual artistic antecedents have been overlooked in the process. The pursuit of these antecedents is difficult, requiring not only cooperation on the viewer's part with regard to vast time and space diffusion, but an acceptance of comparisons that seem unorthodox in the context of a European close-knit, documentary approach to art historical method.

Writings on Northwest Coast art have in recent years shifted emphasis from symbolism (animal design identification) and analysis of heraldic design conventions, to a more creative and empathic reconstruction of the process of design. The scholar-artist Bill Holm has followed creative realization step by step, line upon line.[2] But this method also has its limits, since so much Northwest Coast art is not applied design but sculpture of strongly three-dimensional character and great formal articulation. The flat animaloid designs exist in basic tension with the sculptural dimensions of masks, boxes and bowls. Even this dualism reminds one of ancient Asia. What is needed is greater appreciation of all phases of the art, from the carving of such fragile objects as walking sticks and jewelry to heavy-duty architectonic carvings of the housepost and totem pole variety, to masks of highly plastic refinement that could only be motivated by complex mythologies.

Such an admission opens to view the comparison of objects of the widest possible range within the Northwest Coast style — armor, headdresses, grave posts, bowls, and feast dishes, as well as ceremonial boards and figural sculptures. How did these objects get to look the way they do? In construction and elaboration they do not resemble the rest of Amerindian art. The purpose here is to point out how inextricably coastal carving is imbedded in certain time-hallowed, traditional early Asiatic sculptural forms. Along the northern part of the Coast in particular it paralleled its Pacific Basin origins so persistently that the evidence is amazingly well preserved in carvings executed within the last 150 years.

Style comparison gives connecting links between objects differing in context, despite obvious changes in meaning, content and usage. We are not dealing with what is "Northwest" in this art, but with its visible roots in trans-Pacific, partly alien prototypes. The connections are not intended literally. They

89 Sisiutl ceremonial board of the Kwakiutl, by Dick Price, 1920

hint at cultural cross-connection at some ancient time. The objects may belong to collateral branches extending from a tradition we can project but can never uncover. It is not necessary to visualize Asiatics landing at Yakutat Bay to demonstrate the persistence of orientalism in the visual arts of the recent Haida or Tlingit Indians. We are uncovering roots that run too deep for anything other than archeological visibility. Nonetheless they are current enough to affect how a Tlingit chief of 70 years ago wore his headdress, or to tell us why an animal is a beaver and not a bear on a 19th century Haida bowl.

One of the most powerful motifs on the Northwest Coast is the double-headed snake — the Sisiutl — which appears on ceremonial belts, drums, and other ceremonial paraphernalia. It reaches its most eloquent embodiment in Kwakiutl ceremonial carvings which sometimes reach a length of 20 feet and in which the staccato painted elements do violence to the flat board-like silhouette. One can imagine the effect of these monstrous serpent images seen looming above the spectators attending a winter ceremonial in flickering interior firelight. The Sisiutl board illustrated (fig. 89) was carved by the Southern Kwakiutl master Ya-hua-qua-lae (Dick Price) in 1920, and is complete with painted fins and claws. What haunts the observer, however, is the astonishing profile of the huge Siamese snake as it spreads outward from the human-monster center. Now, where else does a relative of this singular motif occur? Clearly — in fact, only — in Chinese early medieval sculpture, where it enframes the niches of northern and western Wei Buddhist steles of the 6th century A.D. (fig. 90). Such ancient Chinese double serpents also have an arched body, scroll noses, parallel rows of teeth in profile, and clawed feet, as in the stele illustrated. In other Wei steles the serpent's body twists over the top of the sculpture like a rope, perhaps the far away origin of the rows of scales along the shoulder edges of Dick Price's Sisiutl.

The Wei serpents possess none of the Sisiutl's dramatic impact. To compare one with the other is like contrasting a domesticated chimera with a wild boa constrictor. But the chameleon-like transformation is present in both, subordinated to a Buddhist humanistic concept on one hand and presented with naked animalism on the other. In Kwakiutl Indian art the oriental double-headed serpent survived, and its venerable Chinese parallel negates, so far, any other known source in the New or Old World. When it is realized that the double serpent can be traced further back to the gate-protective Makara of India and was in Wei-period China already an appropriation, its presence in the 1920s on Vancouver Island strikes us as miraculous. Its forceful and purely animistic presence makes pale, adulterated survivals of the pagan gods in Western civilization.

An equally fascinating parallel is provided by an ancient Chinese sculpture of lacquered wood, so far unique, unearthed after the second World War in the Ch'u state tombs at Hsin-Yang (Honan) (fig. 91). Compare it with a 19th century Haida carved wood bowl depicting a beaver (fig. 92). In Haida work the beaver identification is strong and clear, because of the volumetric character and incisive handling of the carving by the artist. The beaver is always depicted holding a stick in

90 Buddhist sandstone stele, Northern Wei Dynasty, ca 520, The Nelson Gallery of Art

91 Horned animal of lacquered wood, excavated at Ch'ang-Tsi-Kuan, Hsin-Yang District, Honan

his mouth, its ends supported by outstretched paws. The two upper incisors are enlarged. The beaver pose appears frozen, as if locked in time and space. Indeed the pose is an ancient, oriental one, as the horned animal clearly attests (fig. 91). By the time of the Warring States (481-221 B.C.) it was already a stereotype. In the Chinese sculpture a snake is being eaten, but the paws hold it exactly like a stick, and the tongue seems about to retract into protruding teeth. There is forebearance which stresses ritual over naturalism. Here again there are no other New World parallels.

Of course the differences are as revealing as the similarities. The characteristic Northwest Coast eye and eyebrow form, so prominent in the Haida bowl, are not present in ancient Chinese art. The technique of the Chinese carving is less geometric and, though both appear to belong to the same sculptural tradition, there is not here any question of a direct line of influence, considering the enormous time lag. The Warring States animal was not known at the time the bowl was carved. No one would call the Haida bowl anything other than an indigenous work. Rather, we must postulate a transmittal of the guardian animal in eating pose from South China to the Pacific via Indonesia and Melanesia in several distinct but unknown stages, and finally to the Northwest Coast side of the Pacific Basin — there to crop up like a ghost to haunt our misty vision of the origins of Northwest Coast art.

The Indian snake or Makara was an architectural feature on the four gates of the Sanchi Stupa, as Nelson Wu has pointed out (fig. 93).[3] This architectonic interpretation was reduced to a two-dimensional emblem in the later Chinese Buddhist stele. Therefore one might suppose the architectural function of the snake to have been completely suppressed long before its re-emergence on the Coast. Extraordinarily enough, this is not the case. A number of Kwakiutl plank houses depicted by the Canadian artist Emily Carr early in this century displayed a Sisiutl entablature carried across the top of the facade supported by as many as four uprights, so that the house front was in effect a filled-in architectural gate (fig. 94). In the Kwakiutl graveyard at Fort Rupert there actually existed a giant freestanding weathered Sisiutl cantilevered from three carved posts, with tongues protruding from the terminal serpents rather like the upturned ends of a Japanese tori gate (fig. 95). Another existed, freestanding, with a curvature to the serpent's body that returned to the arched profile of the Wei type stele niche surround. In these cases the snake-monster reverts to the generalized protective role which it played during its mythic beginnings, existing in graveyard markers as a continuum apart from specific Sisiutl legends, which varied markedly from one locale to another.

Japanese sculpture contributes an indication of the source of a prominent Northwest Coast feature in costuming: the wearing of projecting animal headdresses, carved of wood and

92 Haida wood bowl, 19th century

93 Sanchi stone stupa, East Gate, 1st century B.C.

embellished with paint, abalone shell and felt. In the southern part of the Coast, sea wolf masks were worn which projected forward over the forehead. There is a whole class of these objects, including several collected by Captain Cook on Vancouver Island, and many more recent examples. In more northerly reaches a sophisticated type of clan hat occurred, particularly among the Tlingit and Tsimshian. Figure 96 shows such a clan hat as an integral part of a costume (projecting above a human face as apex to a ceremonial panoply); figure 153 illustrates it as a separate piece of sculpture. A dry lacquer sculpture from Nara (Asaka period, 7th century A.D.) depicting a kingly attendant of the god of healing (Yakashi), is one of a set of similar Buddhist kings, some of whom have animal headdresses (fig. 97). An elephant, with trunk partly missing, surmounts the head like a helmet. Since the elephant was traditionally a symbol of strength, the wearing of animal crests on the Northwest Coast would also seem related to the old idea of power protectivity.

Such an origin encourages looking to Siberian ethnology, especially among the tribes on the Amur River north of Manchuria, for a means of transmittal of art types to the Northwest Coast. (By "type" is meant a basic form of mask, furniture, or pictorial convention.) Undoubtedly there are links, and further study of them is needed, but on the whole there is less concordance than one might suspect. There is, however, a trencher used at feasts, here called the "canoe" type, which can be found both among the historical Siberian Gilyak and the Tlingit of the Alaskan Panhandle. It consists of a hollowed-out "hull" with decorated flanges at bow and stern. The Gilyak examples are more box-like and are decorated with motifs also found on this tribe's vestments. The Tlingit ones are more gracefully shaped with the suggestion of the flare of a canoe's hull, and decorated with animal crests, traditionally a brown bear. Nowhere else on the Coast does one find this particular type of canoe trencher — only with the northernmost tribe. A fairly

94 Double-headed Sisiutl of the Kwakiutl, by Emily Carr (after Barbeau), 1912, National Museum of Canada

95 Sisiutl wood carving from Fort Rupert graveyard

96 Tsimshian clan hat worn as part of ceremonial costume   cat no 453

97 Nara, hollow lacquer Deva King, 7th century

recent cultural contact might be suggested here, indicative of a process perhaps often repeated in the past, with the roots going back to Asiatic spirit-canoe shamanism.

Tlingit armor also shows affinities with the slat armor complex found in Japanese depictions on clay Haniwa tomb figures (4th to 6th century A.D.) but used as late as the Edo period. A Tlingit suit at Leningrad, collected in part between 1839 and 1845, has more affinity with the armor shown on proto-historic Haniwa models and the iron suit uncovered at Nagamochayama, Osaka prefecture (figs. 98, 99) than with Imperial Edo pieces, suggesting that the Tlingit war costumes are wooden skeomorphs of the ancient Japanese iron-leather slat armor rather than a fairly recent development. Here the root must have been broken off early, to develop independently. The evil spirit head and neck protectors of the Tlingit armor hark back to Haniwa helmets which also had fish and animal designs indicating rank. It is fascinating to think that the Tlingit defenders of the site of present-day Sitka, who expelled the Russians in 1804, were wearing slat armor of an Asiatic tradition older than anything the "Asiatic" invaders could comprehend.

Of course it is important to cite ways of change as well as connections so that parallels are kept in proportion. Over the centuries the Northwest Coast has been influenced by phenomena of change, among them intermarriage and intercoastal travel. Can these affect an area's art style? In the case of about eight turn-of-this-century Chilkat blankets woven by the Tongass Tlingit Mrs. Mary Hunt, after her marriage into the Kwakiutl Hunts of Fort Rupert, the evidence is clearly affirmative (fig. 118). Mrs. Hunt took her pattern board with her and set up her loom far to the south. But her textiles, which exactly follow Chilkat design, abandoned the set coloration of cream yellow, pale blue, natural, and black in favor of the bright green, yellow, and reds of the highly expressionistic Kwakiutl mask paints, giving them something of the vibrant contrast of the colors of Dick Price's Sisiutl. The result is an unexpectedly offbeat Chilkat-Kwakiutl wearing blanket. One can only speculate how much style has been altered in the past by travel and interchange along the Coast. (Frederick Dockstader cites the case of a partly Hawaiian Haida figure in his pictorial survey of American Indian art.)[4] Again we confront the specter of sea contacts. As the 19th century brought the China-Pacific trade to the front door of these Indians, as they in turn canoed from the Queen Charlotte Islands and Alaskan villages to Europeanized settlements such as Victoria, B.C., it is little wonder that they took advantage of iron tools, commercial paint (trade vermilion is found on masks of the 1840-50 period) and varnish, as well as sheet copper and trade cloth. Their art became acculturated, influenced from without.

Acculturation is a term usually used to indicate debasement of an American Indian style. One can wonder, however, if the Indians of the Coast do not enjoy the last laugh in this matter. In the first place, their styles, however traditional, do have eclectic roots, and I suspect an adaptive or imitative facility (an Asian characteristic) was part of their creativity. Trading was always part of their life, both material and ceremonial. The export art of argillite carving among the Haida, produced from the 1820s on and still intact today at Skidegate, was increasingly less influenced by Russian-American sailor motifs and became totally "native" in inspiration as time went on. This reverse acculturation appears to be a highly compressed version of what happened to Asiatic prototypes as they developed according to tribal usage.

In historical times the Coastal artist has made intelligent use of new materials and ideas. He was discriminating in using outside sources, taking exactly what suited; the results were often creative and are considered "Indian" today. All was not lost with the coming of the white man, despite the considerable attrition caused by misguided administrative and religious zealots. After all, Kwakiutl carving of large-scale masks reached its apogee in the 1920s, after the totem poles of the Haida villages had been largely decimated. Belief in traditional ways is shrinking, but the artistic strain survives in a very healthy condition in the work of artists Dan Cranmer, Joseph Seaweed, Rufus Moody, Bill Reid and others. Even with unsympathetic conditions, the survival mechanism persists today as it did in the time of tribal hegemony.

Consider the following comparison: of two Northwest Coast carved seats, one traditional in shape and one shaped after a Europeanized example, both carved long ago — which is really superior (figs. 100, 101)? One, a backrest, has time-honored conventions painted upon it, including a hawk with beaver tail cross-hatching. In the other, the silhouette of a European chair replaces the traditional backrest and a beaver tail is substituted for the splat (originally derived from Chinese furniture). A beaver is spreadeagled in relief upon the seat with incisors and mouth carried over the front edge. While one cannot deny the efficacy of the pristine backrest, one cannot help but applaud the imagination and vigor of the aberrant chair, with its ingenious handling of imagery. The acculturated chair is also every inch a product for Indians, and it represents the ability to cope with new ideas. Northwest Coast art was not static despite its traditionalism.

Among the factors influencing art of the historical period was Indian art from the interior. Ironically enough, while this influence was not transmitted by whites, the designs in question were based on floral patterns perhaps initially taught to Woodland Indians, far away to the east, by French nuns, or grafted onto an earlier tradition.[5] As late as 1966, at a major American Indian art exhibition at Cologne, a floral beaded "octopus" bag, as these pieces are familiarly called, was labeled Cree. The distribution of this type of pouch has not so far been defined. An example, on exhibition at the Jefferson Memorial, Saint Louis, was collected by Henry Lewis on a voyage up the Missouri in 1848. The Lewis piece has beaded designs that recall Great Lakes type motifs. Many examples of this type of pouch are actually from the interior behind the Northwest Coast and are found among the Thalton (fig. 10). These floral bags explain how botanical elements intrude into the beadwork borders of Tlingit ceremonial costumes. In fact, the bags themselves were imported into the Coast proper and worn as chest adornments by chiefs, as old photographs attest.[6] Tlingit shaman's collars (fig. 102) were ornamented in such a way that flower patterns at times almost destroy the bilateralism. At the University of Kansas Museum of Anthropology there is a Tlingit felt and beaded panel in which floral patterns mingle with a killer whale motif, a veritable marriage of a Woodland pattern with the sea mythology

98 Tlingit armor of wooden slats, Museum of Anthropology and Ethnography at the Leningrad Academy of Sciences

99 Haniwa armored clay figure, late Tomb Period, from Kuai, Nitta County, Gumma, Tokyo National Museum

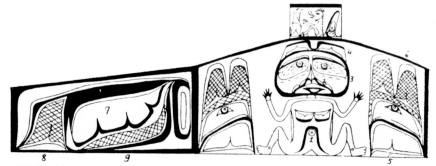

100 Kwakiutl settee, cross section drawing (after Boas)

101 Haida painted wood seat

of immemorial derivation. In general, however, floral beadwork is intrusive in the Northwest Coast and confined to somewhat peripheral aspects of costume. This fact emphasizes the dominance of the original Asiatic-derived art style as the foundation upon which all subsequent development rests, until the footings were all but submerged.

We have only spot-checked possible sources and their interaction. How many oriental traditions must have remained unknown to these people on their remote coast? How many others were merged into new identities along the way? The evidence is scattered, incomplete, fragmented and of inconsistent stages with regard to acculturation and stylistic evolution. The whole problem is extremely complex. We have not even dealt with parallels elsewhere, such as the association of a three-faced serpent with Inca kingship, or concurrences elsewhere in North America. In back of it all resides a world view that was truly cosmological in its acceptance of animal as the guardian and mentor to man's relationship to natural forces. It also serves as a warning to those who admire Indian art because it is merely novel in their experience or because of guilt associations concerning white appropriation of the Indian's land. We cannot set aside past abuses. Neither should we neglect the world view implicit in the original sources, let alone the giant act of acclimatization engendered by the interchanges and positive reactions which have obtained in Northwest Coast and other Amerindian arts. When Indian art is no longer "new" to public taste these enduring values will remain.

(1) Geldern, Robert Heine, "Chinese Culture in the Pacific and in America" (lecture at the Viking Fund, 1949, New York). See Miguel Covarrubias, *The Eagle, the Jaguar, and the Serpent* (vol I), Alfred A. Knopf, 1954, pp 189, 190, for a list of Asiatic and Pacific traits in Northwest Coast art. Carl Schuster, "Joint-marks, a possible index of cultural contact between America, Oceania and the Far East," Med. XCLV, *Afdeling Culturele en Physische Antropologie,* no 39, Amsterdam, Koninklijl Instituut voor de Trpen, 1951.

(2) Holm, Bill, *Northwest Coast Indian Art, an Analysis of Form,* University of Washington Press, 1965, particularly chapter on "Elements of the Art," pp 26 ff.

(3) Wu, Nelson, unpublished material given in lecture form. Makara also appear at Borobudur, Java.

(4) Dockstader, Frederick, *Indian Art in America,* New York Graphic Society, 1961, note accompanying illustration number 80.

(5) Ritzenthaler, Robert E. and Pat, *The Woodland Indians of the Western Great Lakes,* The Natural History Press, 1970, p 74, for a short discussion on the problem of the antiquity of floral patterns in Woodland Indian art.

(6) See Andrews, Ralph W., *Indian Primitive,* Bonanza Books, 1960, illus, pp 97, 101.

Ralph T. Coe is Assistant Director, William Rockhill Nelson Gallery of Art, Kansas City, Missouri. Mr. Coe's interests include painting, architecture, primitive art and ethnology. In 1962 he organized "The Imagination of Primitive Man," an exhibition tracing the stylistic evolution of the non-literate peoples of the world, and this year prepared an American Indian art exhibition, "Indian Art Comes of Age," for the Nelson Gallery.

102 Tlingit beaded cloth collar

103 Eskimo carved and painted wood shaman's mask — represents the sun, moon and helping dog spirits

(LM/UC/B cat no 2-4603)

Eskimo Sculpture

Dorothy Jean Ray

Eskimos have created some of the world's most unusual art, a word that does not exist in their language because the making of beautiful objects was intertwined with all aspects of their lives, especially religion, ceremonialism and magic. They made objects to honor or to personify numerous spirits and deities in an effort to lessen anxiety toward the unknown universe and to assure their well being and safety in a vast, often unpredictable environment.

Some sculptures, like dolls and uniquely shaped household items, were made for the joy of creating, but the bulk of traditional Eskimo art was religious. (Even many of the dolls belonged to the shaman.) Though we cannot ascertain the uses of prehistoric objects classified as "unidentified," we fortunately know enough about ceremonial objects of 19th century Alaska to believe that they had comparable uses. Based on ideas that he had received during visions and dreams, the Alaskan angutkuk (medicine man or shaman) made masks, house and boat protectors in bird and animal shapes, and painted designs on wooden dishes, trays and spoons, for religious or magical purposes.

Included in the term Eskimo art are decorated and sculptured objects made by numerous tribes from Greenland to East Cape, Siberia. They represented varied ways of life and covered a time span of roughly 3,000 years (although Eskimo culture may be 5,000 years old). Our knowledge of prehistoric art depends upon the success of archeologists in finding sites in this vast area; yet the sampling so far has revealed that the most active artists, those who made the largest number of sculptures and conceived the most intriguing forms, lived in the western Eskimo area. From St. Lawrence Island came ornamented "winged objects" and harpoon heads that look like bird beaks in the Okvik and Old Bering Sea periods; from Point Hope, the abstract sculptures of the Ipiutak culture; and from various places in northern Alaska and at Cape Denbigh, the many figurines of the Nukleet and Thule periods, the latter extending into historical times. The huge Canadian Arctic has produced nothing comparable, although there is a distinctive style of human and animal sculpture in the Dorset period in Eastern Canada, represented by only about 115 objects in a million square mile area.[1]

The 18th and 19th century peoples of Canada, who were the direct descendants of the Thule people, apparently had little inclination toward producing art. This has also been said — erroneously — of their contemporaneous relatives in Northern Alaska. Numerous ivory, bone and wooden sculptures used in connection with whale, seal and caribou hunting and ceremonials, and attached to everyday utensils, have come to light in many museum and private collections, which represent hundreds of pounds of carved walrus ivory, much of it purchased from Eskimos who had looted their own sites to sell to northern travelers as long ago as the 1880s and 1890s.

An interesting point about the most plentiful and best art of pre-19th century sites is that metal tools apparently were used; at least, small pieces of iron were found in all such sites. There may be a relationship between the eastward spread of metal from its Asiatic origin to American Eskimo tribes, and the more abundant and technically superior objects of the Western Alaskan Eskimos. Later on, of course, from the early 1700s, knives and other tools were systematically traded from Siberia across the Bering Strait. It cannot be denied that the use of metal tools enabled artists to make more objects with greater efficiency, but the possession of good tools, or even metal, did not necessarily mean there would be a development of art.

The small size of both prehistoric and historic sculptures has been stressed repeatedly in writings about Eskimos, some authors emphasizing the nomadic character of Eskimo life as a reason for the portable character of amulets and similar carvings. Others have considered that the small size of these objects resulted from limitations of their raw materials — walrus ivory, bone and wood. Although both reasons undoubtedly restricted the size of some objects, I think that the determining factor was the function of the object, and was therefore a preferential, cultural factor. For example, the Northern Canadian Eskimos, who moved around the most, made comparatively few sculptures; yet the Western Alaskan Eskimos who lived in permanent winter villages and moved to seasonal camps only at certain times of the year, made a dazzling array of small ivory objects. These same Alaskan Eskimos also made masks, massive memorial monuments, and huge ceremonial dishes from driftwood that had piled high on their treeless rivers and ocean shores. They took many of their small objects with them to the camps, but stored the wooden ceremonial ones in their winter villages. (At Point Hope, a cache of 50 wooden masks, dating from the 19th century, was found under the planks of a dance house.)[2]

Walrus ivory, of course, limits the size of an object, since tusks are rarely more than 36 inches in length, but the Eskimo craftsman was selective about his material: he chose ivory for a specific purpose and use, and wood when he wanted larger sculptures. Certain ivory objects in the shape of birds, fish and animals were made small because they had to be small: they were hung on clothing as amulets or fastened to boats, tents and permanent dwellings as spiritual protectors, or were used as bucket handles, belt fasteners, float plugs, needle cases and the like, some with a magical purpose. The most durable, beautiful and easily carved pieces of driftwood were sought on the beaches for larger sculptures. Sometimes river driftwood, which was not impregnated with salt, was traded to people living on the coast. It would be more accurate to say that the Eskimo artist worked within the limitations of his tools and the uses for his objects, than within the limitations of his materials and his subsistence routine. However, the relative absence of prehistoric and early historic art in Canada and Greenland may well have been the sum of all these restrictions.

The lack of efficient metal tools probably accounts for the comparatively small number of masks found in early 19th century Eskimo sites — it cannot be attributed entirely to poor preservation because pieces of wood have been preserved in many older sites, including the Dorset of Canada. It has been assumed that Eskimos learned mask-making from the Northwest Coast Indians, but since there is no evidence of mask-making by the Indians in prehistoric times, it is possible that the borrowing may have been in the other direction, or more likely, that each grew independently.

A very poetic, but completely unrealistic assumption espoused by some writers about Canadian Eskimos is that the art objects were involuntary, self-generating creations, that arose entirely from

104 Eskimo carved wood mask, Point Hope, early 20th century (LM/UC/B cat no 2-29415)

the form of the material without a plan. According to this notion the artist did not impose an idea on the material, but the subject and shape spontaneously came to life in the carver's hands with no reason but "to be." From explorers' records and the Eskimos' own traditions, we know that all objects had definite purposes, and were made, not because the material held prisoner a seal or a walrus, but because the carver found it necessary to transform a religious, spiritual, or practical idea into visual form. Masks and many wooden sculptures of ordinary or legendary figures were made according to a shaman's exact specifications, often for his own use. An idea was transformed into art regardless of the material, although a mask-maker would often choose a piece of wood with unusual grain, color, or shape to enhance the meaning and form. Perhaps this self-generating theory has been confused with the fact that every Eskimo artist has to make a choice of subject matter from his own experience for a specific piece of stone or ivory. Being a practical man — as has been demonstrated throughout Eskimo history — the carver tried to use a piece best adapted to his chosen subject. In other words, he imposed his practicality onto the material, rather than the other way around. In Alaska, carvers have "released" infinite numbers of subjects from walrus ivory, a monotonous and sometimes very stubborn substance, because their ideas took precedence over the material.

Eskimo masks were used principally in religious ceremonies that honored and propitiated the spirits of game animals and tutelaries (personal helping spirits) to assure hunting success. These unique sculptures, surely some of the most imaginative in the world, were the embodiment of a shaman's vision, each mask different from

another because of the almost infinite variety of visions from shaman to shaman and village to village. In Eskimo cosmology, almost every object, animate or inanimate, possessed a spirit; thus, a blade of beach grass, a rock, or a walrus could be the whole subject or a portion of a mask, vastly extending the range of creative possibilities. Masks were extremely complicated both conceptually and formally in one of their favorite forms, the depiction of an angutkuk's trip to the spirit world. In such a mask, the shaman reported his experiences for re-enactment in a public dance honoring the various spirits carved symbolically into the mask. Separate objects attached to, or painted on the mask represented the spirits of game animals feted at the ceremony, the shaman's tutelary, or the spirits of his dogs, his kayak, and the hunting implements taken along on the journey. Since all animals had the ability to change into a human being at will, the masks were often made as an animal-human face to show the human part of a spirit. This duality was not only rooted in tradition — there are many half-men/half-animal beings in folktales — but it permitted the angutkuk to converse freely and with credibility to the spirits — man to man.

Many of the masks were great works of art, ranging from free forms to realistic human portraits or animal faces, and from small ones fitting only part of the wearer's face to large ones almost four feet high, which were hung from the ceiling. They were usually carved by the shaman who had conceived the idea, but if he was not a good carver, he employed a more skillful carver to make it within the style that had developed in each village. Masks north of St. Michael were made more simply than those south of it, although the variety of forms at Point Hope and King Island was extensive. The making of masks permitted the artist to soar to imaginative heights, and though some masks were made with a disregard for artistic quality, the majority of carvers strove for a well-finished product, and delighted in using red, white, black and blue earth paints in various combinations, and numerous auxiliary decorations — feathers, hoops, fur, rawhide, stones, bird-beaks and claws, ivory figurines, baleen (whalebone), pieces of metal, wood — for percussion effect or to add movement to the mask's more or less static quality.

Some of the masks have been called grotesque, and indeed, the distorted facial configurations associated with certain supernatural beings or spirits do look grotesque in daylight or in the artificial light of a museum, but in the wavering dimness of a seal oil lamp or wood fire, accompanied by drumming, singing, and appropriate gestures, masks fit the mood for which they were made.

Almost every mask, wooden figurine, or ivory amulet, and the designs on hunting implements, were fashioned to influence specific spirits and therefore one of the important aspects of religious art was the effort to create as esthetically pleasing an object as possible. George Swinton, Canadian painter and art critic, who has described and analyzed Canadian Eskimo soapstone sculpture,[3] has argued that an object can be appreciated without knowing what it meant to the artist or his culture, and that its meaning to the carver was irrelevant to its appraisal as a work of art. (He later somewhat modified this stand in an article where he attributed almost all of Dorset art to the shaman.)[4] Although an object can be enjoyed as a piece of sculpture according to non-Eskimo standards, the beauty,

105 Eskimo carved and painted wood mask with feathers, St. Michael (LM/UC/B cat no 2-6918)

strength and imagery of objects like masks are enhanced by knowing their ceremonial meaning and role in the lives of both artist and performer. It seems impossible that the meaning of a mask — or any other ceremonial object — would have been irrelevant to the carver or shaman in view of his total preoccupation with making it acceptable to a spirit. The meaning of the object would have had considerable influence in guiding the artist toward making the best form that would permit him — an Eskimo intermediary living in a precarious subsistence economy — to bring about a liaison with important spirits that controlled the food supply and even the universe. Meaning in that case was not only tantamount to its success as a piece of art, but to life and death as well.

The well-worn statement that traditional Eskimo sculptures were made to be viewed from all angles was only partly true. A mask was made and worn so that the audience could not see the back, although markings were occasionally made on the reverse side for a spirit's benefit. Hundreds of other ivory objects, like birds and animals, were also made with a flat base, which was obscured when attached to containers, hunting visors, skin boats and kayaks.

Traditional Eskimo sculptures are no longer made within a religious or magical framework, but Eskimo sculptors continue to produce new art for a commercial market. The most striking and best known today is the soapstone sculpture from various northern Canadian villages around Hudson Bay and Baffin Bay. Their material and often massive size have set them apart from other Eskimo art since the beginning of their production in 1948 when a new arts program was inaugurated to increase the Eskimos' economic self-sufficiency. The results of this program exceeded all hopes. The pieces are known throughout the world, and many sculptures of subjects traditionally belonging to Eskimo life exemplify the age-old Eskimo proclivity for adaption, reinterpretation and perception. Over the years, the themes, styles and forms have become as varied as the masks of the Alaskan Eskimos, though they are more realistic in form, and of course, are made by anyone who now wants to carve; even women are participating in a heretofore traditionally male activity.

These soapstone objects have overpowered the small ivory sculptures of the Northern Alaskan Eskimos, a style begun during the 1920s. The ivory sculptures, like those of soapstone, originated from and have been nurtured by suggestions from the white man, a fact that considerably upsets the "purists" who do not consider it real "Eskimo art." What they do not know is that Eskimo art has been influenced to a direct degree by the white man since the middle of the 1800s (metal tools were used long before that), and many "traditional" objects collected during the 19th century were made to sell after the enterprising Eskimos saw the ships' officers and sailors eagerly snapping up their objects as souvenirs. The art of the 1970s is Eskimo art as much as the 19th century pieces, or the art of prehistory, because the carver is still an Eskimo, speaking his own language, and living as an Eskimo of his time.

The Northern Alaskan Eskimo carver has often been criticized as being a carver of souvenirs, and in studying "Eskimo art" critics have passed by the small animal, bird and human sculptures with no more than a superficial glance. The realistic forms and

106 Eskimo carved and painted wood mask with feathers   cat no 628

107 Eskimo carved and painted wood mask (LM/UC/B cat no 2-6474)

108 Eskimo carved and painted wood mask, may be from Nushagak (LM/UC/B cat no 2-4584)

the smooth, polished finish have also blinded many critics (who want to keep Eskimo art a "primitive art" or who want it to be something altogether different) to the fact that hundreds of these figurines are powerful interpretations of their subject matter, and actually are far from realistic. The prolific production over the years has also led many to think of this sculpture as merely copy work. The Eskimos of Siberia and Greenland, producing similar sculptures, are faced with the same criticisms. To be sure, a carver's bears, foxes and human figures begin to take on a look-alike mien, but it is repetition, not copying, because every object is conceived anew in the carver's mind. He creates each sculpture without a model and without any plan or drawing except a few pencil marks to indicate proportions. Even the imaginative, bizarre "tupilaks" of East Greenland fail to satisfy the critics. Tupilaks were made as concrete models of traditional tutelaries for Europeans who asked to see what these spirits looked like, and they have been repeated over and over since then. This figure is not to be confused with the Alaskan billiken, which was copied in ivory in 1909 from an "ornamental design" patented on October 6, 1908 by a Kansas City art teacher as a good luck figurine. All carvers hate to make billikens, which are still made along the lines of the original figure, but a man must eat, and billikens emerge when nothing else can be coaxed from bits of ivory.

In the 1970s probably more Eskimos are producing works of art — or at least creating objects for esthetic reasons — than ever before in their history. Not every man can create the best, but in Eskimo culture skillful craftsmen proportionately exceed those coming from almost any other area. In the ever-changing world, Eskimo sculpture is performing a function similar to that of more traditional days, but with a greater participation for all, not just the experts, in invoking forms and designs from their life, to keep step with their world in which preservation in a new economy is as important as it was in the uncertain world of spirits in a quixotic land. Their art is a response to life and a preserving influence in Eskimo culture, a record of the 20th century, another period in Eskimo history.

(1) Taylor, William E., Jr., "Prehistoric Dorset Art: The Silent Echoes of Culture," The Beaver, Autumn, Outfit 298, 1967, pp 36, 38.

(2) Rainey, Froelich G., "The Vanishing Art of the Arctic," Expedition Okvik, Old Bering Sea, and Ipiutak Art, 1959, vol 1 no 2, p 11.

(3) Swinton, George, Eskimo Sculpture, Toronto, Montreal, McClelland and Stewart, Ltd., 1965.

(4) Swinton, George, "Prehistoric Dorset Art: The Magico-Religious Basis," The Beaver, Autumn, Outfit 298, p 39.

Dorothy Jean Ray has written many professional papers on the history and art of the Eskimo — her principal publications include: Artists of the Tundra and the Sea, 1961; Eskimo Masks: Art and Ceremony, 1967; and Graphic Arts of the Alaskan Eskimo. (See Bibliography, this catalogue.) She is presently serving as a consultant and editor for various anthropological studies.

The objects in this section of illustrations are arranged in the same sequence as the Catalogue of the Exhibition (see p 117).

109 Delaware beaded hide bandoleer bag

cat no 2

111 Chitimacha split cane twilled baskets and covers

cat nos 57, 58, 59

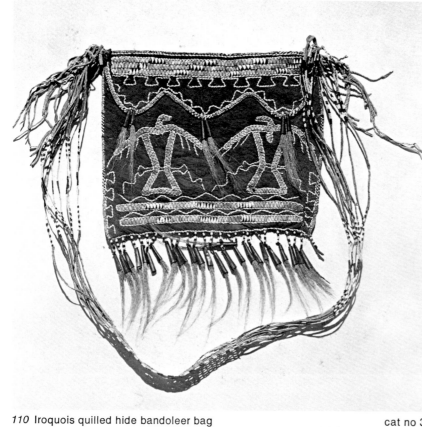

110 Iroquois quilled hide bandoleer bag

cat no 3

112 Apache (Western) coiled willow basket

cat no 62

113 Luiseno or Cahuilla willow basket tray   cat no 84

115 Tulare willow basket   cat no 91

114 Pomo willow basket with feathers and shells   cat no 88

116 Skokomish twined basket   cat no 81

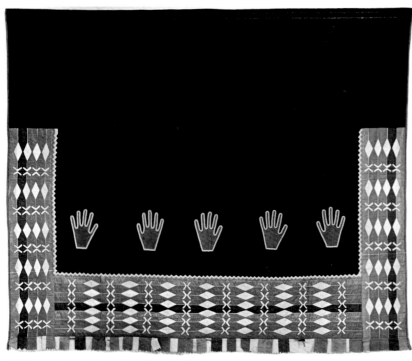

117 Osage beaded and appliqued blanket   cat no 109

119 Kaskaskia carved wood beaver bowl   cat no 139

118 Tlingit (Chilkat) blanket   cat no 136

120 Haida carved wood dish   cat no 150

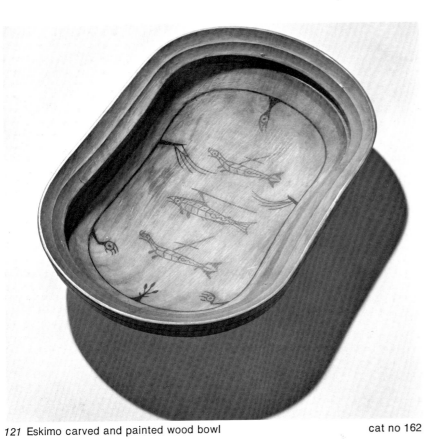

121 Eskimo carved and painted wood bowl   cat no 162

123 Tlingit carved and painted wood chest   cat no 180

122 Huron quilled birchbark box   cat no 164

124 Delaware housepost (longhouse centerpost)   cat no 182

125 Pueblo (Zuni) stone bear fetish   cat no 196

126 Pueblo (Zuni) carved wood war god   cat no 193

127 Haida carved and painted chief's seat   cat no 209

128 Kwakiutl carved and painted wood figure   cat no 211

129 Kwakiutl carved wood potlatch figure   cat no 217

131 Nootka painted wood screen   cat no 220

130 Kwakiutl painted wood puppet   cat no 219

132 Eskimo carved ivory drum handle   cat no 743

133 Sioux rawhide cutout   cat no 238

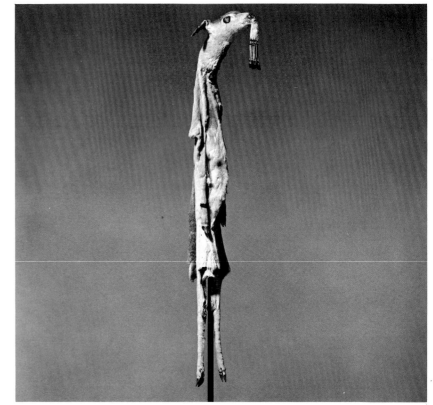

135 Yurok ceremonial staff   cat no 260

134 Pueblo (Hopi) dance wands   cat nos 244, 253, 255

136 Tlingit painted ceremonial copper   cat no 266

137 Micmac chief's coat   cat no 280

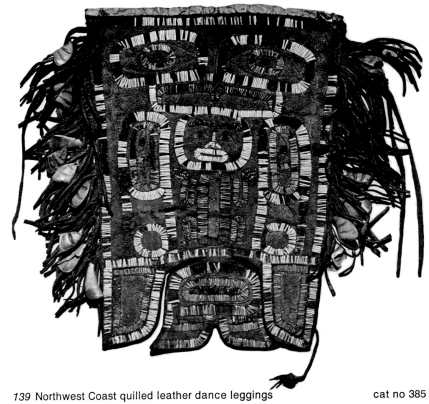

139 Northwest Coast quilled leather dance leggings   cat no 385

138 Sioux girl's beaded dress   cat no 341

140 Pueblo (Hopi) manta   cat no 374

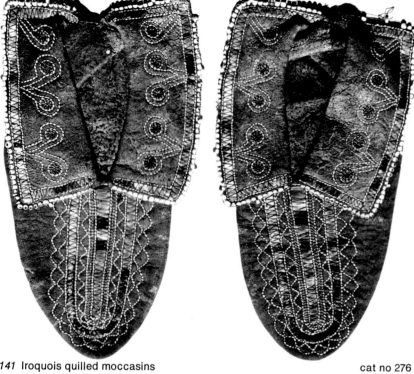

141 Iroquois quilled moccasins   cat no 276

143 Menomini beaded sash   cat no 279

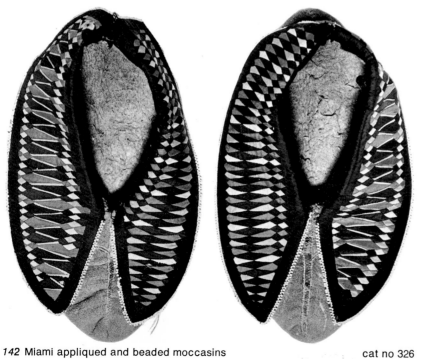

142 Miami appliqued and beaded moccasins   cat no 326

144 Pueblo (Acoma) shawl   cat no 369

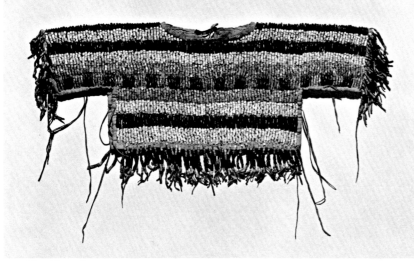

145 Blackfeet dance cape   cat no 295

147 Sioux beaded buckskin vest   cat no 364

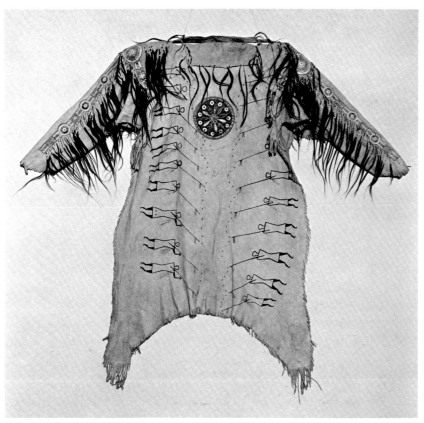

146 Crow buckskin shirt   cat no 316

148 Cocopa painted terra cotta doll   cat no 411

149 Sioux feather headdress   cat no 417

151 Pomo woman's ceremonial feather headdress   cat no 426

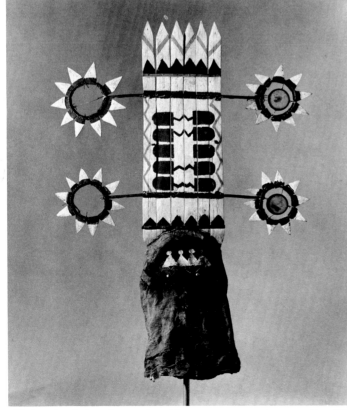

150 Apache Gahan Dancer headdress   cat no 418

152 Haida painted wood clan helmet   cat no 434

153 Tsimshian clan hat   cat no 453

155 Sioux painted buffalo robe   cat no 465

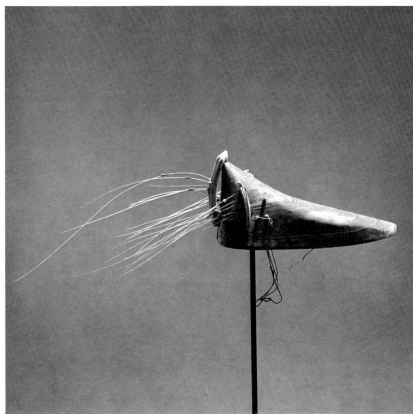
154 Aleut man's painted wood hat   cat no 458

156 Pueblo (Hopi) humming bird kachina   cat no 484

157 Pueblo (Zuni) shalako kachina   cat no 523

159 Tlingit carved and painted mask   cat no 612

158 Northwest Coast carved wood helmet   cat no 456

160 Eskimo mask/seal decoy   cat no 622

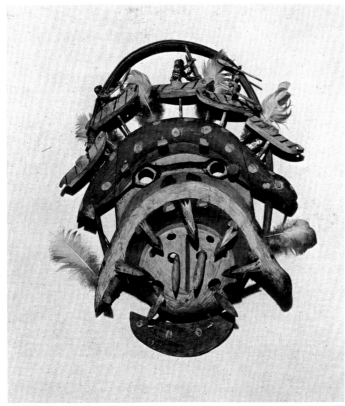

161 Eskimo (Kashunak) dance mask   cat no 631

163 Cherokee gourd mask   cat no 559

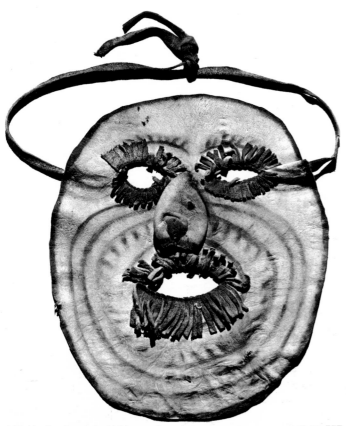

162 Naskapi painted hide mask   cat no 557

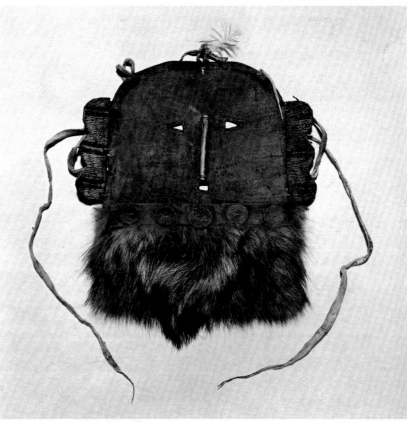

164 Navajo painted hide mask   cat no 563

111

165 Kwakiutl wild man of the woods mask   cat no 591

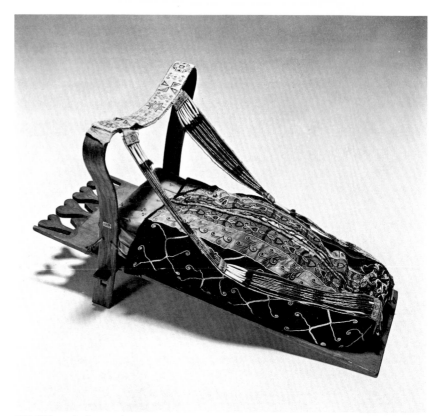

167 Ojibwa baby carrier   cat no 637

166 Nootka carved and painted wood mask   cat no 599

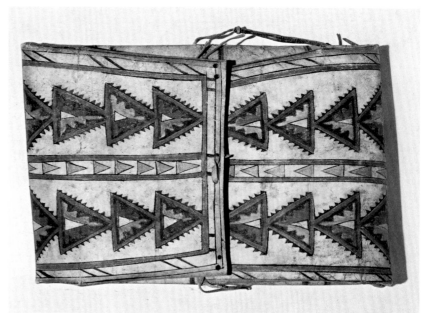

168 Plateau painted rawhide parfleche   cat no 674

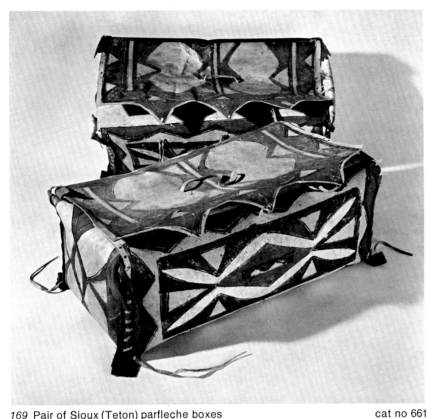

169 Pair of Sioux (Teton) parfleche boxes   cat no 661

171 Haida carved horn ladle   cat no 692

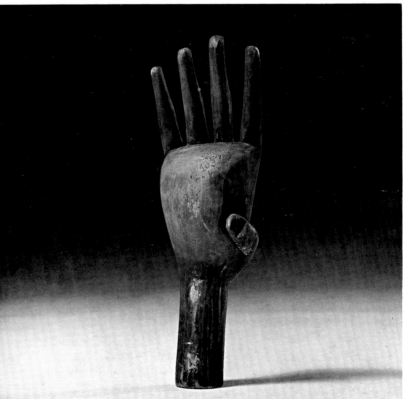

170 Menomini man's saddle   cat no 636

172 Iroquois (Seneca) carved wood rattle   cat no 714

173 Tlingit (Chilkat) double-face rattle   cat no 732

175 Sioux muslin pictograph   cat no 747

174 Alaskan or British Columbian crane rattle   cat no 741

176 Sioux ledger drawing   cat no 751

177 Pueblo (Acoma) painted pot   cat no 786

179 Great Lakes carved wood war club   cat no 826

178 Pueblo (Hopi) painted pot by Nampeyo   cat no 791

180 Haida carved wood fish club
cat no 691

181 Tlingit iron and ivory fighting knife
cat no 850

115

182 Arapaho Ghost Dance shirt

cat no 293

Catalogue of the Exhibition

Names of lenders appear on the last line of each entry, and are abbreviated as follows:

The American Museum of Natural History (AMNH)
The Brooklyn Museum (BM)
Ralph T. Coe (COE)
Cranbrook Institute of Science (CIS)
Earle De Laittre (DE LAITTRE)
Carl S. Dentzel (DENTZEL)
The Denver Art Museum (DAM)
Field Museum of Natural History (FMNH)
The Heard Museum (HM)
E. Adamson Hoebel (HOEBEL)
Joslyn Art Museum (JAM)
Logan Museum of Anthropolgy, Beloit College (LMA/BC)
Lowie Museum, University of California, Berkeley (LM/UC/B)
Milwaukee Public Museum (MPM)
The Minneapolis Institute of Arts (MIA)
Minnesota Historical Society Museum (MHSM)
Museum of Cultural History, University of California, Los Angeles (MCH/UC/LA)
Museum of New Mexico (MNM)
Museum of Northern Arizona (MNA)
The Museum of Primitive Art (MPA)
Museum of the American Indian, Heye Foundation (MAI/HF)
National Museum of Man (NMM)
National Museum of Natural History, Smithsonian Institution (NMNH/SI)
Nebraska State Historical Society (NSHS)
The W. H. Over Dakota Museum (ODM)
Peabody Museum, Harvard University (PM/HU)
Peabody Museum (PM)
Philbrook Art Center (PAC)
Royal Ontario Museum (ROM)
The Science Museum of Minnesota (SMM)
Mr. and Mrs. Morton I. Sosland (SOSLAND)
Southwest Museum (SM)
The State Historical Society of Wisconsin (SHSW)
The Taylor Museum, Colorado Springs Fine Arts Center (TM/CSFAC)
Betty Toulouse (TOULOUSE)
The University Museum, University of Pennsylvania (UM/UP)
Walker Art Center (WAC)
Woolaroc Museum (WM)

All dimensions are given in inches. Height precedes width precedes depth. If only one dimension is given, it indicates height or length. Circular objects are indicated with the abbreviation "diam." for diameter.

Bold face numerals indicate catalogue number; italicized numerals indicate illustration number; numerals in regular type, preceded by the letter "p" indicate the page on which the illustration appears.

An asterisk preceding catalogue number indicates object is on view at Walker Art Center.

Objects are listed alphabetically according to type (from bags through weapons). Each object category is organized into geographic areas as follows: Woodlands, Southeast, Plains, Southwest, Plateau/Basin, California, Northwest Coast, Northern Athabascan, Arctic Coast. Within each geographic area objects are listed alphabetically by tribe. (See map p 146)

Bags

1 Pouch, Algonkian
Northeastern United States, late 18th century
$11\frac{3}{16}$ x 5½ Quillwork and metal on buckskin.
Collection of Mrs. Purinton, Providence, Rhode Island, 1935.
PM cat no E6641

2 Bandoleer Bag, probably Delaware *109*, p 98
18th century
9½ x 9¼ Beadwork on walnut dyed buffalo hide.
Cloth lining.
Collected before Civil War.
Collection of Charles Eagle Plume, Allenspark, Colorado.
DAM cat no BD-21-P

3 Bandoleer Bag, Iroquois *110*, p 98
12 x 9 Quillwork on buckskin.
The designs represent thunderbirds.
Collected by Lord Jeffrey Amherst, 1758-1763.
Gift of Mrs. A. W. F. Fuller, 1964.
FMNH cat no 155563

4 Bag, Menomini
Wisconsin
12½ x 19 Native cord and commercial yarn.
Twined weave.
Collection of American Museum of Natural History, 1913.
NMM cat no 11-N-26

5 Bag, Menomini
Wisconsin
16 x 6¾ Stroud cloth, silk ribbon, seed beads, glass beads, wool. Octopus shape, floral designs on both sides.
Collected by Major Horatio Rust ca 1890.
LMA/BC cat no 1334

6 Bandoleer Bag, Menomini
12½ x 12½ Cloth with woven beadwork, yarn tassels.
Collection of American Museum of Natural History, 1913.
NMM cat no 111-N-9

7 Bandoleer Bag, Ojibwa
Lac du Flambeau, Wisconsin
17½ x 15 Cloth with loom-woven beadwork, wool tassels. Geometric design.
Collected by Albert Green Heath, from Charles Headflier, 1905.
LMA/BC cat no 30564

8 Bandoleer Bag
Great Lakes area
40½ x 10¾ Cloth with beadwork. Floral and geometric designs.
LMA/BC cat no 1450-3

9 Bandoleer Bag, Ojibwa
White Earth Reservation, Minnesota
39 x 13 Cloth with woven and sewn beadwork.
Collected 1918.
MHSM cat no 268/E-64

10 Bandoleer Bag, Ojibwa *51*, p 52
43 x 11½ Trade cloth, beadwork.
Collected by G. W. Haskell.
NMNH/SI cat no $\frac{175283}{29.809}$

11 Bag, Ojibwa
Minnesota
16½ x 8¼ Cloth with beadwork and fringe.
Octopus shape, floral design.
MAI/HF cat no $\frac{15}{4671}$

12 Bag, Ojibwa
Northwest Territories, Canada
11⅝ x $6\frac{11}{16}$ Buckskin with drill, silk, beadwork and woven quillwork.
Collected by Charles H. Stevens.
UMUP cat no 45-15-812

13 Bag, Ojibwa *50*, p 51
18¼ x 23½ Native cord and commercial yarn.
Twined weave.
MPM cat no $\frac{5110}{2207}$

14 Bag, Ojibwa
20½ x 22 Native cord and commercial yarn.
Twined weave.
MPM cat no $\frac{5070}{2207}$

15 Pouch, Ojibwa
7½ x 8½ Commercial cord and yarn. Twined weave.
MHSM cat no 67.199.4

16 Bandoleer Bag, Ojibwa
41 x 12¾ Buckskin with woven and sewn beadwork.
Collected 1923.
MHSM cat no 6333.6

17 Bandoleer Bag, Ojibwa
White Earth Reservation, Minnesota
36 x 12 Cloth with woven and sewn beadwork.
Collected 1918.
MHSM cat no 285/E81

18 Bandoleer Bag, Ojibwa
38 x 13 Cloth with sewn beadwork.
MHSM cat no 9606

19a Bandoleer Bag, probably Ojibwa
Ontario or Manitoba
20 x 14¼ Velvet with sewn and woven beadwork.
Collected by W. D. Wallis, 1914.
NMM cat no V-E-170

19b Fire Bag, Ojibwa
Lake Winnipeg, Canada
18 x 9
Collected 1850-1875.
ROM cat no 960.115.2

20 Bag, Sauk/Fox
20 x 30½ Commercial cord and yarn.
Twined weave.
DAM cat no RSF-10-P

21 Storage Bag, Winnebago
Nebraska
16 x 20 Basswood bark.
Eccentric-warp twine with braided lip.
Used for corn-hulling.
Acquired from Oliver LaMere (Winnebago), 1928.
LMA/BC cat no 48

22 Woven Bag, Winnebago
Wisconsin
27 x 20 Zig zag warp twine. Patterns of
thunderbirds, angular meanders, five-pointed
stars and diamonds.
Collected by Albert Green Heath, from Mrs. H. P. R.
Wyeville in 1942.
LMA/BC cat no 30089

23 Woven Bag, Winnebago   9, p 13
18 x 23¼ Eccentric warp twine. Great
Lakes type.
Collection of Albert Green Heath, Chicago, 1936.
DAM cat no RWin-1-P

24 Woven Bag, Winnebago
Nebraska, before 1850
7¾ x 10 Probably nettle fiber.
Zig-zag warp. Central panel with diamonds and
eight-armed figure on side, different patterns
on obverse.
Collected from Oliver LaMere (Winnebago), 1928.
LMA/BC cat no 47

25 Bandoleer Bag, Winnebago or Sauk/Fox
Southern Lakes area
44 x 14½ Cloth with beadwork. Floral design
with bird.
Collected by Albert Green Heath from John Roy on
Ojibwa reservation at Lac du Flambeau, Wisconsin.
LMA/BC cat no 30667

26 Bandoleer Bag
Woodlands
35½ x 13 Beadwork. Geometric and floral designs.
MHSM cat no 6333/6

27 Pouch
Great Lakes area
5¼ x 6 Commercial cord and yarn. Twined weave.
Collected 1930.
MHSM cat no 6874/20

28 Bandoleer Bag, Creek or Seminole
ca 1825
31¼ English wool baize (called bayeta in the
Southwest) with beadwork.
Collection of F. H. Douglas, Denver, 1954.
DAM cat no BSe-6-G

* 29 Saddle Bag, Apache
50⁷⁄₁₆ x 15 Buckskin with rawhide fringe,
cloth. Geometric design.
PM cat no E31633

* 30 Saddle Bags, Arapaho or Sioux
Late 19th century
14 x 16½ Deerskin with quillwork, beadwork,
feathers, metal tinklers, horsehair.
SMM cat no 49-195a/b

31 Pouch, Cheyenne
Montana
10½ x 7¼ Quillwork and feathers on buckskin.
Collected by Mrs. Louis Jerome Gillespie
(Wahtawaso Tetrault Gillespie).
SM cat no 611-G-760

32 Pipe Bag, Cheyenne
ca 1870
39 Buckskin with beadwork, fringe, quillwork, bells.
Collection of Mrs. V. J. Evans, 1948.
DAM cat no BChy-56-P

33 Pipe Bag, Cheyenne
29 Buckskin with beadwork, cornhusk, feathers.
Formerly in the Bumstead Collection.
DAM cat no BChy-33-PD

34 Pipe Bag, probaby Cree
Northern Plains
25¾ x 8⅝ Hide with flannel, quillwork, beadwork
and copper ornaments. Collected among the Arapaho.
Collection of Sir H. Sloane 1753.
Gift of A. W. F. Fuller, 1964.
FMNH cat no 155572

35 Tobacco Pouch, probaby Cree
Central Canada
17½ x 6½ Quillwork on buckskin.
Collection of E. W. Lenders.
UMUP cat no NA5217

36 Pouch, Crow
Southwestern Montana
10⅞ x 7½ Buckskin with quillwork, beadwork,
metal, feathers, glass beads.
Collected by Mr. and Mrs. T. W. Taliaferro.
CIS cat no 1109

37 Bag, Crow
Crow Reservation, Montana
33 x 17 Quillwork, beadwork, wool on buckskin.
Chevron and bar design. Triangular corner tab.
Gift of Robert T. Hatt.
CIS cat no 4071

38 Pipe Bag, Fox (Mesquaki)   59, p 58
Tama, Iowa
26¾ x 9 Buckskin with seed beads and tin. One
side has chevrons and conventionalized leaf design;
obverse has angular geometric pattern.
Collected by Albert Green Heath from Billy
Old Bear.
LMA/BC cat no 30640

39 Pipe Bag, Sioux
ca 1890
28½ x 7½ Buckskin with beadwork and quillwork.
Collected by Mrs. Louis Jerome Gillespie (Wahtawaso
Tetrault Gillespie).
SM cat no 611-G-511

40 Pipe Bag, probably Sioux   60, p 58
23 x 8 Beadwork on buckskin. Floral pattern on
upper section; geometric designs on main section.
HM

41 Pouch, probaby Sioux
Nebraska
15½ x 6¾ Buckskin with quillwork and dyed
animal hair.
Collection of Mrs. Seth Morse, Salem, Massachusetts,
1943.
PM cat no E24119

* 42 Saddle Bags, Sioux
18 x 11½ Deerskin with quillwork, horsehair, metal
tinklers. Geometric design.
SMM cat no 1-784/1-785

43 Pipe Bag, Sioux
ca 1865
40½ x 6 Buckskin, beadwork, quillwork.
MHSM cat no 69.54.14

44 Tobacco Bag, Sioux
Crow Creek Reservation, Montana
33 x 6½ Quillwork on buckskin.
Collected by David W. Clark.
ODM cat no CMC-B2

45 Pipe Bag, probably Sioux
39 x 7 Beadwork on buckskin.
Collected by Russell Crane among the
Shoshoni.
SMM cat no 47-P-66

46 Pouch, Sioux
16 x 5 Quillwork on buckskin. Buffalo
head figure design.
DAM cat no VS-17

47 "Possible" Bag, Sioux
12¼ x 14½ Buckskin with beadwork, hair and
metal fringe. Collected from Stray Calf (Crow),
on the reservation.
DAM cat no Bs-197-P

48 Pipe Bag
Northern Plains
36 x 6 Quillwork and beadwork on smoked
buffalo hide.
Collected by Mrs. Magnus Jemne, Blackfeet
Reservation, Montana.
SMM cat no A68-7-2

* 49 Saddle Bag, Apache (Western)
ca 1900
73-74 x 13¼ -14½ Leather with calico, wool.
DAM cat no LA-7

50 Bag, Nez Perce
Idaho
11¼ x 9¾ Hemp with false embroidery in cornhusk
and yarn. Twined weave.
Collection of Mrs. Seth Morse, Salem, Massachusetts.
PM cat no E24120

51 Bag, Nez Perce
Idaho
22 x 16 Hemp fiber with false embroidery of corn-
husk and yarn.
Collected by Mrs. Magnus Jemne on the Blackfeet
Reservation, Montana.
SMM cat no A68-7-10

52 Sally Bag, Wasco
Near The Dalles, Oregon, ca 1875
7¾ x 7½ Twined basketry.
DAM cat no YWas-1

* 53 Double Saddle Bag, probably Yakima   *76*, p 75
Washington, ca 1870
13 x 55 Buckskin, stroud cloth, beads.
COE

54 Bag, Tlingit
Alaska
21¼ x 10¾ Cloth with beadwork and yarn fringe.
Octopus shape, floral design.
MAI/HF cat no 14/7397

55 Pouch, Aleut
Aleutian Islands, Alaska
5½ x 3 Twined basketry. Two sections. Geometric
designs.
MAI/HF cat no 9/7041

Baskets

56 Basket, Chitimacha
Southeast
6 x 7 Split cane. Double weave.
Collection of Christian Women's Exchange,
New Orleans, 1936.
DAM cat no YChi-39-P

57 Basket and Cover, Chitimacha   *111*, p 98
Southeast
Basket: 3¾ ; 2¾ diam. Cover: 1½ ; 3 diam.
Split cane. Twilled technique.
Collected by G. G. and C. Ogden, 1928.
MPM cat no 35257 ab
                 9158

58 Basket and Cover, Chitimacha   *111*, p 98
Southeast
Basket: 5½ x 4½ ; 4¾ diam.
Cover: 1¾ x 5; 5¼ diam. Split cane.
Twilled technique.
Collected by G. G. and C. Ogden, 1928.
MPM cat no 35245 ab
                 9158

59 Basket and Cover, Chitimacha   *111*, p 98
Southeast
6 x 4¾ x 4¾ Split cane. Twilled technique.
MPM cat no 35251 ab
                 9158

60 Basket, Choctaw
Broken Bow, Oklahoma, 20th century
4½ x 13¾ Plaited weave. Used for sifting
corn meal.
DAM cat no YCho-48

61 Basket, Apache (Western)
Eastern Arizona
15½ x 4 Coiled with wide mouth.
Walls slope inward to rounded bottom.
Collection of Mrs. Ralph Holly.
MNA cat no 2260/E-2090

62 Basket, Apache (Western)   *112*, p 98
ca 1890
27 x 21½ Willow and black devil's claw
seed pods. Three rod coiling technique
in jar shape.
Collection of Mrs. F. C. Smith, San Francisco, 1954.
DAM cat no YA-124-G

63 Basket, Apache (Western)   *64*, p 64
Arizona, 1910-1920
19½ x 3½ Natural and dyed fiber.
Coiled technique. Abstract human and
geometric designs.
MNM cat no 23280/12

64 Basket, Apache (Western)
Arizona
16⅝ x 3¾ Natural and dyed fibers.
Coiled technique. Abstract animal, human
and geometric designs.
MNM cat no 23320/12

65 Basket, probably Havasupai
3¾ x 11½ Natural and dyed willow.
Coil technique. Star design.
WAC cat no B5

66a Basketry Tray, Pueblo (Hopi)
Second Mesa, Arizona, 20th century
14 diam. Coiled technique. Design represents
a kachina.
DAM cat no YH2-42

66b Basketry Tray, Pueblo (Hopi)
Third Mesa, Arizona, 20th century
14 diam. Wicker.
Design represents Crow Wing kachina.
DAM cat no YH3-51

67 Basket, Inyo
4½ ; 10 diam. Coiled technique.
Pendant triangles extending from rim,
two figures as main design.
Fred Harvey Foundation, Fine Arts Collection.
HM cat no 143 BA

68 Basket, Navajo
Arizona, 19th century
15 diam. Coiled technique. Used in
curing ceremony.
DAM cat no YN-6

69 Basket, Papago
Southern Arizona, 20th century
16; 20 diam. Willow and devil's claw.
Coil technique.
DAM cat no YPa-46

70 Basket, Papago
Southern Arizona, 20th century
4; 14½ diam. Willow and black devil's claw.
Coil technique.
DAM cat no YPa-52

71 Basket, Pima
Southern Arizona 1890-1910
15½ x 3½ Dyed cattail fiber with devil's
claw fiber, willow fiber. Geometric design.
MNM cat no 23372/12

72 Basket, Pima
Southern Arizona, 1900-1920
16¼ x 2⅞ Dyed cattail fiber with devil's
claw fiber, willow fiber.
MNM cat no 23381/12

73 Basket, Pima
Southern Arizona, 1890-1910
15½ x 4½ Dyed cattail fiber with devil's
claw fiber, willow fiber. Geometric design.
MNM cat no 23677/12

74 Basketry Jar, Pima
Southern Arizona, 1900-1920
10¾ x 12 Dyed cattail fibers with devil's
claw fiber, willow fiber. Geometric design.
MNM cat no 23681/12

75 Basket, Pima
Southern Arizona, 1910-1920
6½ ; 25 Dyed cattail fibers with devil's
claw fiber, willow fiber. Coiled technique.
Abstract animal and human design.
TOULOUSE

76 Basket, Chemehuevi
Lower Colorado River, Nevada, 20th century
2½ ; 10 diam.
Coiled weave.
DAM cat no YCh-13

77 Basket, Klikitat   *72*, p 70
Washington, late 19th century
14½ ; 11 diam.
Coiled technique. Imbricated decoration.
DAM cat no YKt-21

78 Basket, Klikitat
Plateau
6¾ x 7¼ Grass, cedar or spruce root.
Coiled, imbricated technique. Geometric
design.
WAC cat no B8

79 Wallet, Nez Perce   *74*, p 72
Plateau
25½ x 16 Hemp twine and dyed cornhusk.
DAM cat no YNP-12

80 Baskets, Paiute
Nevada
2½ ; 4 diam. Covered with netted beadwork.
Coiled technique.
DAM cat nos YPu-33, YPu-36

81 Basket, Skokomish   *116*, p 99
13½ ; 12 diam.
Twined weave.
DAM cat no YSKoK-9-P

82 Basket, Achomawi
Pit River, Northeast California
4½ x 6½ Wicker. Geometric designs of
double false embroidery inside and outside.
WAC cat no x.3004

83 Basket, Achomawi
Pit River, Northeast California, early 20th century
4¼ ; 6 diam. Woven with false embroidery both
inside and outside.
DAM cat no YPR-6

84 Basket, Luiseno or Cahuilla 113, p 99
Southern California
3½ ; 23 diam. Willow sewn with mottled
yellow juncus. Shallow coiled tray with
symmetrical design of two snakes pointing
toward center and two lizards.
LMA/BC cat no 57-C
6793

85 Basket, Panamint
Death Valley, California, late 19th century
4; 10½ diam. Close coil technique.
DAM cat no YPan-5

86 Basket, Pomo
California
5½ ; 11½ diam. Willow with feathers and
shell beads. Coiled technique.
Fred Harvey Foundation, Fine Arts Collection.
HM cat no 525 BA

87 Basket, Pomo
Clear Lake, California, ca 1900
2; 12½ diam. Willow with meadowlark feathers,
woodpecker scalp feathers, quail feathers, shell
beads.
Collection of Gotshall.
COE

88 Basket, Pomo 114, p 99
Central California
4 x 14½ ; 14 diam. Willow with feathers,
abalone shell, beads, string. Coiled, single rod.
Collected by Mrs. E. G. Weimer.
TM/CSFAC cat no 1724

89 Basket, Pomo
California
3¼ ; 8½ diam. Willow with feathers and
beadwork. Coiled technique.
MAI/HF cat no 20/8309

90 Basket, Tulare
California
8; 12¾ diam. Willow. Coiled weave.
DAM cat no YTu-18-P

91 Basket, Tulare 115, p 99
California
5½ x 7½ Natural and dyed willow, grass
stems.
WAC cat no B6

92 Basket, Tulare
California
7¼ x 10½ Natural and dyed willow,
grass stems with quail feathers. Geometric
elements and human figures in design.
WAC cat no x.2999

93 Basket, Tulare
California
5¾ x 9¾ Natural and dyed willow,
grass stems. Geometric design.
WAC cat no x.3000

94 Basket, Tulare
California
6½ x 9½ Natural and dyed willow,
grass stems with quail feathers.
WAC cat no x.3001

95 Basket, Washo
California, late 19th century
4½ x 5½ Natural and dyed willow.
Coiled. Geometric design of stepped
rectangles. Circle in center of bottom.
WAC cat no B10

96 Basket, Washo 73, p 72
Late 19th century
8¾ x 6½ x 3¼ Natural and dyed willow.
Coiled weave with designs.
DAM cat no YW-2-P

97 Basket, Yokuts
San Joaquin Valley, California Basin
9¼ ; 19½ diam. Marsh grass, bracken fern
root and redbud bark. Coiled technique.
Two bands of male and female figures
with joined hands.
HM cat no NA-CB-YO-B-38

98 Bottle-Neck Basket, Yokuts
San Joaquin Valley, California Basin
6¾ ; 9 diam. Grass-stem bundle foundation,
marsh grass root, bracken fern root, redbud
bark, flicker feathers, quail top-knots. Coiled
technique.
HM cat no NA-CB-YO-B-9

99 Basket
Central California
5½ x 8¾ Natural and dyed twined wicker.
Horizontal striped pattern.
WAC cat no x.2998

100 Basket, Cowlitz
Lower Puget Sound, late 19th century
13 x 15½ x 12½ Coiled weave. Imbricated
decoration.
DAM cat no YCz-2

101 Basket, Haida
Masset, Queen Charlotte Islands, Canada
4½ x 10; 14¾ diam. Woven with straight
sides. Fish design on inside.
Collected by Thomas Deasy.
NMM cat no VII-B-1135

102 Burden Basket, Lillooet
British Columbia
12¾ x 13½ ; 16½ long. Split cedar roots.
Coiled technique. Rectangular base and
rim, slightly flaring sides. Imbricated
decoration.
Collected by J. A. Teit.
NMM cat no II-E-18

103 Basket and Cover, Makah
Neah Bay, Washington
2½ ; 3¾ diam. Soft, dyed fiber. Twined
technique.
MAI/HF cat no 5
9911

104 Basket, Tlingit
12½ ; 13 diam. Twined weave. Killer
whale figures in false embroidery.
Fred Harvey Foundation, Fine Arts Collection.
HM cat no 74 BA

105 Basket, Tlingit
Alaska
8¼ x 8½ Split roots. False embroidery
technique.
MAI/HF cat no 16
8446

106 Basket and Cover, Tlingit
Alaska
3½ ; 6½ diam. Soft, dyed fiber. Twined
technique.
MAI/HF cat no 22
1932

107 Basket, Aleut
Aleutian Islands, Alaska
3¾ ; 4 diam. Soft fiber. Twined technique.
MAI/HF cat no 20
6472

Blankets

* 108 Blanket, Fox (Mesquaki)
Tama, Iowa
72 x 53 Wool stroud (trade cloth) with
ribbon appliqué and silver brooches.
Geometric patterns.
Collected by Albert Green Heath from
John Young Bear; belonged to his grand-
mother Wah-suh-say (Walks-in-the-Light).
LMA/BC cat no 30414

* 109 Blanket, Osage 117, p 100
58¾ x 67¾ Wool cloth with
appliqué, beadwork. Beaded hands
symbolize sacred will.
Collection of Albert Green Heath, Chicago, 1952.
DAM cat no AOs-13-PD

* 110 Blanket, Osage
Oklahoma
71½ x 60¼ Cloth with ribbon appliqué.
Geometric design.
MAI/HF cat no 21
1987

* 111 Blanket, Pueblo (Hopi)
Arizona
69¼ x 49¾ Wool.
MAI/HF cat no 16/2835

* 112 Chief Blanket, Navajo
Arizona/New Mexico
72 x 59 Wool. Third phase.
SM cat no 47-P-4

* 113 Blanket, Navajo
Arizona
146 x 104 Wool.
MAI/HF cat no 22
2808

* 114 Blanket, Navajo
New Mexico
75½ x 56¼ Wool.
MAI/HF cat no 18
8590

* 115 Blanket, Navajo
New Mexico
93 x 55¾ Wool.
"Evil rug."
MAI/HF cat no 23/130

* 116 Chief Blanket, Navajo
Arizona/New Mexico, ca 1860
84 x 55 Wool. Second phase.
Collected by Governor Arthur Seligman.
TM/CSFAC cat no 3695

* 117 Chief Banket, Navajo   *8, p 12*
Arizona/New Mexico, ca 1870
70 x 50 Wool. Fourth phase.
Collected by Fred Harvey.
TM/CSFAC cat no 3600

* 118 Chief Blanket, Navajo
Arizona/New Mexico, ca 1880
76 x 58 Wool. Fourth phase.
Collected by Governor Arthur Seligman.
TM/CSFAC cat no 3694

* 119 Chief Blanket, Navajo
Arizona/New Mexico, ca 1880
86 x 65 Wool. Fourth phase.
Collected by Gilbert McClurg.
TM/CSFAC cat no 2028

* 120 Chief Blanket, Navajo   *65, p 65*
Arizona/New Mexico, ca 1850
72 x 57 Wool. First phase.
Collected by Governor Arthur Seligman.
TM/CSFAC cat no 3696

* 121 Chief Blanket, Navajo   *66, p 65*
Arizona/New Mexico, ca 1860
55 x 39 Wool. Second phase.
Collected by Gilbert McClurg.
TM/CSFAC cat no 2026

* 122 Chief Blanket, Navajo
Arizona/New Mexico
58 x 45 Wool. Second phase.
SM cat no 202-L-112

* 123 Chief Blanket, Navajo
Arizona/New Mexico
70 x 60 Wool. Fourth phase.
The Herbert S. Zim and Sonia Bleeker Zim
Collection.
LMA/BC cat no 5064
8925

* 124 Rug, Navajo
Arizona, 1885-1900
108 x 144 Germantown yarn.
MNM cat no 46112/12

* 125 Rug, Navajo
ca 1885
42 x 27 Germantown yarn and string warp.
Intricate diamond pattern. Three-ply.
Collected by M. J. Kohlburg.
TM/CSFAC cat no 3628

* 126 Rug, Navajo
ca 1885
60 x 96 Germantown yarn. Cotton string warp.
Over-all pattern of sawtooth-edged concentric
diamonds with a center star and surrounded
with sawtooth zigzag lines. Tightly woven.
Gift of Mrs. Walter Paepke, Larkspur,
Colorado.
TM/CSFAC cat no 3883

* 127 Blanket, Navajo
Arizona/New Mexico, ca 1880
70 x 48 Wool. Classic period.
Gift of Miss Augusta Holm.
TM/CSFAC cat no 6024

* 128 Blanket, Navajo
Arizona/New Mexico, ca 1880
31 x 54 Wool. Classic period.
Collected by R. W. Corwin.
Lent by Colorado College Museum.
TM/CSFAC cat no 6216

* 129 Blanket, Navajo
Arizona/New Mexico, ca 1880
64 x 48 Wool. Classic period.
Collected by Governor Arthur Seligman.
TM/CSFAC cat no 1925

* 130 Blanket, Navajo
Arizona
113½ x 95½ Germantown yarn.
MAI/HF cat no 23/2058

* 131 Blanket, Navajo
New Mexico
48 x 34½ Wool.
MAI/HF cat no 9/9821

* 132 Blanket, Navajo
New Mexico
70¼ x 44½ Wool.
Two Gray Hills Style.
MAI/HF cat no 24/1070

* 133 Blanket, Haida   *88, p 84*
Prince of Wales Island, Alaska
57 x 67¾ Cloth with buttons, dentalium shells.
Represents a bear.
MAI/HF cat no 16
2769

* 134 Blanket, Kwakiutl
Early 1900s
57½ x 69 Stroud with buttons, abalone shell.
Collar neckpiece is Art Deco-20th century
material — possibly a replacement.
COE

* 135 Blanket, Tlingit (Chilkat)
Alaska
38½ x 53½ Painted caribou skin.
Collected in 1900 at Klukwan.
MAI/HF cat no 5
6905

* 136 Blanket, Tlingit (Chilkat)   *118, p 100*
ca 1940
49 x 58 Cedar bark and mountain goat
wool. Woven by Mary Hunt (Tlingit) after
marriage to Kwakiutl husband; Chilkat style.
SOSLAND

* 137 Blanket, Tlingit (Chilkat)
Alaska
68¹⁄₁₆ x 36¼ Cedar bark and mountain goat
wool.
Collected 1891.
Gift of Wyman K. Flint, 1928.
PM/HU cat no 28.24.10
98343

* 138 Button Blanket, Tsimshian
54½ x 73 Stroud with cloth button appliqué.
Worn in dances.
Collected by Lieut. G. T. Emmons, 1916.
AMNH cat no 16.1/1614

Bowls

* 139 Bowl, probably Kaskaskia   *119, p 100*
Southern Illinois, late 1700s
14 x 15; 40 long. Carved ash root.
Represents a beaver.
Collected by Judge George Turner before 1795.
Gift of heirs of David Kimball, 1899.
PM/HU cat no 99.12.10
52998

* 140 Bowl, Winnebago
Black River Falls, Wisconsin
13; 11 diam. Carved hardwood burl.
Represents a human head on rim.
Collected by Albert Green Heath from
John Blackhawk before 1920.
LMA/BC cat no 30061

* 141 Effigy Bowl, Winnebago
1½; 6¾ diam. Carved wood.
Represents a human head on rim.
Collection of Albert Green Heath.
DAM cat no QWin-1

* 142 Effigy Bowl, Winnebago
Sioux City, Iowa
2¾ x 4¾; 3⅜ long. Carved
wood with brass tacks.
Represents a lodge. Double ridge exterior
bowl border.
Collected by Milford G. Chandler, 1922.
CIS cat no 2249

* 143 Ceremonial Bowl, Sioux
Crow Creek Reservation, South Dakota
6 x 11½ x 3; 12 long; 12¾ diam.
Carved wood with brass nailheads.
Represents bird's head.
Collected by H. Burt.
David W. Clark Collection.
ODM cat no CMC-C8

* 144 Ceremonial Bowl, Sioux (Yankton)   *56, p 57*
Crow Creek Reservation, South Dakota
7 x 12; 20½ long. Carved wood with
brass nailheads.
Represents an opossum.
Collected by H. Burt, ca 1885.
David W. Clark Collection.
ODM cat no CMC-C7

* 145 Bowl, Yakima
Washington
7 x 5½ x 4¾ Carved horn.
Represents skeletons.
MAI/HF cat no $\frac{10}{5467}$

* 146 Dish, Haida
12⅛ Carved wood, inlaid abalone shell.
Represents a seal.
Collection of E. E. Ayer, 1897.
FMNH cat no 14408

* 147 Bowl, Haida
Queen Charlotte Islands, Canada
16 x 7½ Carved wood with shell, opercula,
glass beads.
Represents a seal with four flippers.
LMA/BC cat no 1888

* 148 Bowl, Haida
Queen Charlotte Islands, Canada
13⅜ x 8¹⁄₁₆ x 5⅛ Carved wood.
Represents a seal. Used for grease.
Collected by Lieut. G. T. Emmons, 1917.
Purchased with Wolcott Fund, 1917.
PM/HU cat no $\frac{17.62.10}{87246}$

* 149 Food Dish, probably Haida
10⅞ x 3¾ x 3½ Carved wood.
Represents a double-headed mosquito, one
with stinger.
Gift of the heirs of David Kimball, 1899.
PM/HU cat no $\frac{99.12.10}{53091}$

* 150 Dish, probably Haida   *120, p 100*
British Columbia, ca 1870
7⅜ x 3⅜ x 2¼ Carved wood.
Represents a raven with a man on his back.
Collection of J. T. Hooper, Birmingham Museum, 1870s.
MPA cat no 65.10

* 151 Ceremonial Dish, Haida
Queen Charlotte Islands, British Columbia
4 x 4¾ ; 5¼ long. Carved wood.
Represents a bear.
MAI/HF cat no $\frac{9}{8038}$

* 152 Ceremonial Dish, Haida
British Columbia
20¼ x 11 x 8¼ Carved wood with shell inlay.
Represents a seal.
MAI/HF cat no $\frac{14}{9621}$

* 153 Grease Dish, Niska
Au Keedae, Nass River, British Columbia
9¼ x 5¾ x 3½ Carved wood.
Represents a frog.
MAI/HF cat no $\frac{1}{4275}$

* 154 Food Bowl, Haida
British Columbia
10 Carved wood. Represents an
anthropomorphic recumbent figure.
Collected before 1934.
Gift of the Wellcome Trust.
MCH/UC/LA cat no x65-7474

* 155 Food Bowl, Haida
British Columbia
4 x 6 x 7 Carved mountain sheep horn.
Design of conventionalized hawk faces.
Collected before 1934.
Gift of the Wellcome Trust.
MCH/UC/LA cat no x65-7476

* 156 Feast Bowl, Kwakiutl
14 x 22 x 8½ ; 48 long. Carved and
painted wood.
Represents a beaver.
Collected by Barrett expedition, 1915.
MPM cat no $\frac{17751}{4615}$

* 157 Feast Bowl, Kwakiutl (Koskimo)
16 x 14¾ x 37 Carved and painted wood.
Represents a whale.
Collected by George Hunt, 1899.
AMNH cat no 16/6895 a,b

* 158 Feast Dish, Kwakiutl
Vancouver Island, British Columbia
13⅜ ; 32¾ long. Carved wood.
Represents a killer whale. Blow hole at top
of snout, projecting dorsal fin, teeth indicated
by rope design carving.
BM cat no x274.4

* 159 Bowl with Eagle, Kwakiutl
British Columbia, probably late 19th century
Bowl: 25 diam; 76½ wingspread. Carved
and painted wood. Used at potlatches.
Represents an eagle.
Collected by Stewart Edward White.
Gift of Harwood A. White.
LM/UC/B cat no 2-19569

* 160 Bowl
Northwest Coast
9½ x 7 x 4¾ Sheep horn with
abalone shells.
Represents a panther.
Collected by H. R. Bishop, 1869.
AMNH cat no 16/AI/60

* 161 Feast Bowl
Northwest Coast
13½ x 15 x 45 Carved and painted wood.
AMNH cat no 16/4690

* 162 Bowl, Eskimo   *121, p 101*
Nunivak Island, Alaska
11¼ x 2¾ x 7½ Carved and
painted wood.
MPA cat no 57.276

Boxes

163 Box, Algonkian
Golden Lake, Ontario, Canada
4½ x 5; 5½ long. Scraped birchbark. Floral and bird designs.
MAI/HF cat no $\frac{15}{4438}$

164 Box, Huron   *122, p 101*
9¾ x 6 x 5 Birchbark with quillwork.
Geometric design.
UMUP cat no NA 3851

165 Box, Micmac
Eastern Woodlands, before 1825
7½ x 4⅞ x 4⅜ Birchbark with
wood base, spruce roots and quillwork.
PM cat no E25686

166 Box, Micmac
ca 1850
7 x 11 Birchbark with quillwork.
COE

167 Box, Micmac
Shubenacadie, Nova Scotia
7¾ x 4¾ x 4 Birchbark with
quillwork.
Collected by C. MacMillan, summer 1911.
NMM cat no 11-F-80

168 Box, probably Micmac
Maine or Nova Scotia, ca 1850
7¼ x 5½ x 6½ Wood covered with
birchbark, porcupine quillwork.
Geometric designs.
LMA/BC cat no 7505

169 Box, Micmac
Nova Scotia, before 1882
2⅝ x 3¾ Birchbark with quillwork.
Symmetrical floral design. Lined with
newspaper dated 1882.
LMA/BC cat no 6930

170 Box, Micmac
Nova Scotia
4¾ x 8 x 6¾ Birchbark with
quillwork.
LMA/BC cat no 7404

171 Box, Micmac
Nova Scotia
3¾ x 8 x 6¼ Birchbark with
quillwork.
LMA/BC cat no 7406

172 Box and Cover, Ojibwa
Lake Temagami, Ontario, Canada
7 x 6 x 5½ Scraped birchbark.
Floral designs.
MAI/HF cat no $\frac{14}{3057}$

173 Box, Passamaquoddy
Maine, late 19th century
8⅞ x 6¾ Birchbark and pine with
porcupine quillwork and spruce root.
Collected by Dr. Kinsman.
Collection of Robert Abbe Museum,
Bar Harbor, Maine.
PM cat no E27779

174 Box and Cover, Haida
Skidegate, British Columbia
15 x 9¼ x 11¼ Carved argillite.
MAI/HF cat no $\frac{8}{3210}$

175 Covered Box, probably Haida
British Columbia
7¾ x 9¼ Carved and incised wood.
Convex sides.
Collected before 1940.
Gift of the Wellcome Trust.
MCH/UC/LA cat no x65-4264

176 Box, probably Haida
British Columbia
25½ x 18 Carved and painted wood.
Heraldic designs.
Collected before 1934.
Gift of the Wellcome Trust.
MCH/UC/LA cat no x65-4254

177 Box, Haida
Skidegate, British Columbia
10¼ x 10⅝ x 11 3/16 Painted wood.
Collected by J. G. Swan, 1883.
Smithsonian Institution exchange, 1888.
PM/HU cat no 88.51.10/50481

178 Chest, Haida
Queen Charlotte Islands, Canada
44 x 23¼ x 27¼ Carved wood.
Collected by Stewart Culin and C. F. Newcombe, John Wanamaker expedition, 1900.
UMUP cat no 37733

179 Box, Kwakiutl
British Columbia
8½ x 7 5/16 x 6⅝ Incised wood.
Collected by C. F. Newcombe, Peabody Museum expedition, 1917.
PM/HU cat no 17.17.10/87135

180 Chest, Tlingit *123,* p 101
Alaska, 19th century
20¼ x 30⅝ x 20½ Carved and painted wood.
MPA cat no 56.270

181 Box, Tlingit
Alaska
10⅝ x 16½ x 11 9/16
Painted wood, leather.
Collected by Edward G. Fast, 1867-68.
PM/HU cat no 69.30.10/2182

Carvings

* **182 Housepost, Delaware** *124,* p 101
Copan, Oklahoma, ca 1874
46 x 12 x 17½ Carved wood. Two faces.
May have been painted. Longhouse centerpost.
Collected by Clark Field.
PAC cat no 60.11.1

* **183 Housepost, Delaware**
Copan, Oklahoma, ca 1874
15¼ x 8¾ Carved and painted wood.
Collected by Fred Washington.
WM cat no 710

* **184 Sun Dance Buffalo Carving, Cheyenne**
18th century
7 x 2⅞ ; 8¾ long. Carved wood with fiber-tuft tail and inset carved wooden horn.
Collected by Roberta Campbell Lawson.
PAC cat no MI 2277

* **185 Sun Dance Buffalo Carving, Cheyenne**
18th century
6½ x 2¾ ; 8¼ long. Carved wood with hide, hair and black feathers.
Collected by Roberta Campbell Lawson.
PAC cat no MI 2278

* **186 Fertility Figure, Pueblo (Taos)**
Taos Pueblo, New Mexico
13; 5½ diam. Carved wood.
Collected by H. H. Garnett.
TM/CSFAC cat no 3198

* **187 Bear Fetish, Pueblo (Zuni)**
Zuni Pueblo, New Mexico
6½ x 2 x 3¼ Basalt with turquoise.
TM/CSFAC cat no 3197

* **188 Bird Fetish, Pueblo (Zuni)**
Zuni Pueblo, New Mexico
6 x 3½ x 4¼ Black basalt with turquoise and shell.
Collected by C. G. Wallace and H. H. Garnett.
TM/CSFAC cat no 3151

* **189 Human Figure Fetish, Pueblo (Zuni)**
Zuni Pueblo, New Mexico
5½ x 2½ ; 1½ diam. Black basalt.
Male altar fetish.
Collected by C. G. Wallace and H. H. Garnett.
TM/CSFAC cat no 3142

* **190 Buffalo Head, Pueblo (Zuni)**
Zuni Pueblo, New Mexico
10¾ x 7½ x 11¼ ; 8 diam. Painted cottonwood and horsehair. From the altar of the Buffalo Clan, used during Shalako dances.
Collected by H. H. Garnett, Denver Art Museum, 1937.
TM/CSFAC cat no 1549

* **191 Bird Fetish, Pueblo (Zuni)**
Zuni Pueblo, New Mexico
5½ x 2 Black basalt with turquoise.
Collected by C. G. Wallace and H. H. Garnett.
TM/CSFAC cat no 3162

192 War God, Pueblo (Zuni)
New Mexico
23⅝ x 2 1/16 Carved wood.
Collected by Stewart Culin, museum expedition, 1904.
BM cat no 04.192

193 War God, Pueblo (Zuni) *126,* p 102
New Mexico
30¼ x 9⅞ Carved wood.
Acquired by Stewart Culin, museum expedition, 1903.
BM cat no 03.124

194 War God, Pueblo (Zuni)
New Mexico, ca 1860
27½ Carved wood, sticks. Carved from lightning struck wood.
DAM cat no QZu-44

* **195 Fetish, Pueblo (Zuni)**
New Mexico
5 x 2 x 2¾ Carved stone with small stones attached.
MAI/HF cat no 9/3769

* **196 Fetish, Pueblo (Zuni)** *125,* p 102
New Mexico
2¼ x 6¾ x 1½ Carved stone.
Represents a bear.
MAI/HF cat no 21/5038

197 Effigy of Pock-San-E (Place in Meadow), Klamath *75,* p 73
Southwest Oregon, early 1900s
21⅝ x 9 x 7⅛ Carved wood with feather necklace.
To be placed on top of a shaman's house.
Carved by Dr. John, a leading medicine man.
Collected by Miss Nicholson and Mr. Hartman, 1910.
Gift of Lewis H. Farlow, 1910.
PM/HU cat no 10-21-10/76535

198a Plaque, Bella Bella
25 x 23½ Carved and painted wood.
Collected 1902.
ROM cat no 23139

* **198b Eagle Grave Monument, Bella Coola**
Bella Coola, British Columbia
18 x 24 x 36 Carved and painted wood.
Wings outspread. Original legs missing.
Collected by H. I. Smith.
NMM cat no VII-D-233

199 Carving, Haida
Queen Charlotte Islands, Canada
5¼ x 2¼ x 5½ Argillite.
MAI/HF cat no 23/6103

200 Carving, Haida
ca 1875
7⅛ x 8 Slate. Figure group with Raven Woman.
DAM cat no QHI-96-ex

201 Figure, probably Haida
Northwest Coast
7⅝ x 3 3/16 x 2 3/16 Carved and painted wood, hair. Effigy of woman with labret.
Gift of heirs of David Kimball, 1899.
PM/HU cat no 99.12.10/53093

202 Carving, Haida
Skidegate, Queen Charlotte Islands, Canada
6¼ x 2¼ ; 10¾ long. Argillite.
Depicts man and two bears.
Collected by Dawson, 1885.
NMM cat no VII-B-751

203 Cemetery Totem Pole, probably Haida
British Columbia
31½ x 4 Carved wood. Full human
figure base; otters' heads above human
head; full otter figure above.
Collected by H. S. Pingree, 1887.
CIS cat no 1940

204 Figure, probably Haida
Northwest Coast
18 x 5⅛ x 3⅜ Carved wood
and hair.
Gift of heirs of David Kimball, 1899.
PM/HU cat no 99.12.10
53094

205 Mask Accessory, probably Haida
7¼ x 2½ x 2½ Carved and painted wood,
cloth, hair. Figure with bow and arrow.
AMNH cat no 16.1/2540

206 Man and Woman, Haida
Masset, Queen Charlotte Islands, Canada,
before 1890
9½ x 13¼ Carved and painted wood.
Represents a kneeling man killing a
crouching female.
Collected by Mrs. Roderick F. Dodd.
Gift of Dr. W. Barclay Stephens.
LM/UC/B cat no 2-15545

207 Kneeling Figure, Haida
British Columbia
8½ x 3½ Carved argillite with
shell inlay. Represents a chief
with a box.
MAI/HF cat no 7
42

208 Human Figure with Two Bears, Haida
Queen Charlotte Islands, Canada
5¾ x 2½ x 5½ Carved argillite. Represents the
legend of a berry picker.
MAI/HF cat no 23
6103

* 209 Chief's Seat, probably Haida   *127, p 102*
26; 108¼ long. Carved and painted wood.
Three parts.
Collected by C. F. Newcombe, 1902.
FMNH cat no 79595

* 210 Dentsik Board, Kwakiutl
47½ x 34¾ Painted wood. Used in
dances of the Toxuit or Woman's Society.
Collected by George Hunt, 1892.
FMNH cat no 19884

* 211 Figure, Kwakiutl   *128, p 102*
57 x 9 Carved and painted wood.
Collected by Barrett expedition, 1915.
MPM cat no 17382
7615

* 212 Figure, Kwakiutl
Vancouver Island, British Columbia
88½ Carved and painted wood.
Set over house during a potlatch.
Collected by Ralph C. Altman.
TM/CSFAC cat no TM 3990

* 213 Chief Sculpture, Kwakiutl
Vancouver Island, British Columbia
50 Carved and painted wood with copper.
Collected by Ralph C. Altman.
TM/CSFAC cat no TM 3973

* 214 Grave Monument, Kwakiutl
Hopetown, British Columbia
60 x 21 Carved and painted wood.
Collected by W. H. Birmingham, 1950-70.
NMM cat no V I I-E-767

* 215 Potlatch Figure, Kwakiutl
Vancouver Island, British Columbia
42⅞ Carved and painted wood with beads.
BM cat no X274.3

* 216 Potlatch Figure, Kwakiutl
57 Carved and painted wood. Typical
speaker's figure used at potlatches.
Collection of Tozier, 1875-1915.
DAM cat no QKW-31-P

* 217 Potlatch Figure, Kwakiutl   *129, p 103*
53⅞ x 13¾ x 6 Carved wood.
Roll of hair or headdress represented
on top of head.
BM cat no X274.1

218 Copper Breaking Anvil, Kwakiutl
37 x 22 x 11½ Carved and painted wood.
Represents "Tsckish," a sea monster.
Collected by C. F. Newcombe at Alert Bay, 1905.
DAM cat no QKw-19-Ex

* 219 Articulated Puppet, Kwakiutl   *130, p 103*
British Columbia
38 x 12 Carved and painted wood, fur.
Used in Winter Dance ceremonies.
Collected by Barrett expedition, 1915.
MPM cat no 17372a
4615

* 220 Screen, Nootka   *131, p 103*
Qualicum Bay, Vancouver Island, British Columbia,
mid-19th century
43 x 64¾ x ⅝ Painted wood.
Gift of Mr. and Mrs. Robert W. Campbell.
MPA cat no 69.30a-c

221 Pair of Figures, Tlingit
Alaska, before 1898
16½ Carved and painted cedar wood with
human hair. Represent shaman's messenger
spirits. Carved forms on figure of a
land otter.
Gift of Alaska Commercial Company.
LM/UC/B cat no 2-4812 and 2-4813

222 Figure with Stick and Frog, Tlingit
Alaska, before 1898
19½ Carved and painted wood. Represents
a man holding a stick; frog on base; hat with
four rings and raven on head; tear line
on cheek.
Gift of Alaska Commercial Company.
LM/UC/B cat no 2-4799

* 223 Canoe Ornament, Tlingit   *19, p 22*
52 x 32½ Carved and painted wood.
Collected by Lieut. G. T. Emmons, 1902.
FMNH cat no 79320

* 224 Shaman's Staff, Tlingit (Chilkat)
47 x 4 x 6 Carved and painted wood with
human hair. Represents a crane, a devil
fish, land otter and two spirits.
AMNH cat no 19/1228

225 Figure, Tlingit
17¾ x 3¾ x 2¾ Carved and painted
wood, human hair, inlaid abalone. Shaman's
guardsman. The back of the man is carved
to represent a ground shark.
AMNH cat no 19/308

226 Shaman's Comb, Tlingit
5 x 2½ Baleen with human hair rope.
Carved to represent a bear, two salmon, an
owl and a crow.
AMNH cat no 19/448

227 Frog Carving, Tlingit
Southwest Coast, Alaska, 19th century
4½ x 1¾ Bone.
Collection of Harry E. Wood.
MIA cat no 28.117

228 Human Figure Eating Frog, Tlingit
Southwest Coast, Alaska, 19th century
4 x 3¼ x 1¾ Stone.
Collection of Harry E. Wood.
MIA cat no 28.116

229 Shaman's Figure, Tlingit
Northwest Coast
8¼ x 11. Wood with human hair, leather,
bone.
Collected by Dickerman.
TM/CSFAC cat no 4910

230 Wolf Figure, Tlingit
Southwest Coast, Alaska, 19th century
5 x 2 x 1 Stone.
Collection of Harry E. Wood.
MIA cat no 28.115

231 Owl
Columbia River Valley, 19th century
3½ x 5⁵⁄₁₆; 7½ long. Stone.
Owl's face carved at one end, curvilinear
grooves on sides indicate wings and
feathers.
BM cat no 64.161.1

* 232 Ceremonial Board
Lake Washington, Seattle, Washington
84 Painted cedar board. Used in the
Spirit Cause Ceremony.
Collected by George Dorsey, 1899.
FMNH cat no 55960

* **233a Theatrical Dentsik**
Northwest Coast
138 x 35½ Carved and painted wood, painted fabric. Used by a woman's society in the Winter Dance ceremonies.
Collected by George Hunt, 1904.
AMNH cat no 16/9584

233b Puppet
Northwest Coast
22 Carved wood, articulated.
In form of a skeleton.
ROM

Ceremonial Objects

* **234 Dancer's Feast Stick, Ojibwa**
White Earth Reservation, Minnesota.
19½ Carved wood. Used by lead dancer at a feast to strike the kettle from which food is to be served.
Collected 1918.
MHSM cat no E97/301

* **235 Dance Wand, Winnebago** *16*, p 19
30 Stick with beaded pouch. Hand design in beadwork.
Collected by Thomas R. Roddy before 1908.
SHSW cat no 1954.1860/E466

236 Cutout, Crow
9 x 8 Painted rawhide. Elk with antlers.
Part of a pipe bundle.
Collected by Albert Green Heath from Chief Crooked Horn.
LMA/BC cat no 31140

237 Dance Fan, Kiowa
Plains, ca 1900
16 Buckskin with beadwork, feathers.
DE LAITTRE

238 Cutout, Sioux *133*, p 104
Near Pine Ridge, South Dakota, before 1882
13⅛ x 8½ Rawhide figure of man. Hung from center pole of Sun Dance Lodge during dance.
Collected by Miss A. C. Fletcher, 1882.
PM/HU cat no 82.45.10/27498

* **239 Dance Club, Sioux (Hunkpapa)**
Standing Rock Reservation, North Dakota
34 x 2 Carved wood with horsehair, bells, feathers, hide. Used in dance to represent horse ridden in battle.
MAI/HF cat no 20/1294

* **240 Ritual Club, Sioux**
29¼ Carved stone with rawhide, wood.
Represents a mountain goat and a turtle.
Collection of Omaha Public Library.
On permanent loan since 1948.
JAM cat no 698.1949

241 Kachina Dance Wand, Pueblo (Hopi)
Arizona
18⅞ x 5 Carved and painted wood.
Carried by members of the Marau, a women's society.
Collected by Fred Harvey, 1910.
AMNH cat no 50/9276b

242 Kachina Dance Wand, Pueblo (Hopi)
Arizona
20 x 10¼ Carved and painted wood.
Collected by Fred Harvey, 1910.
AMNH cat no 50/9278

243 Kachina Dance Wand, Pueblo (Hopi)
Arizona
21¾ x 8 Carved and painted wood.
Collected by Fred Harvey, 1910.
AMNH cat no 50/9282

244 Kachina Dance Wand, Pueblo (Hopi) *134*, p 104
Arizona
21⅞ x 9½ Carved and painted wood.
Collected by Fred Harvey, 1910.
AMNH cat no 50/9284

245 Pair of Kachina Dance Wands, Pueblo (Hopi)
Arizona
20⅝ x 5⅛ Carved and painted wood.
Collected by Fred Harvey, 1910.
AMNH cat no 50/9291A/B

246 Kachina Dance Wand, Pueblo (Hopi)
Arizona
17 x 6⅜ Carved and painted wood.
Collected by Fred Harvey, 1910.
AMNH cat no 50/9341

247 Tablet, Pueblo (Hopi)
Northern Arizona
$17\frac{5}{16}$ x $13\frac{1}{16}$ Carved and painted cottonwood with rawhide, raffia, feathers.
(Naktci of Palahikomana.) This personage appears in women's ceremony called Mamzrauti.
Collected by J. Walter Fewkes and Thomas V. Keam, 1892.
Gift of the estate of Mary Hemenway, 1945.
PM/HU cat no 45.25.10/28713

248 Bullroarer, Pueblo (Hopi)
Shongopovi, Arizona
6 x 2 Painted cottonwood with string.
MAI/HF cat no 23/6129

249 Dance Wand, Pueblo (Hopi)
Oraibi, Arizona
21¾ x 4¾ Carved and painted wood.
Represents an Alosaka kachina.
MAI/HF cat no 9/575

250 Dance Wand, Pueblo (Hopi)
Oraibi, Arizona
21 x 8¼ Carved and painted wood.
Represents a Hu kachina.
MAI/HF cat no 9/579

251 Dance Wand, Pueblo (Hopi)
Arizona
21¾ x 8½ Carved and painted wood.
Represents a kachina.
MAI/HF cat no 16/1956

252 Prayer Board, Pueblo (Hopi)
Arizona
23⅝ x $13\frac{3}{16}$ Carved and painted wood.
Collected by J. M. Johnson.
CIS cat no 3871

253 Kachina Dance Wand, Pueblo (Hopi) *134*, p 104
First Mesa, Arizona
21⅞ x 4¼ Carved and painted wood.
Collected by Robert H. Lowie, 1916.
AMNH cat no 50.2-19A

254 Kachina Dance Wand, Pueblo (Hopi)
First Mesa, Arizona
20½ x 6 Carved and painted wood.
Represents a Hemis kachina.
Collected by J. J. Spinden, 1912.
AMNH cat no 50.1/6816

255 Kachina Dance Wand (Marau Baho), Pueblo (Hopi) *134*, p 104
22⅛ x 8 Carved and painted wood.
Collected by Fred Harvey, 1910.
AMNH cat no 50/9277

256 Kachina Dance Wand, Pueblo (Hopi)
14 x 5⅞ Carved and painted wood.
Collected by Fred Harvey, 1910.
AMNH cat no 50/9339

257 Ceremonial Wand, Pueblo (Hopi)
ca 1920
25½ x 6¾ Carved and painted wood with yarn, feathers. Designs on both faces; scalloped at one end.
MNA cat no 2519/E-4001

258 Kachina Dance Paddle, Pueblo (Zuni)
Western New Mexico
12¼ x 6¾ Carved and painted wood.
Represents Shalako Mana.
Fred Harvey Foundation, Fine Arts Collection.
HM cat no 909-C-1

* **259 Dance Wand, Karok**
California
23½ Wood with obsidian point, woodpecker head, feathers.
MAI/HF cat no 15/1928

* **260 Ceremonial Deerskin, Yurok** *135*, p 104
Northwest California
41 Deerskin with woodpecker scalps, feathers.
Used in White Deerskin Dance.
Collected by Dr. A. L. Kroeber.
Exchanged with Department of Anthropology, University of California, Berkeley.
PM/HU cat no 04.28.10/63484

261 "Soul Catcher," Niska
Nass River, British Columbia
6¼ x 1 Carved ivory with haliotis shell inlay.
Represents a double-headed mythical water animal.
MAI/HF cat no 9/7936

262 Shaman's Charm, Tlingit
Alaska
4 x 1¼ Carved ivory. Represents an animal head
and a raven head with spirit figures.
MAI/HF cat no 4/1659

263 Shaman's Charm, Tlingit
Alaska
4½ x 1¾ Carved ivory. Represents a spirit
figure.
MAI/HF cat no 4/1671

264 Shaman's Charm, Tlingit
Sitka, Alaska
4¾ x 2 Carved ivory inlaid with haliotis shell.
MAI/HF cat no 9/7949

* 265 Doctor's Wand, Tlingit
20½ Carved and painted wood, human hair trim.
Doctor's dance wand. Represents an otter, a
Tlingit spirit, a devil fish and a doctor's spirit.
AMNH cat no E/2454

266 Copper, Tlingit   *136*, p 104
Alaska, mid-19th century
34¼ x 21 x ⅛ Painted copper.
Collection of Chief Kyan.
MPA cat no 65.104

267 "Soul Catcher," Tsimshian
Nass River, British Columbia
6¾ x 1¼ Carved ivory inlaid with
haliotis shell.
MAI/HF cat no 5/5069

268 Copper
Northwest Coast
30½ x 17½ Painted copper.
SOSLAND

269 Copper
Northwest Coast
30 x 21¼ Painted copper. Beaver design.
Collected by Fred Harvey.
Collection of E. E. Ayer, 1893.
FMNH cat no 19022

* 270 Medicine Man's Wand
Quilleute, Washington
15¼ x 3¼ Carved and painted wood, cloth.
Represents guardian spirit.
MAI/HF cat no 5/7575

271 Charm, Eskimo
Point Barrow, Alaska
3 x ¾ Carved ivory. Represents a man.
MAI/HF cat no 5/4551

272 Charm, Eskimo
Point Barrow, Alaska
1¾ x ½ Carved ivory. Represents a seal.
MAI/HF cat no 5/4766

273 Charm, Eskimo
Point Barrow, Alaska
2 x 1½ Carved ivory. Represents a human head.
MAI/HF cat no 7/754

Clothing

* 274 Woman's Moccasins, Fox (Mesquaki)
Iowa
9½ Buckskin with beadwork.
Collected by Albert Green Heath from Young Bear.
LMA/BC cat no 30781

* 275 Sash, Huron
Oklahoma
18½ x 4 Braided commercial yarn with
beadwork, tassels.
Collected by John Cochrane.
Collection of Millicent Nichols.
PM cat no E30723

* 276 Moccasins, Iroquois   *141*, p 106
Late 18th century
9½ x 4½ Buckskin with quillwork.
Collection of Mrs. A. W. F. Fuller.
FMNH cat no 155557

* 277 Sash, Iroquois
Early 19th century
63 x 7⅛ Braided yarn with beadwork, fringe.
Collection of Mrs. Helen Russell.
PM cat no E13,649

* 278 Pair of Garters, Menomini
Menomini Reservation, Wisconsin, before 1887
2¾ wide. Loom beadwork with yarn fringe.
Geometric design.
Collected by Charles Edwin Kelsey at
Keshena, Wisconsin, 1887-1895.
SHSW cat no 50.718a

* 279 Sash, Menomini   *143*, p 106
33 x 4 Loom beadwork with yarn fringe.
Geometric design.
SHSW cat no 46.1005

* 280 Chief's Coat, Micmac   *137*, p 105
Tobique Point, New Brunswick, mid-1800s
43 x 18¼ Cloth with beadwork. Double
curve designs.
Collection of Frank Francis, Chief of the
Amalecite Indians at Tobique Point, New Brunswick.
Purchased 1894.
PM/HU cat no 94.15.10/50793

* 281 Garment, Micmac
Nova Scotia
24 x 10 Velveteen with beadwork,
sequins, glazed chintz, cloth tape.
Floral design.
Collected by Albert Green Heath.
LMA/BC cat no 30450

*282 Leggings, Ojibwa
Mid-19th century
26½ x 10¾ Trade cloth, embroidered
and appliquéd decoration.
MHSM cat no 8303.1

* 283 Moccasins, Ojibwa
9 Buckskin with beadwork, velvet.
SMM cat no 62-89

* 284 Vest, Ojibwa
Minnesota
20½ x 18½ Black velvet with beadwork.
Collected 1923.
MHSM cat no 6333/13

* 285 Moccasins, Potawatomi
Mayetta, Kansas
9½ Buckskin with beadwork.
Floral design.
Collected by Milford G. Chandler.
CIS cat no 3061

* 286 Moccasins, Potawatomi   *47*, p 48
10½ Buckskin with beadwork.
Separate sole is unusual.
Collection of Mrs. O. S. Perkins,
Allenspark, Colorado.
DAM cat no BPw-4-P

* 287 Vest, Potawatomi
Northern Wisconsin
21 x 21 Wool with beadwork,
lined with calico and wool.
Floral designs.
Collected by H. L. Mumm.
SHSW cat no 1954.811

* 288 Breech Cloth, probably Winnebago
Nebraska
55 x 18 Trade cloth with beadwork.
Collected by Thomas R. Roddy before 1908.
SHSW cat no 50.6415/E192

* 289 Man's Sash, Winnebago
Wisconsin
31½ x 3¾ Loom beadwork with
native fiber, wool fringe. Geometric design.
Collected by Major Horatio Rust.
LMA/BC cat no 1361

* 290 Sash, Choctaw
Early 19th century
Trade cloth with braided yarns, beadwork,
beaded fringe.
PM cat no E25963

* 291 Man's Belt, Seminole
Florida
33½ x 2½ Woven beadwork with yarn fringe.
MAI/HF cat no 1/7927

* 292 Dress, Arapaho
Wyoming
60 Painted buckskin with fringe, down
and magpie feathers. Worn in Ghost Dance
Society. Thunderbird or magpie figures
on one side, crescents and crosses on obverse.
Collected by Albert Green Heath from Little Raven.
LMA/BC cat no 30449

* **293 Shirt, Arapaho** *182*, p 116
31 x 21½ Painted buckskin with fringes.
Birds, stars, turtle and man, naturalistic
representations. Used in Ghost Dance.
MAI/HF cat no 2/1133

* **294 Dance Cape, probably Assiniboin**
ca 1900
26 x 28 Beadwork. Worn over cloth shirt.
COE

* **295 Dance Cape, Blackfeet** *145*, p 107
ca 1900
9¼ x 23 Bugle beads. Worn
over cloth shirt.
COE

* **296 Woman's Leggings, probably Blackfeet**
Northern Plains
13 x 14 Buckskin with beadwork, cotton,
deerskin. Geometric design.
SMM cat no 49-78

* **297 Moccasins, Blackfeet**
Montana
10¼ Buckskin with quillwork and beadwork.
SMM cat no 63.1.1

* **298 Man's Shirt, probably Blackfeet or Assiniboin**
Northwestern Plains
30½ x 17½ Painted and dressed skin
with beadwork, feathers, ermine tails.
Bequest of Victor J. Evans estate, 1931.
NMNH/SI cat no 357,516/113,605

* **299 Man's Shirt, probably Blackfeet**
Northern Plains, late 19th century
25½ Buckskin with quillwork.
SMM cat no 49-92

* **300 Man's Shirt, Blackfeet**
After 1860
33 Buckskin with beadwork, flannel,
weasel skins. Geometric design.
Collected by L. W. Hill.
SMM cat no 1-1112

* **301 Man's Shirt, Blackfeet**
1911
33 Buckskin with quillwork.
Geometric design.
SMM cat no 49-95

* **302 Man's Shirt, Blackfeet**
Late 19th century
26 x 22 Woolen trade cloth
with beadwork, buckskin, quillwork.
Collected by L. W. Hill.
SMM cat no 1-1044

* **303 Man's Shirt, Blackfeet**
Late 19th century
36½ x 29 Painted buckskin with
quillwork, beadwork.
SMM cat no 1-1040

* **304 Dress, Cheyenne**
Oklahoma
60 Buckskin with beadwork, fringe and
metal cones. Worn in Ghost Dance Society.
Collected by Albert Green Heath from
Hattie Black Wolf, Oklahoma, 1912.
LMA/BC cat no 30413

* **305 Dress, Cheyenne (Northern)** *62*, p 60
Montana
48 x 33 Cloth with cowrie and
dentalium shells.
MAI/HF cat no 21/2563

* **306 Moccasins, Cheyenne**
Early 20th century
10½ Buckskin with beadwork.
MHSM cat no 6333.9

* **307 Moccasins, Cheyenne**
10½ Buckskin with beadwork.
Purchased at Cheyenne Agency, Montana, 1922.
MHSM cat no 8387

* **308 Moccasins, Cheyenne**
ca 1930
10¾ Buckskin with beadwork.
MHSM cat no NPR

* **309 Coat, probably Cree**
ca 1865
37½ x 33 Buckskin with silk embroidery.
Made in imitation of a European coat.
MHSM cat no 66.271

* **310 Scout Coat, Plains Cree**
Manitoba or North Dakota
43 x 23 Buckskin with quillwork, fringe.
Cut in the style of a Prince Albert coat.
MHSM cat no 8303/2

* **311 Woman's Leggings, Cree**
Central Canada
22 x 9½ Wool with velvet, beadwork.
Floral design.
Collected by Albert Green Heath.
LMA/BC cat no 30454

* **312 Moccasins, Cree**
10 x 3¾ Buckskin with quillwork,
moose hair.
Collection of Mrs. W. H. Miller, 1916.
UMUP cat no NA 4946

* **313 Woman's Leggings, probably Crow**
17½ x 16 Buckskin with beadwork.
DAM cat no BCr-64-G

* **314 Dress, Crow**
Montana
45 x 25 Cloth with imitation elk teeth
covering almost entire garment.
MAI/HF cat no 12/6407

* **315 Shirt, Crow**
Montana
36 x 23½ Painted Buckskin with
beadwork, scalp locks.
Collected by S. C. Simms, 1901.
FMNH cat no 69578

* **316 Shirt, probably Crow** *146*, p 107
Northern Plains, ca 1840
52⁹⁄₁₆ x 25³⁄₁₆ Painted buckskin with
quillwork, scalp locks. Figures represented
are enemies killed by the warrior.
Gift of American Antiquarian Society of
Worcester, Massachusetts, 1890.
PM/HU cat no 90.17.10/49309

* **317 Man's Leggings, Gros Ventre**
32 x 14 Buckskin with beadwork.
SMM cat no 1-1056a/b

* **318 Moccasins, Kickapoo**
10¼ Buckskin with beadwork.
DAM cat no BKp-6-P

* **319 Woman's Belt Set, Kiowa**
39 Buckskin with commercial leather,
crackerjack coins, beadwork.
DAM cat no BK1-19-PQ

* **320 Dress, Kiowa**
Oklahoma
60 Painted buckskin with fringe.
Crescent and star designs.
Worn in Ghost Dance Society.
Collected by Albert Green Heath.
LMA/BC cat no 30416

* **321 Shirt, Mandan**
North Dakota
38 x 31½ Painted buckskin with
quillwork, horsehair, human hair.
Geometric designs.
MAI/HF cat no 16/5277

* **322 Leggings, Miami**
Wabash, Indiana
34½ x 14³⁄₁₆ Broadcloth with
beadwork.
Collected by Milford G. Chandler.
CIS cat no 2209

* **323 Leggings, Miami** *52*, p 52
Wabash, Indiana
24¹⁄₁₆ x 9¹⁄₁₆ Broadcloth
with beadwork.
Collected by Milford G. Chandler.
CIS cat no 2210

* **324 Moccasins, probably Miami**
Indiana, mid-19th century
Buckskin with
beadwork, quillwork, cloth cuffs.
PM cat no E6644

* **325 Moccasins, Miami**
Indiana
9½ x 5½ Buckskin with quillwork
and beadwork.
PM cat no E3707

* **326 Moccasins, Miami** *142*, p 106
Wabash, Indiana
9⁷⁄₁₆ Buckskin with silk appliqué,
beadwork.
Collected by Milford G. Chandler
from family of Meshinga Mezhas.
CIS cat no 2207

* 327 Woman's Robe, Osage
Oklahoma
62¼ x 57½ Cloth with ribbon
appliqué. Geometric designs.
MAI/HF cat no 2
             796

* 328 Robe, Osage
Oklahoma
57 x 60 Wool list cloth with silk
ribbon appliqué.
Collected by Albert Green Heath.
LMA/BC cat no 30400

* 329 Sash, Osage
87 Braided yarn with beadwork.
Finger weave.
Collection of Albert Green Heath,
Chicago, 1949.
DAM cat no ROS-7-P

* 330 Shirt, Osage
Oklahoma
29 x 23½ Cloth with beadwork.
MAI/HF cat no 10
             3014

* 331 Shirt, Ponca
42 x 24 Painted buckskin with scalps.
Worn by a tribal leader on war expeditions.
Belonged to Standing Bear.
Collection of Omaha Charley Bristol, 1876.
NSHS cat no 338-03

* 332 Man's Leggings, probably Shoshoni   77, p 75
Northern Plains
30¼ x 13 Buckskin with beadwork.
SMM cat no 49-64

* 333 Breastplate, Sioux
Plains
19¾ x 12½ Quillwork with
feathers, tin cones. Chevron designs.
HM cat no NA-PL-So-C-25

* 334 Breastplate, Sioux
Mid-19th century
18¼ x 8½ Bone, hair pipes, plum
seeds, trade beads and rawhide.
PM cat no E22019

* 335 Breastplate, probably Sioux
Crow Creek Reservation, South Dakota
46¼ x 11¾ Hair pipe with beadwork,
leather. Worn by men and women.
Collected by and collection of David W. Clark.
ODM cat no CMC-K-21

* 336 Dress, Sioux
Northern Plains
50 x 63½ Buckskin with beadwork,
fringe and tin danglers.
Bequest of Victor J. Evans estate, 1931.
NMNH/SI cat no 357,534
              113,605

* 337 Dress, Sioux
Northern Plains
57 x 61½ Buckskin with beadwork
and fringe.
Bequest of Victor J. Evans estate, 1931.
NMNH/SI cat no 357,535
              113,605

* 338 Dress, Sioux
66 Painted elkskin with beadwork.
Yoke solidly beaded with lazy stitch
and geometric designs.
SMM cat no 1-1113

* 339 Dress, Sioux
North Dakota
53¾ x 37 Painted buckskin with feathers.
Used in Ghost Dance. Eagle with rainbow
representations.
MAI/HF cat no 2
             7308

* 340 Girl's Dress, Sioux (Teton)
Standing Rock Reservation, North Dakota
27¾ x 24 Buckskin with heavily
beaded yoke. Geometric designs.
MAI/HF cat no 12
             6152

* 341 Girl's Dress, Sioux   138, p 105
28¾ x 25½ Buckskin with
beadwork and fringe.
Collected by Emile Granier.
NMNH/SI cat no 00633
              34005

* 342 Girl's Dress, Sioux (Eastern)
43 x 32 Sinew-sewn doeskin with
buckskin yoke, beadwork and fringe.
Tailored.
Gift of Dr. Willem Van Royen.
NMNH/SI cat no 394,432
              214,357

* 343 Leggings, Sioux
South Dakota, 1870s
30 Buckskin with beadwork.
War exploit designs.
HM cat no NA-PL-SO C-37/WUN-12/1229

* 344 Half Leggings, probably Sioux
Minnesota
18 x 13 Buckskin with ribbon, cotton
duck, beadwork. Floral design. Worn over
cloth trousers.
LMA/BC cat no 1288

* 345 Half Leggings, probably Sioux
Minnesota
21 Buckskin with cotton duck, beadwork,
brass bells. Floral design. Worn over
cloth trousers.
LMA/BC cat no 1281

* 346 Loincloth, probably Sioux
Lower Brule Reservation, South Dakota
18 x 9 Buckskin, quillwork, beadwork fringe.
Collected by L. C. Walker, ca 1875.
Collection of David W. Clark.
ODM cat no CMC-D-24

* 347 Moccasins, Sioux
Poplar, Montana, late 19th century
Buckskin with quillwork.
Collection of Mr. Willard C. Cousins, 1946.
PM cat no E25830

* 348 Moccasins, Sioux (Eastern)
Minnesota, 1869
9½ Buckskin with beadwork.
MHSM cat no 8419.22

* 349 Moccasins, Sioux
Cheyenne River Reservation, South Dakota, ca 1900
10 Buckskin with beadwork.
MHSM cat no 9859.50a/b

* 350 Moccasins, Sioux
ca 1900
10¾ Buckskin with beadwork, quillwork.
MHSM cat no NPR

* 351 Moccasins, Sioux
10¾ x 4 Buckskin with quillwork, horsehair, metal tinklers.
SMM cat no 1-1089

* 352 Child's Moccasins, Sioux
6 Buckskin with beadwork.
Collected 1930.
MHSM cat no 6874/23

* 353 Shirt, Sioux   7, p 12
19th century
50 x 43⅜ Painted buckskin with
beadwork, scalp lock. Bear claw design.
The Dick S. Ramsay Fund.
BM cat no 38.629

* 354 Shirt, Sioux
28 Painted buckskin.
Collected by Carter Harrison III.
Collection of Mrs. Richard D. Stevenson, 1970.
FMNH cat no 257209

* 355 Man's Shirt, Sioux
Crow Creek Reservation, South Dakota
34½ x 23¼ Buckskin with quillwork,
eagle feathers. Owned by Arrow, Big Bend.
Collected by and collection of David W. Clark, 1940.
ODM cat no CMC-D41

* 356 Man's Shirt, Sioux
ca 1850
51 x 54 Buckskin with quillwork.
MHSM cat no 69.54.2

* 357 Shirt, Sioux (Oglala)
South Dakota
29½ x 18½ Painted buckskin with
fringe. Used in a dance. Large horse
represented in center front.
MAI/HF cat no 11
             4622

* 358 Man's Shirt, probably Sioux
Northern Plains, late 19th century
33 Buckskin with beadwork, scalp
locks, green felt.
SMM cat no 49-89

* 359 Man's Trousers, probably Sioux
36¼ x 10 Buckskin with quillwork,
beadwork, cotton cloth. Geometric design.
SMM cat no 49-65

* 360 Vest, Sioux
20 x 18¼ Deerskin with beadwork.
Horse and triangle design.
SMM cat no 61-5

* 361 Vest, probably Sioux   58, p 58
20 x 17½ Deerskin with quillwork.
Flag and horse design.
SMM cat no 61/345

*** 362 Vest, probably Sioux**
ca 1880
21 x 17 Buckskin with quillwork.
Floral design.
MHSM cat no 9539.4

*** 363 Vest, Sioux**
1900
20½ x 20 Buckskin with beadwork,
lined with cloth, thong attachments.
Geometric design.
SMM cat no 49-85

*** 364 Vest, Sioux** *147,* p 107
19 x 19 Buckskin with beadwork, fringe.
According to White Bear (Sioux), this
vest belonged to John White Wolf.
DAM cat no BS-103-G

*** 365 Child's Vest, Sioux**
ca 1900
17 x 13 Buckskin with beadwork, fringe.
Two naval amulets attached.
MHSM cat no 65.36.1

*** 366 Girl's Dress**
Northern Plains
28 x 27½ Buckskin with beadwork and fringe.
Bequest of Victor J. Evans, 1931.
NMNH/SI cat no 357,531
113,605

*** 367 Moccasins**
Plains, after 1860
11 Buckskin with quillwork, beadwork.
SMM cat no 1-1082a/b

*** 368 Moccasins**
Northern Plains, before 1850
10½ x 5 Buckskin with beadwork.
DAM cat no B-155-P

*** 369 Shawl, Pueblo (Acoma)** *144,* p 106
Acoma Pueblo, New Mexico
48 x 57 Two-strand fiber weave with
embroidery. Natural dyes.
Collected by Governor Arthur Seligman, 1937.
Gift of Alice Baylor.
TM/CSFAC cat no 3827

*** 370 Kilt, Pueblo (Hopi)**
Arizona
61½ x 45 Wool embroidery on cotton.
SM cat no SWM-1

*** 371 Kilt, Pueblo (Hopi)**
61½ x 45 Cotton with wool embroidery.
SM cat no 1

*** 372 Dance Kilt, Pueblo (Hopi)**
45 x 23 Painted buckskin. Serpent design.
TM/CSFAC cat no TM5133

*** 373 Kilt, Pueblo (Hopi)**
24 x 37¼ Painted leather with deer hoofs.
AMNH cat no 16.1/1510

*** 374 Manta, Pueblo (Hopi)** *140,* p 105
20th century
50 x 80 Commercial cotton thread with
embroidery in commercial yarns.
Collection of Alfred I. Barton.
DAM cat no RHc-92

*** 375 Woman's Leggings, Ute**
14¾ x 8¾ Buckskin with beadwork.
DAM cat no BU-62-PD

*** 376 Sisiutl Belt, Kwakiutl**
British Columbia, 19th century
53 x 10¼ Carved and painted
wood with oiled cloth.
SOSLAND

*** 377 Cloth Apron, Tlingit**
Alaska
24¾ x 34¼ Painted cloth
with tinklers.
MAI/HF cat no 6539

*** 378 Man's Coat, Tlingit**
Southeast Alaska, before 1867
30¾ x 25⅝ Painted deerskin with
gabardine. Worn by Sitka Jack at his
potlatch, 1877. Designs are family crests.
Gift of Lewis H. Farlow, 1904.
PM/HU cat no 04.10.10
62978

*** 379 Shaman's Robe, Tlingit**
Chatham Straits, Admiralty Island, Alaska
46 x 24½ Painted rawhide. Slit for
neck, poncho shape.
MAI/HF cat no 11
274

*** 380 Man's Shirt, Tlingit (Chilkat)**
Alaska
45 x 22½ Woven wool.
MAI/HF cat no 18
7902

*** 381 Shirt, Tlingit**
Alaska
33¼ x 51 Cloth with buttons.
Design represents a bird.
Used in a dance.
MAI/HF cat no 16
1720

*** 382 Shirt, Tlingit**
1890s
42 x 59 Felt with seed beads.
Design represents a bear.
COE

*** 383 Shirt, Tlingit**
Alaska
38½ x 25¼ Cloth with beadwork.
MAI/HF cat no 21
6806

*** 384 Dance Skirt, Tlingit (Chilkat)**
28 x 42 Woven mountain sheep wool.
Collected by H. R. Bishop, 1869.
AMNH cat no 16/A1/348

*** 385 Dance Leggings** *139,* p 105
Northwest Coast
$14\frac{9}{16}$ x 16½ Leather with quillwork,
puffin beaks.
Collected by Mrs. Davies Gilbert.
Collection of Mrs. A. W. F. Fuller, 1964.
FMNH cat no 155568/155569

*** 386 Dress, Cree** *15,* p 18
Saskatchewan, Canada
47⅜ Painted buckskin with beadwork.
Linear designs in unusual early pattern.
Collected by Lewis and Clark 1804-06.
Gift of heirs of David Kimball, 1899.
PM/HU cat no 99.12.10
53046

*** 387 Moccasins, Dogrib**
Northwest Territories, Canada
10 Mooseskin with silk thread embroidery.
Collected by Nancy Lurie.
MPM cat no 59586 ab
20874

Dolls

*** 388 Pair of Jugger Dolls, Menomini**
Wisconsin
9 x 2¼ Carved and painted wood, cloth.
Collected by Samuel A. Barrett, Menomini
Reservation, Wisconsin, 1919.
MPM cat no 24991 a/b

*** 389 Pair of Medicine Dolls, Ojibwa** *14,* p 17
Leech Lake, Minnesota
6 Used as love charms.
Collected by Albert Green Heath from
Jine Fine Day, 1927.
LMA/BC cat no 31154

*** 390 Doll, Ojibwa**
Michigan
17¼ x 4¾ Carved wood, articulated joints.
Ceremonial use.
MAI/HF cat no 22
8524

*** 391 Doll, Ojibwa**
9 x 3½ Trade cloth and beads.
MHSM cat no E32

*** 392 Doll, Ojibwa**
13 x 4½ Cloth and beads.
MHSM cat no 8014

*** 393 Pair of Love Dolls, Ottawa**
Michigan
3¾ Wood. Used as love charms.
Collected by Albert Green Heath.
LMA/BC cat no 30844

*** 394 Male Love Doll, Potawatomi (Prairie)**
Crandon, Wisconsin
$9\frac{1}{16}$ Carved wood with wool, nails.
Collected by Milford G. Chandler, 1920.
CIS cat no 3058

*** 395 Pair of Dolls, Winnebago**
Wisconsin, 1890s
Female: 8, Male: 8½ Cloth with
buckskin, silver brooches.
Made by Mable St. Cyr in Nebraska, 1890s.
LMA/BC cat no 30595

*** 396 Doll, Seminole**
Florida
31½ x 8½ Dressed in typical
Seminole man's costume.
MAI/HF cat no 20
3611

* 397 **Doll, Seminole**
Florida
28½ x 9 Dressed in typical Seminole
woman's costume.
MAI/HF cat no   20
1140

* 398 **Matching Pair of Dolls, Gros Ventre**
Montana
12 Deerskin with beadwork, horsehair
braids, fur, yarn. Made by Juanita Tucker,
Fort Belknap, Montana.
SMM cat no 52/5a/b

* 399 **Doll, Sioux**
12 Deerskin with hair.
Collected at Standing Rock Agency, 1865-1890.
SMM cat no 1-754

* 400 **Doll, Sioux**
14 x 4 Buckskin with beadwork.
MHSM cat no 8034.6

* 401 **Doll, Sioux**
8½ x 3 Buckskin with beadwork.
MHSM cat no 61.83.7

* 402 **Doll, Apache (Western)**
Arizona
15 Cloth with sticks, buckskin,
beadwork, metal dangles.
Collected by Charles L. Owens, 1901.
LMA/BC cat no 1236

* 403 **Toy Cradle, Apache (Western)**
White River, Arizona
7⅝ Wood with buckskin, beadwork.
Rag figure of baby.
Collected by Charles L. Owens, 1901.
LMA/BC cat no 1234

* 404 **Doll, Mohave**
Southern Arizona
7 Pottery with bead dangles, cotton cloth.
LMA/BC cat no 1535

* 405 **Doll, Mohave**
Rio Colorado, California, 1854
9⅞ x 3¾ x 2 Painted pottery.
Collected by Jules Marcou, 1854.
PM/HU cat no 72.26.10
7062

* 406 **Doll, Mohave**
ca 1880
6⅜ x 3¼ x 1⅝ Painted pottery
with beads, hair.
Gift of Miss Nellie M. Betteley, 1905.
PM/HU cat no 05.22.10
64869

* 407 **Doll, Mohave**
Southern Arizona
5 Pottery with wool flannel, beads.
LMA/BC cat no 1532

* 408 **Doll, Mohave**
Southern Arizona
7 Pottery with bead dangles, cotton cloth.
LMA/BC cat no 1534

* 409 **Doll, Mohave**
Southern Arizona
3 Pottery with beads.
LMA/BC cat no 1537

* 410 **Doll, Mohave**
Southern Arizona
6¾ Painted pottery with cloth and beads.
LMA/BC cat no 1531

* 411 **Doll, Cocopa**   *148*, p 107
Southern California, early 1900s
10; 5¼ diam. Painted terra cotta
with bead earrings.
Collected by Miss Grace Nicholson, 1912.
Gift of Lewis H. Farlow, 1912.
PM/HU cat no 12.29.10
84105

* 412 **Doll, Eskimo**
Alaska
5½ x 1¾ Ivory.
Collected by Mercier, Norton Sound
to Point Barrow, 1886.
NMM cat no IV-E-353

* 413 **Doll, Eskimo**
Melville Peninsula, Canada
3 x ¾ Carved ivory.
MAI/HF cat no   18
5051

Hats and Headdresses

414 **Dance Headdress, Blackfeet**
Late 19th century
35 x 7½ Buckskin with weasel strips,
wool, eagle feathers.
SMM cat no 1-1103

415 **Man's Society Headdress,**
Hidatsa or Mandan   *55*, p 56
Fort Berthold Reservation, North Dakota, mid-1800s
36½ x 7⅛ Clipped crow feathers, wool, trade
cloth, Venetian glass beads, split buffalo horns,
quillwork, fur.
Collected by Rev. C. L. Hall, 1886.
Gift of Professor William James, 1887.
PM/HU cat no 87.11.10
40898

416 **Feathered Bonnet, Sioux**
63¾ x 24¼ Cloth with bison horns, eagle
feathers, down.
Collected by E. Adamson Hoebel, 1935.
HOEBEL

417 **Headdress, probably Sioux**   *149*, p 108
Central Plains
70½ Beadwork, eagle feathers, down, buckskin,
flannel.
Collected by Fred K. Hinchman.
SM cat no 535-9-1110

418 **Gahan Dancer Headdress, Apache**   *150*, p 108
San Carlos, Arizona
35 x 25¾ Cloth, wood, paint, metal,
mirror, cord.
Collected by E. H. Davis in 1910-1911.
Collection of Museum of the American Indian,
Heye Foundation.
MPA cat no 66.11

419 **Hat, Apache (White Mountain)**
Arizona
5; 10 diam. Painted hide with feathers.
Ceremonial use.
MAI/HF cat no   9
4592

420 **Headdress, Apache (White Mountain)**
Arizona
5½; 10¼ diam. Painted deerskin with feathers,
beadwork.
MAI/HF cat no   20
8055

421 **Tableta, Pueblo (Hopi)**
Walpi, Arizona
19¼ x 13 x ⅜ Painted wood with leather straps.
Headdress with carved steps on top and cut out bird
in center. Used in Butterfly Dance.
Fred Harvey Foundation, Fine Arts Collection.
HM cat no 332-C-1

422 **Tableta, Pueblo (Hopi)**
ca 1920
18 x 26½ Carved wood and paint, cord.
Made by attaching cut pieces of wood to door-shaped
frame with cord strung through drill holes. Sun-
flowers and clouds on one side, corn and clouds
on opposing face. Used in Butterfly Dance.
MNA cat no 2519/E-4002

423 **Headdress, Hupa**
California
9; 37¼ long. Hide with feathers.
Used in a dance.
MAI/HF cat no 1210

424 **Plume, Karok**
California
25½ Feather. Used in Brush Dance.
MAI/HF cat no   15
1917

425 **Woman's Ceremonial Headdress, Pomo**
Upper Lake, California
15⅜ x 3 x 5⅛ Rawhide wrapped in otter fur,
beads and small feather mats held by wire; quillwork,
cotton twine, shell and ribbon.
Collected by Grace Nicholson, 1905.
PM/HU cat no 05.7.10
65637

426 **Woman's Ceremonial**
Headdress, Pomo   *151*, p 108
Upper Lakes, California, late 1800s
42 Rawhide wrapped in otter fur, beads and
small feather mats held by wire; shell, quillwork,
yarn, wool tape, beaded projections.
Gift of Mrs. Thomas B. Bishop, 1908.
PM/HU cat no 08.14.10
73080

427 **Feather Hair Ornaments, Pomo**
Northern California
21¼ x 5½ Shafted flicker tailfeathers
with woodpecker, oriole, bluebird and quail feathers.
DAM cat no FPO-8-PD

428 Feathered Ear Plugs, Pomo
Northern California
14⅛ Shafted flicker tailfeathers with woodpecker, oriole, bluebird and quail feathers.
DAM cat no FPO-10-PD

429 Feathered Pin, Pomo
Northern California
20¼ Shafted flicker tailfeathers with crane's wishbone (hairpins), woodpecker, oriole, bluebird and quail feathers.
DAM cat no FPO-14-Ex

430 Head Ring, Yurok
California
8½ diam. Deer hair and woodpecker scalps on hide.
MAI/HF cat no 15
7029

* 431 Basketry Hat, Haida
1884
7; 17 diam. Spruce root fiber and paint.
Motif of eyes, ears, wings and claws.
Collected by Alex Mackenzie.
NMM cat no VII-B-891

* 432 Basketry Hat, Haida
1884
8¼ ; 21 diam. Spruce root fiber and paint.
Narrow cylindrical crown, flaring brim, crest designs.
Collected by Alex Mackenzie.
NMM cat no VII-B-892

* 433 Potlatch Hat, Haida
12; 13½ diam. Carved and painted wood with basketry rings, copper, abalone shell, brass nails, fur.
UMUP cat no NA 11740

* 434 Clan Helmet, Haida   152, p 108
Queen Charlotte Islands, Canada
10⅝ x 15⅝ Painted wood. Bear shape.
Collected by Stewart Culin, museum expedition, 1905.
BM cat no 05.274

* 435 Frontal Dance Headdress, Tlingit (Chilkat)
7¼ x 6¼ x 2½ Carved wood, ermine skins, wool, walrus whiskers, abalone shell inlay and tail feathers.
Gift of A. Lewisohn, 1905.
AMNH cat no 16. 1/304

* 436 Shaman's Frontal Headdress, Tlingit (Chilkat)
4½ x 3¾ x 2½ Carved and painted wood with human hair trim, abalone shell inlay. Represents the spirit of the devilfish.
AMNH cat no 19/920

* 437 Headdress, Tlingit
Angoon, Admiralty Island, Alaska
9¾ x 10 Carved and painted wood, cloth, fur, feathers.
MAI/HF cat no 14
9607

* 438 Frontal Headdress, Tlingit
6¾ Carved and painted wood, swansdown, human and animal hair, feathers.
AMNH cat no 19/911

* 439 Frontal Headdress, Tlingit
5½ x 4½ x 4 Carved and painted wood, swansdown, bald eagle feathers. Represents an eagle spirit.
AMNH cat no E/916

* 440 Frontal Headdress, Tlingit
5½ x 4⅝ x 2¾ Carved and painted wood, swansdown, feathers, bone carvings. Small wooden mask represents a Tlingit spirit.
AMNH cat no E/943

* 441 Frontal Headdress, Tlingit
5¼ Carved and painted wood, swansdown, human hair, fur, feathers. Small wooden mask represents the spirit of a dead Tlingit.
AMNH cat no E/944

* 442 Frontal Headdress, Tlingit
7¾ x 6¼ x 2 Carved wood, ermine, wool cloth, walrus whiskers.
Used in a dance.
AMNH cat no E/1062

* 443 Frontal Headdress, Tlingit
Angoon, Alaska
8 x 6¼ x 2½ Carved wood, ermine, wool cloth, walrus whiskers, abalone and haliotis shell inlay. Used for ceremonial dance. Represents a beaver sitting up, gnawing a piece of wood.
AMNH cat no E/1559

* 444 Hat, Tlingit
Southeastern Alaska
13½ ; 13½ diam. Carved and painted wood, human hair, copper. Represents "Raven of the Roof."
Collected by Louis Shotridge, 1925.
UMUP cat no NA 10511

* 445 Helmet, Tlingit
10¼ ; 15 diam. Carved and painted wood.
Collected by Louis Shotridge, 1917.
UMUP cat no NA 5740

* 446 Headdress, Tlingit
8¼ x 8¼ x 11½ Carved and painted wood with hide and metal. Represents a kingfisher and frog.
AMNH cat no E/2364

* 447 Headdress, Tlingit
Alaska
9 x 7¾ x 6¾ Carved and painted wood, copper, abalone shell, walrus hide, human hair, animal teeth.
Collected by Louis Shotridge, 1926.
UMUP cat no NA 10832

* 448 Raven Clan Hat, Tlingit
Alaska, 19th century
14 x 13½ x 20½ Carved and painted wood, abalone shell inlay, heavy skin, stroud cloth.
SOSLAND

* 449 Ceremonial Hat, Tlingit
Alaska
10½ x 13⅜ x 10⅞ Carved and painted wood, human hair.
Collected by Louis Shotridge, 1926.
UMUP cat no NA 11741

* 450 Frontal Headdress, Tlingit
Klukwan, Alaska
5½ Carved and painted wood, moose tail, ermine, opercula teeth, human hair, swansdown, abalone shell inlay, brass tack eyes, feathers, caribou tail. Spruce twig framework. Used by doctor. Mask represents a spirit.
AMNH cat no E/2372

* 451 Helmet, Tsimshian
Kitkatla, British Columbia, 1895-1901
17 x 12½ Carved and painted wood, shell, bear canines. Depicts small man on sea lion.
Collected by C. F. Newcombe.
NMM cat no VII-C-273

* 452 Frontal Headdress, Tsimshian
Nass River, British Columbia
7⅞ x 6½ x 3 Carved and painted wood, abalone shell inlay with inscription: "Owl from Nass River." Represents the white owl.
Collected by Franz Boas, 1895.
AMNH cat no 16/967

* 453 Clan Hat, Tsimshian   153, p 109
British Columbia, 19th century
8½ x 8¼ Carved and painted wood, abalone shell inlay.
SOSLAND

* 454 Frontal Headdress, Tsimshian
Northwest Coast
5⅛ x 6¾ x 8½ Carved and painted wood. Used by a doctor. Represents a raven's head and a spirit. Over the head are many heads representing spirits possessed by the doctor which assist him.
AMNH cat no E/2512

* 455 Crown
Northwest Coast
5½ x 15½ Leather, human hair, inlaid copper. Con Goush — from Kehk country. Worn by chief as fighting headdress or for feast or ceremony.
AMNH cat no E/725

* 456 Helmet   158, p 110
Northwest Coast
13½ x 10 x 11 Carved wood.
UMUP cat no 37945

457 Hat, Aleut
Aleutian Islands, Alaska
15 x 8½ x 9 Painted wood with ivory, walrus whiskers, glass beads.
MAI/HF cat no 14
4871

458 Man's Hat, Aleut   154, p 109
Aleutian Islands, Alaska, before 1867
16¹¹⁄₁₆ x 8⅝ x 7¾ Painted wood, sea lion whiskers.
Originally loaned by Boston Marine Society, 1869.
PM/HU cat no 69.20.10
1263

459 Hunting Visor, Eskimo
Kuskokwim River, Alaska, late 19th century
12 x 7⅞ Carved and painted wood with feathers, carved and incised walrus ivory. Ivory represents human heads, bird heads; incised representations of caribou, hunters, sleds.
Collected by Charles L. Hall, ca 1895.
LM/UC/B cat no 2-81

Hides

* 460 Buffalo Robe, Ojibwa   11, p 14
Great Lakes, Eastern Woodlands, late 1800s
81 x 72¼ Painted hide. Rare example,
only a dozen or so known.
Gift of Mr. William Barbour, 1910.
PM/HU cat no 10.46.10
                            76789

* 461 Tipi, Cheyenne
216; 240 diam. Painted cowhide.
Bear paw designs; buffalo image on flaps.
Collected by J. Mooney, 1904.
FMNH cat no 96787

* 462 Hide, Comanche
Oklahoma
30½ x 37½ Painted hide.
MAI/HF cat no 2/2169

* 463 Buffalo Robe, Mandan   4, p 10
North Dakota, 1797
79½ Painted hide. Illustrates battle
fought between Sioux and Arikara against
Mandans and Hidatsa in which combatants are
represented on horseback, 1797.
Collected by Lewis and Clark expedition, 1805.
Gift of the heirs of David Kimball, 1899.
PM/HU cat no 99.12. 10
                            53121

* 464 Hide, Shoshoni
Wyoming
65 x 66½ Painted elkhide.
Design relates to Sun Dance.
MAI/HF cat no 23/6400

* 465 Buffalo Robe, Sioux   155, p 109
Central Plains
93½ x 74 Painted hide. Sunburst design
with border.
MPA cat no 63.82

* 466 Buffalo Robe, Sioux
South Dakota, 1870
74 x 92 Painted hide. Black Bonnet design.
DAM cat no PS-39-P

* 467 Hide, Apache
Arizona
54 x 31 (center) x 57 (base). Painted bear
hide. Scenes of "the life of Mr. Touzalin."
Shows hunters, dancers, warriors, white men,
a tipi, a church and a centipede.
Collected by and gift of Lidas M. Touzalin.
TM/CSFAC cat no 1550

* 468 Playing Cards, Apache
Arizona
3¾ x 2¼ Painted rawhide.
MAI/HF cat no   6
                      4597

* 469 Hide, Pueblo (Zuni)
Zuni Pueblo, New Mexico
63¼ x 33 Painted deerskin.
Used in a kiva.
MAI/HF cat no 21/8666

* 470 Poncho, Tlingit
Northwest Coast
67 x 23¾ Painted skin. Cut into fish
shape. Represents sharks.
Collected by Ralph C. Altman.
TM/CSFAC cat no 3985

Kachinas

471 Aha (Silent) Kachina, Pueblo (Hopi)
North Central Arizona
14 x 4½ Carved and painted wood, cloth,
feathers. Case mask, belt, skirt, moccasins,
wand and rattle.
Fred Harvey Foundation, Fine Arts Collection.
HM cat no 781-C-1

472 (Badger) Kachina, Pueblo (Hopi)
North Central Arizona
13 x 6 Carved and painted wood with cloth.
Case mask, pop-eyes, snout, badger paws on face,
skirt, rattle, concho belt, sash.
Fred Harvey Foundation, Fine Arts Collection.
HM cat no 850-C-1

473 (Bear) Kachina, Pueblo (Hopi)
Oraibi, Arizona, 1920s
15 Carved and painted wood with fur. Made
by White Bear's father, Charles Fredericks.
SM cat no 491-P-3493

474 Chakwaina Kachina, Pueblo (Hopi)
Arizona
10⅝ Carved and painted wood with horsehair.
MNA cat no 2563/E-3758

475 (Cross Crown) Kachina, Pueblo (Hopi)
North Central Arizona
14 x 6 Carved and painted wood with cloth.
Ruff, bow, rattle, sash.
Fred Harvey Foundation, Fine Arts Collection.
HM cat no 776-C-1

476 (Eagle) Kachina, Pueblo (Hopi)
North Central Arizona
11 x 4½ Carved and painted wood with
feathers, yucca cloth. Case mask, headdress,
belt, skirt. In dancing position.
Fred Harvey Foundation, Fine Arts Collection.
HM cat no 915-C-1

477 Hakto Kachina, Pueblo (Hopi)
Arizona
12 Carved and painted wood with feathers, yarn.
Case mask with beads, kilt, ceremonial sash.
Appears in Bean Dance at First Mesa. Style of
a Zuni kachina.
MNA cat no 2563/E-3873

478 Heheya Kachina, Pueblo (Hopi)
First Mesa, Arizona, 1920s
12¾ Carved and painted wood with turquoise,
silver, velvet.
Elizabeth Compton Hegemann Collection.
Originally McGill Collection.
MNA cat no 2277/E-2289

479 Ho-e Kachina, Pueblo (Hopi)
Arizona,1920s
8¾ Carved and painted wood with lambskin,
cloth. Zuni-type with movable arms and
removable kilt.
Elizabeth Compton Hegemann Collection.
Originally McGill Collection.
MNA cat no 2277/E-2301

480 Holi Kachina, Pueblo (Hopi)
North Central Arizona
15½ x 8½ Carved and painted wood, cloth.
Headdress, pop-eyes, snout, skirt and robe,
belt, moccasins.
Fred Harvey Foundation, Fine Arts Collection.
HM cat no 816-C-1

481 Hololo Kachina, Pueblo (Hopi)
North Central Arizona
16 x 6½ Carved and painted wood, feathers,
yucca fiber, cloth.
Fred Harvey Foundation, Fine Arts Collection.
HM cat no 802-C-1

482 Hololo Kachina, Pueblo (Hopi)
Arizona, 1920s
8½ Carved and painted wood. Case mask,
pop-eyes, kilt, moccasins, arm bands.
Elizabeth Compton Hegemann Collection.
Originally McGill Collection.
MNA cat no 2277-E-2286

483 Hu (Whipper) Kachina, Pueblo (Hopi)
North Central Arizona
13 x 7 Carved and painted wood with fox skin,
yucca cloth. Case mask, belt, loincloth.
Fred Harvey Foundation, Fine Arts Collection.
HM cat no 854-C-1

484 (Hummingbird) Kachina, Pueblo (Hopi) 156, p 109
Arizona
7 x 5¾ Carved and painted wood, cotton cord.
Early example.
Collected by George Wharton James.
SM cat no 421-G-136

**485 Kohonin Putchko (Rabbit) Kachina,
Pueblo (Hopi)**
Arizona
14¾ Carved and painted wood, cloth, feathers.
Crown, spider web ears, canvas kilt, muslin belt,
wool wristlets.
Collected by John L. Nelson.
SM cat no 640-G-162

486 Kokleh Kachina, Pueblo (Hopi)
Arizona
6¼ Carved and painted wood with feathers.
Early example.
Collected by John L. Nelson.
SM cat no 640-G-152

487 Konin Kachina, Pueblo (Hopi)
Arizona, 1920s
7 Carved and painted wood. Flat rectangular
board, rectangular mouth. Baby's kachina.
Elizabeth Compton Hegemann Collection.
Originally McGill Collection.
MNA cat no 2277/E-2299

488 Koyemsi (Mudhead) Kachina, Pueblo (Hopi)
Arizona, 1930
8¾ Carved and painted wood. Kilt, scarf at neck; circular eyes and mouth; knobs on head.
MNA cat no 1343/E-985

489 Kwa (Eagle Dance) Kachina, Pueblo (Hopi)
Oraibi, Arizona, 1940s
18 x 17½ Carved and painted wood with feathers, cotton. Made by Otto Pentewa and Charles Fredericks.
SM cat no 491-P-3494

490 Lagan (Squirrel) Kachina, Pueblo (Hopi)
Second Mesa, Arizona
9⅞ Carved and painted wood. Case mask, round eyes, snout mouth with teeth, bandoleers across shoulders, kilt, concho belt.
MNA cat no 2563/E-3786

491 (Longhair) Kachina, Pueblo (Hopi)
North Central Arizona
11 x 4½ Carved and painted wood with hair, cloth. Case mask, belt, skirt.
Fred Harvey Foundation, Fine Arts Collection.
HM cat no 837-C-1

492 (Longhair) Kachina, Pueblo (Hopi)
North Central Arizona
15 x 4½ Carved and painted wood with cloth. Face mask, hair and beard, belt, skirt, moccasins.
Fred Harvey Foundation, Fine Arts Collection.
HM cat no 826-C-1

493 Omau (Cloud or Swaying) Kachina, Pueblo (Hopi)
Sichomovi, Arizona, 1960
15½ Carved and painted wood with feathers. Peeping Out Man (Na Ui Kui Taka). Made by Earl Mumziwan. Corn cob in one hand; rattle in the other.
SM cat no 491-P-3495

494 Owa or Kawa Kachina, Pueblo (Hopi)
Arizona
8½ Carved and painted wood.
Baby's kachina.
MNA cat no 2563/E-3811

495 Paiyi Kala (Three Horned) Kachina, Pueblo (Hopi)
Arizona, 1920s
29 Carved and painted cottonwood with tin, feathers. Protruding eyes, ears and snout. Conventional dance kilt decoration.
Collected by John L. Nelson.
SM cat no 640-G-146

496 Palhik Mana (Butterfly Maiden) Kachina, Pueblo (Hopi)
Oraibi, Arizona, 1920s
23½ Carved and painted wood with down, feathers. Spreading headdress. Made by Kocha Honawa (White Bear).
SM cat no 491-P-3496

497 Palhik Mana (Butterfly Maiden) Kachina, Pueblo (Hopi)
Arizona
10⅞ Carved and painted wood. Cloud tableta.
MNA cat no 2563/E-3751

498 Palhik Mana (Butterfly Maiden) Kachina, Pueblo (Hopi)
Arizona
11½ Carved and painted wood, feathers.
MNA cat no 2563/E-3741

499 Palhik Mana (Butterfly Maiden) Kachina, Pueblo (Hopi)
Arizona, 1920s
12¾ Carved and painted wood. Dress, maiden's shawl, boots, elaborate tableta.
Elizabeth Compton Hegemann Collection. Originally McGill Collection.
MNA cat no 2277-E-2284

500 Palhik Mana (Butterfly Maiden) Kachina, Pueblo (Hopi)
Mishongnovi, Arizona
11 x 5¼ Carved and painted wood. Woman's dress, robe, belt and boots.
Fred Harvey Foundation, Fine Arts Collection.
HM cat no 304-C-1

501 Palhik Mana (Butterfly Maiden) Kachina, Pueblo (Hopi)
North Central Arizona
18½ x 15¼ Carved and painted wood. Elaborate tableta, dress, cloak.
Fred Harvey Foundation, Fine Arts Collection.
HM cat no 765-C-1

502 Politaka (Cloud) Kachina, Pueblo (Hopi) *63, p 62*
Arizona
15¼ x 9¾ Carved and painted wood.
Collected in 1890s.
DAM cat no QH-200

503 Quia Kachina, Pueblo (Hopi)
North Central Arizona
13½ x 3 Carved and painted wood, cloth, fox skin, metal.
Fred Harvey Foundation, Fine Arts Collection.
HM cat no 876-C-1

504 Sio Hemis Kachina, Pueblo (Hopi)
Arizona, ca 1890
6¾ x 4¼ Carved and painted wood. Flat candy-striped body with projecting eye-shade and tableta headdress.
Collected by George Wharton James.
SM cat no 421-G-128

505 Sio Shalako Kachina, Pueblo (Hopi)
Arizona, 1920s
7 Carved and painted wood. Mask with band around pop-eyes, horns and dance kilt.
Collection of Elizabeth Compton Hegemann. Originally the C. Viera Collection.
MNA cat no 2277/E-2270

506 Sip-ikne (Zuni Warrior) Kachina, Pueblo (Hopi)
Arizona
6½ Carved and painted wood. Case mask, flower ears, tube mouth, eyes joined together.
MNA cat no 2563/E-3818

507 Tata-nga-ya (Hornet) Kachina, Pueblo (Hopi)
Second or Third Mesa, Arizona
9½ Carved and painted wood with feathers. Case mask with datura flower ears, pot hook eyes.
MNA cat no 2563/E-3750

508 Tsvaiyo (Bogy-Man) Kachina, Pueblo (Hopi)
Arizona
11 Carved and painted wood with fur, horsehair, feathers. Protruding eyes and snout, flat ears.
Collected by John L. Nelson.
SM cat no 640-G-268

509 Tuma-oi (White Chin) Kachina, Pueblo (Hopi)
Arizona
9⅝ Carved and painted wood with string.
Baby's kachina.
MNA cat no 2563/E-3752

510 Tungup Kachina, Pueblo (Hopi)
Third Mesa, Arizona, 1917
6½ Carved and painted wood with horsehair. The Tungup kachina flogs the candidates for initiation with yucca whips. Carved by Chaveyo.
Collected by A. C. Vroman.
SM cat no 30L-X45-ACV

511 Wukokala (Big Forehead) Kachina, Pueblo (Hopi)
Oraibi, Arizona
15 x 5½ Carved and painted wood, cloth, beads. Case mask with snout nose, skirt, rattle.
Fred Harvey Foundation, Fine Arts Collection.
HM cat no 833-C-1

512 Wupomo Kachina, Pueblo (Hopi)
Arizona, 1920s
8 Carved and painted wood with leather. Yucca sifter mask, pop-eyes, long bill, kilt, moccasins.
Elizabeth Compton Hegemann Collection. Originally McGill Collection.
MNA cat no 2277/E-2275

513 Hemis Kachina, Pueblo (Zuni)
New Mexico
19 x 6 Carved and painted wood with cloth kilt and cloth arm bands.
Fred Harvey Foundation, Fine Arts Collection.
HM cat no 761-C-1

514 Hil'li Kachina, Pueblo (Zuni)
Western New Mexico
14 x 5 Carved and painted wood with hair, feathers, cloth. Arms hinged, sun symbol on top of mask.
Fred Harvey Foundation, Fine Arts Collection.
HM cat no 1686-C-1

515 (Home Dancer) Kachina, Pueblo (Zuni)
New Mexico
18 x 6 Carved and painted wood, cloth. Right arm movable, holds rattle. Zuni version of a Hopi kachina.
Fred Harvey Foundation, Fine Arts Collection.
HM cat no 764-C-1

516 Ho Pocheala Kachina, Pueblo (Zuni)
Western New Mexico
15 x 5 Carved and painted wood with cloth, leather, feathers. Ruff, pants, skirt, moccasins.
Fred Harvey Foundation, Fine Arts Collection.
HM cat no 1685-C-1

517 Kohonind (Rain Priest of the North) Kachina, Pueblo (Zuni)
Western New Mexico
12½ x 7 Carved and painted wood, cloth, horn. Case mask, rectangular eyes, bow and quiver, sash, belt, skirt and moccasins.
Fred Harvey Foundation, Fine Arts Collection.
HM cat no 787-C-1

518 Pawik (Duck) Kachina, Pueblo (Zuni)   *68, p 67*
New Mexico
12¾ Carved and painted wood with horsehair. Case mask with duck bill, staff, rattle, armband and moccasins.
MNA cat no 2563/E-3726

519 Sai-astasana (Rain Priest of the North) Kachina, Pueblo (Zuni)
Western New Mexico
11 x 7½ Carved and painted wood, cloth, horn, fox skin. Case mask with robe, bow, quiver and dance paddles.
Fred Harvey Foundation, Fine Arts Collection.
HM cat no 839-C-1

520 Saiatasha Kachina, Pueblo (Zuni)
New Mexico
15½ x 7 Carved and painted wood, cloth, buckskin, hair, horn, cloth. Boots, bow and dance paddles.
Fred Harvey Foundation, Fine Arts Collection.
HM cat no 1687-C-1

521 Salimopia Kachina, Pueblo (Zuni)
Zuni Pueblo, New Mexico
12¾ x 3 Carved and painted wood. Initiates children. Prototype for Hopi Cipikne.
MNA cat no 2434/E-1941

522 Shalako Kachina, Pueblo (Zuni)
Western New Mexico
22 x 8 Carved and painted wood, cloth, feathers, leather.
Fred Harvey Foundation, Fine Arts Collection.
HM cat no 1688-C-1

523 Shalako Kachina, Pueblo (Zuni)   *157, p 110*
Western New Mexico
21 x 5 Carved and painted wood, cloth, feathers.
Fred Harvey Foundation, Fine Arts Collection.
HM cat no 1689-G-1

524 Shalako Kachina, Pueblo (Zuni)
New Mexico, early 20th century
15¾ Carved and painted wood.
Collected by Stewart Culin, museum expedition, 1903.
BM cat no 03.129

525 Tsola Witche Kachina, Pueblo (Zuni)
Arizona, ca 1890
8 Carved and painted wood. Male figure, wrapped stick in right hand.
Collected by A. C. Vroman.
SM cat no 30L-X43-ACV

526 Wakasi (Cow) Kachina, Pueblo (Zuni)
New Mexico, early 1920s
13½ Carved and painted wood, feathers, leather, cloth, goat hair, silver. Movable arms, protruding eyes, cow snout and horns; dressed in complete dance costume; doll can be dressed and undressed.
HM cat no 149-G-34

527 (White Buffalo) Kachina, Pueblo (Zuni)
New Mexico, 1880-1900
11¼ Carved and painted wood with feathers, horsehair, yarn. Case mask, snout mouth, horns.
MNA cat no 2563/E-3768

528 Wotemsa (Mixed Dancer) Kachina, Pueblo (Zuni)
Western New Mexico
16 x 6 Carved and painted wood, feathers. Feather headdress, painted mask and ears, snout, cotton skirt, belt, leather moccasins.
Fred Harvey Foundation, Fine Arts Collection.
HM cat no 1683-C-1

529 Wukoqala (Big Forehead) Kachina, Pueblo (Zuni)
New Mexico, 1880-1900
12½ Carved and painted wood with shell. Case mask, protruding ears; unusual dumbbell club in left hand, rattle in right.
MNA cat no 2563/E-3798

530 Kachina, Pueblo (Zuni)
New Mexico, early 20th century
15¾ Carved and painted wood.
Collected by Stewart Culin, museum expedition, 1903.
BM cat no 03.325.4622

531 Kachina, Pueblo (Zuni)
New Mexico, late 19th century
11¼ Carved and painted wood.
Collected by Stewart Culin, museum expedition, 1903.
BM cat no 03.325.4653

532 Kachina, Pueblo (Zuni)   *67, p 66*
New Mexico, late 19th century
14½ Carved and painted wood.
Collected by Stewart Culin, museum expedition, 1903.
BM cat no 04-297.5372

533 Kachina, Pueblo (Zuni)
New Mexico, late 19th century
14½ Carved and painted wood.
Collected by Stewart Culin, museum expedition, 1907.
BM cat no 07.467.8447

534 Kachina, Pueblo (Zuni)
New Mexico, early 20th century
16 Carved and painted wood.
Collected by Stewart Culin, museum expedition, 1903.
BM cat no 04.297.5354

Masks

535 Mask, Iroquois
Grand River, Ontario
10¼ x 6⅛ Carved and painted wood, tin, horsehair, tobacco offering tied to forehead. "Whistling mask" or "blowing spirit mask." Represents a common face begging for tobacco.
Collected by Stewart Culin, John Wanamaker expedition, 1901.
UMUP cat no 38529

536 Mask, Iroquois
New York
10¼ x 6½ Carved and painted wood with horsehair and metal.
Collected by Albert Green Heath.
LMA/BC cat no 30567

537 Mask, Iroquois
New York
9⅛ x 6½ Carved wood with horsehair.
Collected by Albert Green Heath from Dr. T. S. Hitchcock, Oswego, New York, 1911.
LMA/BC cat no 30570

538 Mask, Iroquois
New York, before 1915
9 x 7 Carved and painted wood with horsehair, brass tacks, buffalo horns. "False face."
LMA/BC cat no 1717

539 Mask, Iroquois
New York
9 x 6¼ Painted wood with horsehair.
Collected by Albert Green Heath from Dr. T. S. Hitchcock, Oswego, New York, 1911.
LMA/BC cat no 30569

540 Mask, Iroquois   *46, p 47*
Six Nations Reserve, Ontario, Canada
11½ x 11½ Braided cornhusk.
Made by Gunuktanyon (Shaking the Bed) Onondaga woman.
SMM cat no 63.11.2

541 Mask, Iroquois
New York
11 x 7 Carved and painted wood with horsehair, tin. "False face," worn by a doorkeeper or a doctor.
MAI/HF cat no 9142

542 Mask, Iroquois
Grand River Reservation, Ontario, Canada
10¾ x 6½ Carved and painted wood with horsehair, tin. "False face."
MAI/HF cat no $\frac{8}{1206}$

543 Mask, Iroquois
New York
Carved and painted wood, hair, metal. "False face."
PM cat no E15167

544 Mask, Iroquois
New York
10½ x 6¾ Carved and painted wood, hair, metal.
Collected by S. A. Barrett, December 31, 1918.
MPM cat no $\frac{24212}{6084}$

545 Mask, Iroquois
Ontario, Canada
10½ x 6½ Carved and painted wood, tin, horsehair, string.
Collected by Roddy, July 25, 1906.
MPM cat no $\frac{3243}{161}$

546 Mask, Iroquois (Cayuga)   *44, p 45*
10½ x 6½ Carved and painted wood, feathers, hair, metal.
PM cat no E24970

547 Mask, Iroquois (Cayuga)
Grand River Reservation, Ontario, Canada
10½ x 6 Carved and painted wood with
horsehair. "False face."
MAI/HF cat no 21
⎯⎯⎯
450

548 Mask, Iroquois (Onondaga)
New York
11 x 8¾ Carved and painted wood with
horsehair.
MAI/HF cat no 8775

549 Mask, Iroquois (Seneca)   *43, p 42*
Cattaraugus Reservation, New York
10¼ x 6¼ Carved and painted wood with
horsehair, tin. "False face," used during
childbirth.
MAI/HF cat no 16
⎯⎯⎯
2029

550 Mask, Iroquois (Seneca)
Genessee Valley, New York
10¼ x 5 Carved and painted wood with
horsehair, tin. "False face," used to purify
the home of a maternity patient and in the
ceremonial sacred fire lighting.
MAI/HF cat no 2
⎯⎯⎯
9601

551 Mask, Iroquois (Seneca)   *45, p 46*
10¾ x 6 Carved and painted wood. "False
face."
DAM cat no NSen-14

552 Mask, Iroquois (Seneca)
Cattaraugus Reservation, New York
9 x 5¾ x 9⁹⁄₁₆ Carved and painted
wood, hair, metal.
Collected by M. R. Harrington, 1904.
Collection of Huntington-Frothingham
Wolcott Fund.
Purchased 1904.
PM/HU cat no 04.23.10
⎯⎯⎯
65440

553 Mask, Iroquois (Seneca)
Cattaraugus Reservation, New York
10⅛ x 5¾ x 4¾ Carved and painted
wood, metal, hair.
Collected by M. Raymond Harrington,
Director, Peabody Museum expedition, 1903,
from Jesse Logan of the Seneca tribe.
PM/HU cat no 03.32.10
⎯⎯⎯
62696

554 Mask, Iroquois (Seneca)
New York
12 x 6 Carved and painted wood with
metal.
MAI/HF cat no 20/2844

555 Mask, Iroquois (Seneca)
Cattaraugus Reservation, New York
10½ x 6¾ Carved and painted wood, tin,
horsehair, tobacco bags. Bi-funnelate
blower-mouth.
Collected by S. A. Barrett, December 31, 1918.
MPM cat no 24205
⎯⎯⎯
6084

556 Mask, Iroquois (Seneca)
Allegany Reservation, New York
11⅝ Carved and painted wood, tin,
horsehair. Represents the Thunder Spirit.
Collection of Dr. Frank G. Speck, 1949.
PM cat no E27992

557 Mask, Naskapi   *162, p 111*
Pennsylvania, 1946
8 Painted caribou skin. Probably for
Clown Dance.
Collection of Dr. Frank G. Speck.
DAM cat no NNs-5-PD

558 Gourd Mask, Cherokee
20th century
9⅝ Painted gourd with fur. Two
parts. Used in the Boogerman Dance.
UMUP cat no 46-G-2

559 Gourd Mask, Cherokee   *163, p 111*
North Carolina
7¼ x 5⅞   Gourd with twine. Elliptical
eyes, linear mouth. Used in the Boogerman
Dance. Represents "Funny Buffalo."
Collected by Dr. Frank G. Speck before 1940.
CIS cat no 1360

560 Mask, Cherokee
Qualla Reservation, North Carolina
11½ x 7¾ Carved wood. Used in the
Buffalo Dance.
MAI/HF cat no 18
⎯⎯⎯
5513

561 Mask, Cherokee
North Carolina
9½ x 7 Carved wood with feathers.
Represents a warrior.
MAI/HF cat no 21
⎯⎯⎯
8638

562 Mask, Navajo
Arizona
12 x 11 Stiff leather concealing neck and
throat. Represents female deities.
Collected by L. Hubbell, 1910.
FMNH cat no 53227

563 Mask, Navajo   *164, p 111*
Arizona
Mask: 15⅝ x 9⅞ Hat: 11⅞ x 11⅞
Painted hide, basketry hat with sticks, woolen
yarn.
Collected by Stewart Culin, museum expedition,
1903.
BM cat no 03.183

564 Dance Mask, Pueblo   *69, p 68*
New Mexico
23¼ x 16; 6⅞ diam. Painted wood
and leather, wicker crest.
Collected by Amelia E. White.
CIS cat no 1712

565 Kachina Mask, Pueblo (Hopi)
Tewa Village, Arizona
8¾ Painted leather with cloth, wood.
UMUP cat no 38720

566 Mask, Pueblo (Santo Domingo)
Santo Domingo Pueblo, New Mexico, 1942
12; 8 diam. Painted leather with feathers,
cotton. Represents Pai-u-tiwa, leader of
Tsai-akyu-it-sa dancers. Made by Martin Herrera.
SM cat no 491-G-1106

**567 Ceremonial Dance Mask, Pueblo
(Santo Domingo)**
Santo Domingo Pueblo, New Mexico, 1942
22; 7¾ diam. Painted leather with feathers.
Used in Good Dance. Made by Martin Herrera.
Collected by Charles MacReeve.
SM cat no 491-G-1105

* 568 Face Mask, Bella Bella   *83, p 80*
9¾ x 8½ x 8¼ Carved and painted wood,
animal hair. Worn in Lao'laxa Ceremony.
Collected by George Hunt, 1899.
AMNH cat no 16/4736

* 569 Mask, Bella Bella
Rivers Inlet, British Columbia, 1923
84 x 10 x 6 Carved wood, deep relief.
Collection of Theodore Roosevelt.
NMM cat no VII-EE-33

* 570 Face Mask, Bella Bella
9¾ x 9½ x 5 Carved and painted wood,
inlaid fur eyebrows, mustache and beard,
movable eyes. Used in the Thunderbird Dance.
Collected by H. R. Bishop, 1869.
AMNH cat no 16/AI/595

* 571 Sun Mask, Bella Coola   *82, p 79*
26 x 25 x 8 Carved and painted wood,
cedar bark, feathers, down.
Collected by George Hunt and
Dr. Franz Boas, 1896.
AMNH cat no 16/1506

* 572 Mask, Coast Salish
Nanaimo, Vancouver Island, British Columbia
17¾ x 10½ Carved and painted wood.
Represents shway (spirit).
MAI/HF cat no 18
⎯⎯⎯
1063

* 573 Mask, Cowichan
Katsey Reserve, Port Hammond, British Columbia
20 x 11¼ x 11 Carved and painted wood,
bark padding. Represents Sxwaixwe, an
ancestor spirit.
Collected by Harlan I. Smith, 1898.
AMNH cat no 16/4662

* 574 Messenger Mask, Dene (Ingalik)
Anvik, Alaska
7¹⁄₁₆ x 4½ Carved and painted wood,
moose hair.
Collected by Leo Dimoski, 1917.
UMUP cat no NA5831c

* 575 Face Mask, Haida
9½ x 8 x 4½ Carved and painted wood, movable
leather brow and eyelids, animal hair trim, fur
mustache and beard. Tarhtchakt, or dancing mask.
Collected by H. R. Bishop, 1869.
AMNH cat no 16/AI/375

*** 576 Face Mask, Haida**
9¾ x 7⅛ x 4 Carved and painted wood.
Represents a woman. Painted and carved by Quaa-Telth, Masset.
Collected by H. R. Bishop, 1869.
AMNH cat no 16/AI/364

*** 577 Mask, Haida**
Queen Charlotte Islands, Canada, 1879
13 x 12 Carved and painted wood with abalone shell inlay for eyes, and opercula shell teeth.
Collected by I. W. Powell.
NMM cat no VII-B-15

*** 578 Mask, Haida**
Masset, Queen Charlotte Islands, Canada, before 1890
9½ x 7¼ Carved and painted wood with seal fur, string. Movable eyelids and mouth.
Collected by Mrs. Roderick F. Dodd.
Gift of Dr. W. Barclay Stephens.
LM/UC/B cat no 2-15550

*** 579 Shaman's Face Mask, Haida (Howkan)**
11½ x 10 x 7¼ Carved and painted wood.
Represents a combination of man and owl's face talking.
AMNH cat no 19/890

*** 580 Mask, Haida (Kaigani)**
Kasaan, Prince of Wales Island, British Columbia
24½ x 17¼ Carved and painted wood. No eye holes. Animal and humanoid characteristics.
Collected before 1924.
Gift of the Wellcome Trust.
MCH/UC/LA cat no x65-4282

*** 581 Face Mask, Kwakiutl** *78,* p 76
1938
51 Carved and painted wood, shredded cedar bark. Main head represents Galakumps, the cannibal spirit in Hamatsa Society dances.
Used by Mungo Martin. All four heads have movable beaks pulled by string.
Made by George Walkus.
DAM cat no NKW-25

*** 582 Mask, Kwakiutl**
23 x 13 Carved and painted wood.
Represents a wolf.
Collected by George Hunt, 1893.
FMNH cat no 19174

*** 583 Female Spectator Mask, Kwakiutl**
British Columbia
14½ x 9½ Carved and painted wood, part of Lao'laxa set.
Collected by Barrett expedition, 1915.
MPM cat no 17302/4615

*** 584 Male Gambler Mask, Kwakiutl**
British Columbia
11½ x 8¼ Carved and painted wood, cloth.
Part of Lao'laxa set.
Collected by Barrett expedition, 1915.
MPM cat no 17305/4615

*** 585 Fool Dancer's Mask, Kwakiutl**
British Columbia
13½ x 9¾ Carved and painted wood, cedar bark. Worn by members of the Nulmal or Fool Dancer Society.
MPM cat no 17358/4615

*** 586 Mask, Kwakiutl**
17 x 9½ x 9 Carved and painted wood with mirror, metal, feathers. Represents a thunderbird.
AMNH cat no 16/4800

*** 587 Mask, Kwakiutl**
Mamalelequala Village, British Columbia
109⅞ x 11⅜ x 14 3/16 Carved and painted wood, cedar bark fronds. Represents Sisiutl (two-headed snake). Used in Winter Dance by members of secret society.
Collected by C. F. Newcombe, Peabody Museum expedition, 1917.
PM/HU cat no 17.17.10/87206

*** 588 Bird Mask, Kwakiutl**
48½ Carved and painted wood.
Collection of Walter Waters, Wrangell, Alaska.
DAM cat no NKW-36

*** 589 Face Mask, Kwakiutl**
13 x 18¾ x 9¾ Carved and painted wood.
Represents an eagle.
Collected by George Hunt, 1899.
AMNH cat no 16/6770

*** 590 Thunderbird Mask, Kwakiutl**
11 x 10½ x 16 Carved and painted wood, swansdown feathers. Ku'uxulal masks of Kunusila, Nimkish Village.
Used in Winter Dance.
Collected by George Hunt, 1898.
AMNH cat no 16/4800

*** 591 Wild Man of the Woods Mask, Kwakiutl** *165,* p 112
ca 1920
13¼ x 10½ Carved and painted wood, fur trim, probably fox. Attributed to Willie Seaweed.
Collection of University of Washington, Seattle.
DAM cat no NKW-33-P

*** 592 Mask, Kwakiutl**
1920s
29½ x 17 Carved and painted wood.
Made by George Walkus.
Collected by Edward Malin.
COE

*** 593 Killer Whale Mask, Kwakiutl** *18,* p 21
British Columbia
49½ x 10½ Carved and painted wood, obsidian eyes, movable jaw.
Collected by Barrett expedition, 1915.
MPM cat no 17365/4615 a,b,c

*** 594 Sea Urchin Mask, Kwakiutl** *81,* p 79
British Columbia, ca 1900
11 x 30 Carved and painted wood.
SOSLAND

*** 595 Wild Man of the Woods Mask, Kwakiutl**
12½ x 8 Carved and painted wood, bearskin.
MPM cat no 17361/4615

*** 596 Mask, Kwakiutl**
British Columbia
15½ x 15 Carved and painted wood, bearskin, horsehair. Represents Tsonoqua, the Cannibal Woman.
Collected by S. A. Barrett expedition, 1915.
MPM cat no 17359/4615

*** 597a Loon Mask, Kwakiutl**
British Columbia
20 x 6½ x 2½ Carved and painted wood with interchangeable attachment feathers.
Collected by Barrett expedition, 1915.
MPM cat no 17324b

*** 597b Mask, Kwakiutl**
13 x 13½ x 6½ Carved and painted wood.
Represents the moon.
ROM cat no HN1367

*** 597c Mask, Kwakiutl**
13½ x 18 x 24 Carved and painted wood.
Represents a wolf. Used in a secret society in the winter ceremonies.
ROM cat no HN1324

*** 598 Mask, Tsimshian (Niska)**
British Columbia
8½ x 7⅜ x 5⅛ Carved and painted wood.
MPA cat no 56.60

*** 599 Mask, Nootka** *166,* p 112
Vancouver Island, British Columbia
12¼ x 10½ x 27¼ Carved and painted wood.
Collected by F. Jacobson, 1897.
AMNH cat no 16/1902

*** 600 Human Face Mask, Nootka** *80,* p 78
Vancouver Island, British Columbia
18 x 11½ Carved and painted wood, black horsehair, bone, bead eyes.
DAM cat no NNu-10

*** 601 Shaman's Face Mask, Tlingit (Chilkat)**
8 x 7⅛ x 4¾ Carved and painted wood.
Represents a wrinkled old man.
AMNH cat no 19/894

*** 602 Shaman's Face Mask, Tlingit (Chilkat)**
8½ x 7¼ x 5¼ Carved and painted wood, opercula teeth. Represents a sleeping man's spirit.
AMNH cat no 19/892

*** 603 Shaman's Face Mask, Tlingit (Chilkat)**
8¼ x 6⅞ x 4½ Carved and painted wood, traces of human hair trim, opercula teeth.
Represents a dead owl.
Obtained from Chilkat shaman.
AMNH cat no 19/864

* **604 Shaman's Forehead Mask, Tlingit (Chilkat)**
4¼ x 4¼ x 3 Carved and painted wood,
inlaid abalone eyes. Represents an eagle
spirit.
AMNH cat no 19/923

* **605 Face Mask, Tlingit (Chilkat)**
9½ x 8½ x 6½ Carved and painted wood.
Taken from shaman's grave below a Chilkat
village.
AMNH cat no 19/850

* **606 Shaman's Face Mask, Tlingit (Chilkat)**
8¼ x 7½ x 5 Carved and painted wood, cut
mirror teeth, glass eyes. Represents an
Eastern Indian.
AMNH cat no 19/859

* **607 Face Mask, Tlingit**
Icy Strait, Alaska
9¾ x 7½ x 6 Carved and painted wood,
fur mustache and beard, glass eyes, opercula
teeth. Doctor's mask.
AMNH cat no E/2356

* **608 Face Mask, probably Tlingit**
8¾ x 6⅞ x 3½ Carved and painted wood.
Represents a spirit used by a doctor when
treating the sick.
AMNH cat no E/343

* **609 Shaman's Face Mask, probably Tlingit**
8¼ x 7 x 4¾ Carved and painted wood,
human hair, opercula teeth, bone ear pendant.
Represents a death head.
AMNH cat no 19/854

* **610 Face Mask, Tlingit**
8¼ x 7½ x 5¼ Carved and painted wood.
Inscription: "Doctors' dancing mask
representing a Nass River Indian."
AMNH cat no 16.1/996

* **611 Face Mask, Tlingit**
Sitka, 1800s
9¾ x 7¼ Carved wood with copper
nostrils and lips, teeth of opercula (sea
snail shells); eyebrows, mustache and beard
of bear's fur. Design on lower face represents
an octopus.
Collected and donated by Dickerman.
TM/CSFAC cat no 5006

* **612 Face Mask, Tlingit**   *159*, p 110
Dry Bay, Alaska
6½ x 7 x 6 Carved and painted wood.
Represents the spirit of a crow. Used
by a doctor.
AMNH cat no E/1566

* **613 Shaman's Mask, Tlingit**
Alaska
11½ x 5¼ Carved and painted wood.
Represents a wolf. Worn when practicing
medicine.
Collected by Lieut. G. T. Emmons, 1902.
FMNH cat no 79254

* **614 Mask (Sea Bear), Tlingit or Haida**   *87*, p 83
British Columbia or Alaska
12 x 8 x 9 Copper, haliotis (abalone),
shell and fur.
MPA cat no 58.329

* **615a Mask, Tsimshian**
Nass River, British Columbia
15½ x 16 x 18 Carved and painted wood.
Articulated eyelids.
Collected 1929.
ROM cat no HN898

* **615b Janus Head, probably Tsimshian**
British Columbia
9 Carved and painted wood with rawhide
straps, animal skin. Strapped to top of
dancer's head.
Collected before 1940.
Gift of the Wellcome Trust.
MCH/UC/LA cat no x65-8554

* **615c Mask, Tsimshian**
British Columbia
8 x 8½ ; 22½ long. Carved and painted wood
with copper, mollusc teeth. Small human figures
represent a dorsal fin of a marine animal.
Used as funeral mask. •
ROM cat no HN1289, 938.26.1

* **616 Face Mask**
9 x 7 x 3½ Carved and painted wood,
divides into two sections.
AMNH cat no 16.1/2247A

* **617 Face Mask**
Admiralty Island, Alaska
9¾ x 8 x 4¼ Carved and painted wood,
traces of human hair with opercula teeth.
Doctor's mask from a grave house.
Represents the face of a dying man
killed in a fight. Worn by a shaman
impersonating the spirit of this warrior.
AMNH cat no E/2501

618 Mask, Eskimo
St. Michael, Alaska, late 19th century
11¼ Carved and painted wood, feathers.
Carved beaver and weasel attached to
back board. Worn while a song was sung.
Represents a spirit.
Collected by H. M. W. Edmonds, M.D., 1890-99.
LM/UC/B cat no 2-6624

619 Mask, Eskimo
Alaska, ca 1880
15 Carved and painted wood, seal thong.
Represents human face emerging from
bird's beak.
Gift of Alaska Commercial Company.
LM/UC/B cat no 2-4597

620 Mask, Eskimo
St. Michael, Alaska, late 19th century
10 x 5¾ Carved and painted wood, goose
feathers, sinew, parchment, fur. Represents
the spirit of the driftwood.
Collected by H. M. W. Edmonds, M.D., 1890-99.
LM/UC/B cat no 2-6926

621 Mask, Eskimo
St. Michael, Alaska, late 19th century
8 x 5¾ Carved and painted wood, quills,
ptarmigan feathers. Represents a sculpin.
Collected by H. M. W. Edmonds, M.D., 1890-99.
LM/UC/B cat no 2-6914

622 Mask/Seal Decoy, Eskimo   *160*, p 110
Kodiak Island, Alaska
6⅝ x 8¼ ; 10 diam. Carved and painted
wood. Worn as a cap to hunt species of seal
called "Nerpa" by the Russians. Hunter hides
among rocks and calls the animal.
Collected by Captain Edward G. Fast, 1867.
Purchased 1869.
PM/HU cat no 69.30.10
                      64700

623 Mask, Eskimo
ca 1880-1890
5 x 19 x 3½ Carved and painted wood.
Collected by Bishop Farrhaut.
COE

624 Medicine Mask, Eskimo
Kuskokwim River, Alaska
11⅜ x 8¼ x 4⁵⁄₁₆ Carved and painted
wood, sinew strap. Heavy-browed, prognathous
mask with elliptical eyes. Wooden-pegged
frontal and broad slit mouth, ear representations.
Collected by G. B. Gordon.
CIS cat no 3225

625 Shaman's Mask, Eskimo
Pastolik, Alaska, late 19th century
14 Carved and painted wood. Long,
curved mouth and single eye.
Gift of Alaska Commercial Company.
LM/UC/B cat no 2-6442

626 Mask, Eskimo
St. Michael, Alaska, late 19th century
8 x 4 Carved and painted wood. Worn
centered in the middle of the face. Represents
mythical half-man.
Collected by H. M. W. Edmonds, M.D., 1890-99.
LM/UC/B cat no 2-6913

627 Mask, Eskimo
Nushagak area, Alaska, late 19th century
20 x 45 Carved and painted wood, baleen.
Probably represents spirits of a sea mammal
and the shaman who possessed that spirit.
Collected by Alaska Commercial Company.
LM/UC/B cat no 2-5852

628 Mask, Eskimo   *106*, p 96
St. Michael, Alaska, late 19th century
14 x 10½ Carved and painted wood, feathers.
Represents the figure of a man with a face
superimposed on his body.
Collected by R. Neumann, Alaska Commercial
Company.
LM/UC/B cat no 2-6476

629 Mask, Eskimo
St. Michael, Alaska, late 19th century
9¼ x 6¾ Carved and painted wood.
Reminiscent of undecorated masks from
the North. Represents a spirit.
Collected by R. Neumann, Alaska
Commercial Company, 1880-90.
LM/UC/B cat no 2-6479

630 Dance Mask, Eskimo (Kashunak)
Near Askinut Mountain, Alaska, ca 1900
15 x 34⅝ x 6⅛ ; 29 long. Carved wood,
feathers tipped with down, cedar bark.
Collected by J. Albert Lee, 1905.
Purchased 1906.
PM/HU cat no 06.25.10
⎯⎯⎯⎯⎯⎯
66315

631 Dance Mask, Eskimo (Kashunak)   *161, p 111*
Near Askinuk Mountain, Alaska
19⅝ x 16³⁄₁₆ Carved wood, feathers and
cedar bark. Hung from the roof of dance house.
Worn by judge who presided over the poison
ordeal, which was trial and execution of persons
accused of witchcraft.
Collected by J. Albert Lee, 1905.
Purchased 1906.
PM/HU cat no 06.25.10
⎯⎯⎯⎯⎯⎯
66314

Miscellaneous Utilitarian Objects

* **632 Cradleboard, Huron**
Canada, before 1850
29¼ x 10½ Carved and painted wood,
rawhide.
HM cat no NA-NE-HUQ-1

* **633 Cradleboard Wrapping, Iroquois (Cayuga)**
Cloth with beadwork.
PM cat no E27437

* **634 Corn Mush Paddle, Iroquois**
Western New York
21 x 4 x 1 Carved wood.
Collected by S. A. Barrett, 1918.
MPM cat no 23944
⎯⎯⎯⎯⎯
6084

635 Heddle for Beadwork Loom, Menomini
Wisconsin
7¾ x 7¾ x ½ Carved and painted wood.
Collected by S. A. Barrett, 1910.
MPM cat no 4532
⎯⎯⎯⎯
2207

* **636 Man's Saddle, Menomini**   *170, p 113*
Menominee, Wisconsin
20 x 13½ x 22½ Leather over wood
frame, brass tacks. Pommel carved as
horse head.
Collected by W. Jones, 1903.
AMNH cat no 50/4848

* **637 Baby Carrier, Ojibwa**   *167, p 112*
Eastern Woodlands
31⅛ x 11¼ Wood with cloth, beadwork,
quillwork, shells, string, wool tassel.
Collections of American Board of
Commissions of Foreign Missions.
PM cat no E25409

638 Fishing Lure, probably Ojibwa
Great Lakes
Fish: 6¾ Carved and engraved wood with
tin. Fish tied to stick with fish line, lead
weight at bottom. Dangled in water to
attract fish to be speared.
Collected by Albert Green Heath.
LMA/BC cat no 30352

639 Spoon, Ottawa
Good Hart, Michigan
Bowl: 5¼ x 1½ Carved deer antler,
cotton tape. Hemispherical bowl, three
drilled holes in nubby handle. Loop of
light brown tape laced through three
upper holes.
Collected by Albert Green Heath from
Sha-wan-nawguet (Blue Sky), 1914.
LMA/BC cat no 30818

640 Belt Loom, Potawatomi
Skunk Hill, Wisconsin
10⅞ x 9⅞ Carved and incised wood.
40 slats and holes, 39 slits. Bear, fish, bird,
otter, diamond and circle figures.
Collected by Milford G. Chandler from Angelina Cook.
CIS cat no 3053

641 Awl, probably Winnebago
Wisconsin
4¾ x 5 Steel point, carved bone. Handle
topped with figure of a bear standing beside
a tree stump. Used by women for sewing
bark and skins.
Collected by Albert Green Heath.
LMA/BC cat no 30309

642 Awl, probably Winnebago
Black River Falls, Wisconsin
3½ Steel point, carved bone. Used by
women for sewing bark and skins.
Collected by Albert Green Heath from
Nellie Eagle.
LMA/BC cat no 30306

643 Awl, probably Winnebago
Wisconsin
4½ x ½ Steel point, carved bone.
Handle with bear on top and weasel
at side. Used by women for sewing
bark and skins.
Collected by Albert Green Heath.
LMA/BC cat no 30310

* **644 Quirt, Winnebago**
Wisconsin
11¾ x 1½ Carved and incised wood.
MAI/HF cat no   2
⎯⎯⎯⎯
9998

* **645 Quirt, Winnebago**
Wisconsin
19¾ x 2½ Carved wood with metal studs,
hide.
MAI/HF cat no   2
⎯⎯⎯⎯
4511

* **646 Crupper, Blackfeet**
Montana or Alberta
52½ x 16 Buckskin with wool, beadwork,
flannel, cotton.
SMM cat no 49/328

* **647 Martingale, Blackfeet**
49 x 6½ Flannel with beadwork, fringe,
bells. Floral design.
SMM cat no 49/289

648 Parfleche, Blackfeet
Gleichew, Alberta
23 x 14½ Painted rawhide.
Collected by H. I. Smith, 1929.
NMM cat no V-B-190

649 Pair of Parfleche, Cheyenne
ca 1880
22 x 15 Painted rawhide.
DAM cat no P Chy-12-P/Chy-13-P

* **650 Saddle Blanket, Cheyenne**
Plains, mid-1800s
74 Buckskin with beadwork. Geometric
pattern.
Collection of Theodore Pitman.
DAM cat no BChy-82-G

651 Gun Case, Crow
Montana
38¾ x 4½ Hide with beadwork and fringe.
Geometric designs.
MAI/HF cat no 9055

* **652 Horse Collar, Crow**
38 Wool cloth with beadwork, calico
tassels, yarn, leather.
Collected by Babitt Bros., Flagstaff,
Arizona, 1936.
DAM cat no BCr-8-PD

* **653 Baby Carrier, Kiowa**
44 x 14 Wood frame with beadwork,
rawhide thongs.
Fred Harvey Foundation, Fine Arts Collection.
HM cat no 81BE

* **654 Baby Carrier, Kiowa**   *2, p 8*
44 x 14 Wood frame with beadwork, rawhide
thongs, metal studs.
Fred Harvey Foundation, Fine Arts Collection.
HM cat no 82BE

655 Parfleche, Ponca
Oklahoma
17¾ x 11 x 7¾ Painted rawhide. Box shape.
Geometric design.
MAI/HF cat no   3
⎯⎯⎯⎯
6594

656 Parfleche, Ponca
Oklahoma
28 x 13¼ Painted rawhide. Geometric
design.
MAI/HF cat no   3
⎯⎯⎯⎯
6732

* **657 Baby Carrier, Sioux**
38 x 10 x 9 Wood supports, beadwork,
metal studs and bells.
Fred Harvey Foundation, Fine Arts Collection.
HM cat no 145BE

* **658 Baby Carrier, Sioux**
Early 20th century
22 x 6 x 10 Leather with beadwork.
MHSM cat no NPR

* **659 Baby Case, Sioux**
Crow Creek Reservation, Montana
10 x 8 Buckskin with quillwork, brass bells, beadwork, cloth.
Collected by H. Burt, ca 1880.
Collection of David W. Clark.
ODM cat no CMC-D-30

660 Parfleche, Sioux
15¼ x 8 Painted rawhide.
Collection of W. C. Cousins, 1948.
PM cat no E27627

661 Pair of Parfleche Boxes, Sioux (Teton) *169*, p 113
Rosebud Reservation, South Dakota
22 x 10 x 8 Painted rawhide.
Collected by A. B. Clark.
Collection of David W. Clark.
ODM cat no CMC-M1 and M2

* **662 Saddle, Sioux**
Portage La Prairie, Manitoba, 1914
22¾ x 12 Leather with beadwork, silk, velvet, wool tassels. Floral design.
Collected by W. D. Wallis.
NMM cat no VE-148

* **663 Saddle Blanket, Sioux**
68 x 38 Buckskin with beadwork.
MHSM cat no 58.9539.3

* **664 Saddle Blanket, Sioux (Sisseton)**
39 x 30 Buckskin with beadwork.
Geometric designs.
Reiff Collection.
SMM cat no 61/349

665 Spoon, Sioux *5*, p 11
6⅜ x 3 Carved buffalo horn, trade beads. Zoomorphic handle carved in the shape of a bird's head and neck, inlaid eyes, neck bent by steaming. Original label reads: "Spoon made of buffalo horn by a wife of Sitting Bull and used by him for two years." Label questionable.
Collected by Rev. G. L. Payne.
PM/HU cat no 970-38-10 / 51263

666 Spoon, Sioux *5*, p 11
9½ x 5 x 1$\frac{13}{16}$ Carved horn.
Gift of Mrs. Charles Fairchild, 1914.
PM/HU cat no 14.40.10 / 85997

667a Spoon, probably Sioux
Rosebud Reservation, South Dakota
11½ x 3½ Carved wood, brass. Represents an owl. Atypical form.
Collected by Aaron B. Clark.
Collection of David W. Clark.
ODM cat no CMC-S-48

***667b Horse Ornament**
Plains
14 x 18 Hide with beadwork.
ROM

668 Shaman's Neck Rest, Pueblo (Hopi)
First Mesa, Arizona
5½ x 6¾ ; 20¼ long. Carved wood.
Collected by Robert H. Lowie, 1916.
AMNH cat no 19/259

* **669 Baby Carrier, Pima** *71*, p 69
Arizona
32 x 7½ x 11 Wood with hide, cloth, dangles, feathers, beadwork.
MAI/HF cat no 20 / 9597

* **670 Baby Carrier, Ute**
41 x 21¼ Painted wood with beadwork, cloth, fringe.
Collection of Emma A. Finney, 1928.
DAM cat no BU-86-G

* **671 Baby Carrier**
Plateau
36 x 14 Buckskin with beadwork, cloth and wooden backboard.
MHSM cat no 8045/1

672 Parfleche, Bannock
Plateau, ca 1890
24½ x 12 Painted rawhide.
Collected by E. Adamson Hoebel, 1934.
HOEBEL

673 Spoon, Wishram-Wasco
Lower Columbia River
3¾ x 4 x 1¾ Carved wood with lead inlay repair. Human figure handle.
Received from The Detroit Institute of Arts, Stearns Collection, 1963.
CIS cat no 1216

674 Parfleche *168*, p 112
Plateau
21½ x 14 Painted rawhide.
UMUP cat no 29-47-184

675 Spoon, Hupa
California
7¼ Carved deer antler. Ovate bowl, handle has longitudinal slot and zig-zag notching on edges, top rectangular. Used by men to eat acorn mush.
Collected by Major Horatio Rust before 1892.
LMA/BC cat no 712-4

676 Spoon, Hupa
California
6¼ Carved deer antler. Ovate bowl, rectangular handle with rounded notches along edges and top, longitudinal slot and top hole for suspension. Used by men to eat acorn mush.
Collected by Major Horatio Rust before 1892.
LMA/BC cat no 712-3

677 Spoon, Hupa
California
7 Carved deer antler. Ovate bowl, straight sided handle with edges notched, two larger flanges at bottom. Used by men to eat acorn mush.
Collected by Major Horatio Rust before 1892.
LMA/BC cat no 712-2

678 Spoon, Hupa *17*, p 21
California
6$\frac{3}{16}$ x 2⅜ Carved deer antler.
Used by men to eat mush from basket bowl.
Collected by Grace Nicholson, 1906.
Gift of Lewis H. Farlow, 1906.
PM/HU cat no 06.5.10 / 66487

679 Spoon, Hupa
California
7¼ Carved deer antler. Ovate bowl with slender zig-zag handle. Used by men to eat acorn mush.
Collected by Major Horatio Rust before 1892.
LMA/BC cat no 712-1

680 Man's Spoon, Karok *17*, p 21
California
7 x 2⅜ Carved elk antler. Bent stem handle, tiny spoon at tip, rectangular decoration near bowl.
Gift of Lewis H. Farlow, 1913.
PM/HU cat no 13.9.10 / 85257

681 Man's Spoon, Karok
California
8⅜ x 2$\frac{5}{16}$ Carved elk antler.
Notched handle.
Gift of Lewis H. Farlow, 1913.
PM/HU cat no 13.9.10 / 85257

682 Man's Spoon, Karok *17*, p 21
California, late 1800s
7⅝ x 2⅝ Carved elk antler.
Handle has two notches near bowl, square handle top.
Gift of Lewis H. Farlow, 1913.
PM/HU cat no 13.9.10 / 85257

683 Man's Spoon, Karok *17*, p 21
California, late 1800s
6½ x 2½ Carved elk antler. Diamond shaped handle with hole in tip, rectangular shape near bowl.
Gift of Lewis H. Farlow, 1913.
PM/HU cat no 13.9.10 / 85257

684 Spoon, Klamath
California
9¾ Carved deer antler. Long oval bowl with zig-zag notched handle. Suspension hole at top. Used by men to eat acorn mush.
Collected by Major Horatio Rust before 1892.
LMA/BC cat no 715

685 Man's Spoon *17*, p 2
Northern California
6½ x 2½ Carved elk antler and thread.
Collected by Miss Grace Nicholson and C. L. Hartman, 1898.
Gift of Lewis H. Farlow, 1908.
PM/HU cat no 08.4.10 / 73140

686 Spoon, Bella Bella
4½ ; 13 long. Carved wood with inlaid
abalone shell. Removable wooden
skull in bowl of spoon.
DAM cat no QBB-3

687 Spindle Whorl, Coast Salish
Vancouver Island, British Columbia, 19th century
1⅛ ; 8⅝ diam. Carved wood. Sisiutl
image (a mythical two-headed plumed snake).
Collected by Dr. C. F. Newcombe, acquired
by Stewart Culin, museum expedition, 1905.
BM cat no 05.262

688 Spindle Whorl, Coast Salish
Duncan, Vancouver Island, British Columbia
7½ ; 6½ diam. Carved wood. Represents a
raven, an eagle, and a salmon.
MAI/HF cat no 15
8957

689 Spindle Whorl, Coast Salish
Duncan, Vancouver Island, British Columbia
7½ ; 6½ diam. Carved wood. Represents a
raven, an eagle, and a field mouse.
MAI/HF cat no 15
8958

690 Spindle Whorl, Cowichan
Vancouver Island, British Columbia
8½ diam. Carved and painted wood.
Collected by W. F. Tolmie, 1884.
NMM cat no VII-G-6

691 Fish Club, Haida   *180*, p 115
Queen Charlotte Islands, Canada
20⁷⁄₁₆ x 2¾ Carved wood.
Represents sea otter. Used to kill fish.
Collected by Stewart Culin, museum expedition,
1905.
BM cat no 05.285

692 Ladle, probably Haida   *171*, p 113
British Columbia 1850-70
17¼ x 5⅛ Carved mountain sheep horn.
Beasley Collection.
MPA cat no 63.138

693 Spoon, Haida
British Columbia
12½ x 3 Carved horn.
MAI/HF cat no   5
3279

694 Apron Ornament, Niska
Nass River, British Columbia
3½ x 1 Carved ivory inlaid with haliotis
shell. Represents a raven.
MAI/HF cat no   9
7961

695 Spoon, Niska
Nass River, British Columbia
10 x 3 Carved sheep horn.
MAI/HF cat no   9
8080

696 Spoon, Niska
Nass River, British Columbia
13 x 3 Carved sheep horn.
MAI/HF cat no   9
8075

697 Halibut Hook, Tlingit
Late 19th century
6½ x 11½ Carved wood.
COE

698 Ladle, Tlingit
Late 19th century
31½ Carved wood.
COE

699 Dagger, Tlingit
Southwest coast, Alaska, 19th century
12 x 2½ x 1½ Wood and iron or steel.
Collection of Harry E. Wood.
MIA cat no 28.106

700 Pendant, Tlingit
Alaska
2 x 1½ Carved ivory with shell inlay.
Represents a raven.
MAI/HF cat no 19
8648

701 Spoon, Tlingit
Northwest Coast
13½ x 3½ Carved and incised
mountain goat horn.
DAM cat no QT1-116

702 Spoon, Tlingit
Southeast coast, Alaska, 19th century
9¼ x 3½ x 2 Carved bighorn sheep
horn and mother-of-pearl.
Collection of Harry E. Wood.
MIA cat no 28.118

703 Spoon, Tlingit
Alaska
10½ x 2¼ Carved goat horn.
MAI/HF cat no 20
6950

704 Spoon, Tlingit
Alaska
21 x 6½ x 3¼ Horn with incised decoration.
MAI/HF cat no 21
4492

705 Grease Dipper
Northwest Coast, late 19th century
18 Carved wood with brass buttons.
Handle represents a bird head.
Gift of Alaska Commercial Company.
LM/UC/B cat no 2-4640

706 Salmon-killing Club
Northwest Coast, before 1858
15½ Carved and painted wood with inlaid
shell. Represents a human figure, hands
clasped over drawn-up left knee; animal
headdress at the top of club.
Gift of Mrs. H. H. Bancroft (presented to
Mrs. Bancroft from Major Van Bokkelan's
collection).
LM/UC/B cat no 2-8873

707 Spoon
Northwest Coast
13 Wood. Totem figures on handle.
Collection of Connecticut Historical Society, 1947.
PM cat no E26, 415

708a Button, Eskimo
Point Barrow, Alaska
1½ x ½ Carved ivory. Represents a halibut.
MAI/HF cat no   5
4741

708b Kayak, Eskimo
Hudson Bay, Canada
168 Wood frame with hide cover.
ROM

708c Snow Goggles, Eskimo
Old Bering Sea, Alaska
Ivory.
ROM

709 Spoon, Eskimo
Alaska
7¾ Horn with carved wood, inlaid mother-
of-pearl.
Collection of Omaha Public Schools.
On permanent loan to Joslyn Art Museum since 1949.
JAM cat no 294.1950

710 Toggle, Eskimo
Point Barrow, Alaska
2 x ¾ Carved ivory. Represents a seal.
MAI/HF cat no 16
7574

711 Toggle, Eskimo
Point Barrow, Alaska
2½ x 1¼ Carved ivory. Represents
the heads of a bear and two seals.
MAI/HF cat no 19
6747

712 Toggle, Eskimo
Point Barrow, Alaska
2½ x ¾ Carved ivory. Represents
a seal.
MAI/HF cat no 19
6749

713 Toggle, Eskimo
Point Barrow, Alaska
1½ x ½ Carved and incised bone.
Represents a seal.
MAI/HF cat no 22
3949

Musical Instruments

714 Rattle, Iroquois (Seneca)   *172*, p 113
Cattaraugus Reserve, New York
10 x 3 Carved and stained wood
in the shape of a right hand.
Collected by Albert Green Heath.
LMA/BC cat no 30371

715 Drum with Standards, Ojibwa
White Earth Reservation, Minnesota
13¾ x 24¾ Wooden barrel with metal wire,
wool, beadwork, cotton braid, copper dangles,
painted skin heads. Used in Dream Dance.
Collected by Albert Green Heath.
LMA/BC cat no 30.058

716 Medicine Drum, Ojibwa *13,* p 16
Great Lakes area
¾; 7 diam. Rawhide laced over a hoop. Eagle represented on one side, a bear on the other. Depicts a "bear walker," or shaman practicing malevolent magic.
Collected by Albert Green Heath.
LMA/BC cat no 31160

717a Drum, Assiniboin
Plains
14; 16 diam. Hide with beadwork.
ROM

717b Song Stick, Osage
Oklahoma
18½ x 1 Carved wood.
MAI/HF cat no 2/937

718 Ceremonial Drum, Pawnee *1,* cover
3¾; 23 diam. Painted rawhide. Double-headed.
Collected by George Dorsey, 1902.
FMNH cat no 71856

719 Grass Dance Whistle, Sioux
Late 19th century
19 Painted wood.
Carried and played by a dance leader.
DAM cat no MS-12

720 Song Stick, Sioux (Sisseton)
South Dakota
13¼ x 2 Incised wood.
MAI/HF cat no 4/418

721 Ceremonial Rattle, probably Sioux
Lower Brule Reservation, South Dakota
48 x 2 Tin can with quillwork, feathers, beadwork.
Design represents horse tracks.
Collected by L. C. Walker.
Collection of David W. Clark.
ODM cat no CMC-G-29

722 Drum and Drumstick, Pueblo
Cochita Pueblo, New Mexico
14¾ x 12½ x 22¾ Painted hide on wood with beadwork on drumstick.
MAI/HF cat no 21/2541

723 Time Beater, Pueblo
New Mexico
10¾ x ½ Carved and painted wood.
MAI/HF cat no 15/3873

724 Time Beater, Pueblo (Hopi)
Arizona
16¼ x 1¼ Carved and painted wood.
MAI/HF cat no 9/377

725 Flute, Yuma
Lower Colorado River
22; ¾ diam. Incised reed or cane. Straight tube with four holes. Bands of diamonds, men and women, and elaborate "lizard" forms.
Collected by Major Horatio Rust, before 1890.
LMA/BC cat no 1617

726 Flute, Yuma
Lower Colorado River
23; ½ diam. Incised reed or cane. Straight tube with four holes. Geometric line patterns, concentric diamonds, parallel zig-zags.
Collected by Major Horatio Rust before 1890.
LMA/BC cat no 1619

727 Drum, Hupa
California
20 x 18¼ Painted rawhide.
MAI/HF cat no 1404

728 Rattle, Haida
Alaska
10¾ x 4 Carved and painted wood.
Represents a human face.
MAI/HF cat no 2/431

729 Rattle, Haida
British Columbia
10¼ x 3 Carved and painted wood.
Represents a bird with a frog.
MAI/HF cat no 4/8463

730 Rattle, Haida
9½ x 5 5/16 x 4 9/16 Carved and painted wood.
Used in a dance.
Collected 1838-1886.
Exchange with Smithsonian Institution, 1888.
PM/HU cat no 88.51.10/50485

731 Raven Rattle, Sitka
12½ x 4½ x 3½ Carved and painted wood.
Represents a crow. On the back is a dead man with protruding tongue in the bill of a kingfisher; on the lower side, an owl and frog.
AMNH cat no 19/803

732 Rattle, Tlingit (Chilkat) *173,* p 114
Alaska
9 x 5¼ x 3 3/16 Copper, wood, leather, shell inlay. Double face.
Gift of Lewis H. Farlow, 1904.
PM/HU cat no 04.10.10/62984

733 Rattle, Tlingit
Alaska
9 Carved and painted wood.
Raven with a man, a frog and a bird head on its back.
Collected by J. E. Standley in Sitka, Alaska, ca 1901.
LMA/BC cat no 1538

734 Rattle/Spoon, Tlingit
Chilkat, Alaska, 1869
17¾ Carved, painted and incised wood.
Fish form with human figure inside, spoon projects from head of fish.
Collected by George Davidson.
LM/UC/B cat no 2-19096

735 Raven Rattle, Tlingit
Alaska
12¼ Carved and painted wood. Anthropomorphic figure with protruding tongue going into bird's bill on back. Carried by chief at public ceremonies.
Gift of Alaska Commercial Company.
LM/UC/B cat no 2-4619

736 Shaman's Rattle, Tlingit
Alaska
3 5/16 x 2⅞ x 9½ Carved and painted wood.
Collected by Edward G. Fast, 1867-1868.
PM/HU cat no 69.30.10/1777

737 Rattle, Tlingit
6½ x 4 x 12½ Carved and painted wood.
Two pieces.
Collected by Lieut. G. T. Emmons, 1904-05.
AMNH cat no 16/9379

738 Rattle, Tlingit
Alaska, 19th century
11¼ x 4 Carved and painted wood.
SOSLAND

739 Raven Rattle, Tsimshian
14¼ x 4½ x 4 Carved and painted wood.
Grasshopper (poorviell) on back.
Collected by H. R. Bishop.
AMNH cat no 16/A1/297

740 Raven Rattle, Tsimshian
5 x 4¼ x 5 Carved and painted wood.
Collected by H. R. Bishop, 1869.
AMNH cat no 16/292

741 Crane Rattle *174,* p 114
Alaska or British Columbia, 1875-1900
8¾ x 5 x 5 Carved wood, fiber, ivory.
Collection of Worthington Hammersley Southwick.
MPA cat no 56.334

742a Rattle
Northwest Coast
11¾ Hammered copper with wood.
Bird on each side.
Collection of Isabel Anderson, 1949.
PM cat no E28234

742b Rattle
Northwest Coast
14 x 8 x 5 Carved and painted wood in shape of a frog.
Collected 1923.
ROM cat no HN-50

743 Drum Handle, Eskimo *132,* p 103
Alaska, 19th century
2 x 4¼ x 3⅛ Carved ivory with beads, hide thongs. Represents a human face.
MPA cat no 57.271

Painted Muslins and Drawings

744 Eight Ledger Drawings, Cheyenne
Fort Marion, St. Augustine, Florida, 1876
8¼ x 10½ Pencil and crayon. Cover titled in ink: "Specimens of Indian sign language, drawn by White Horse." 8 sheets plus 2 covers.
Collected by Noel Atwood, 1876.
Collection of Mrs. J. Barlow Reynolds.
JAM cat no 1949/165

745 Ten Ledger Drawings, Cheyenne (Southern)
12, p 16
Fort Reno, Indian Territory (Oklahoma), ca 1878
16 x 21 Watercolor on paper.
Collected by and collection of Carl S. Dentzel.
DENTZEL

746 Pictograph, Crow
57, p 57
Montana
35 x 85 Painted muslin.
Bequest of Victor J. Evans.
NMNH/SI cat no 358,425
113,605

747 Pictograph, Sioux
175, p 114
ca 1880
67 x 108 Inked muslin (pencil outlines, colored
inks). Two different groups of war exploits,
probably by two different artists.
DAM cat no PS-36-G

748 Pictograph, Sioux
68½ x 34⅞ Painted muslin.
Depicts Battle of Little Big Horn; includes
Sitting Bull, Crazy Horse, Kicking Bear,
Rabbit Stands Up and General George A. Custer.
Painted by Kicking Bear.
CIS cat no 8597

749 Pictograph, Sioux
100 x 69½ Painted muslin. Classic Sioux
example as expressed in the distorted horse forms.
Donated in 1962.
MPM cat no 57783
18707

750 Pictograph, Sioux
Black Hills, South Dakota
72 x 76 Painted muslin.
Obtained by J. H. Van Gassbeek.
NSHS cat no 8182-1

751 Six Ledger Drawings, Sioux
176, p 114
9 x 13½ Ink and pencil on ledger paper.
Dakota Sioux in various activities related
to war.
Purchased from H. H. Hyassen, 1900.
MPM cat no 2063

752 Four Ledger Drawings, Ute
Basin, 1870s
12 x 16 matted. Ink with pencil and water
color on tissue paper. Depictions of Indian
horsemen and cavalrymen, tipis.
Drawn by Yellow Nose.
Collected by Captain John Bourke, 1870s.
Collection of Captain John Bourke and his daughter,
Mrs. A. H. Richardson.
JAM cat nos 1965.183, .184, .185, .186

Pipes

* **753 Pipe, Fox (Mesquaki)**
Tama, Iowa
Stem: 26¼ Bowl: 7⅛ x 3½
Catlinite bowl with carved wood stem.
Naturalistic figure of beaver on stem.
Collected by Albert Green Heath from
John Young Bear.
LMA/BC cat no 30942

* **754 Pipe Bowl, Ojibwa**
Manitoulin Island, Ontario
3½ ; 5 long. Carved and incised stone,
with babbitt metal. Found in grave.
Represents a double-headed hawk or eagle.
Collected by Albert Green Heath.
LMA/BC cat no 30937

* **755 Pipe Bowl and Stem, Ojibwa**
White Earth Reservation, Minnesota
Stem: 29½ Bowl: 3½ x 2½
Carved and painted wood.
Collected 1918.
MHSM cat no E98

* **756 Pipe Bowl**
3½ ; 7½ long. Carved and incised
catlinite. Cylindrical bowl with faceted
anterior projection. Relief figure of
twined snake with diamond designs.
Collected by Albert Green Heath.
LMA/BC cat no 30917

* **757 Pipe Bowl**
Upper Midwest, late 19th century
3½ Carved stone. Four faces in
low relief.
Collected by Dr. Nathan Sturges Jarvis.
The Brooklyn Museum, F. S. Benson,
Henry Batterman Funds.
BM cat no 50.67-141

* **758 War Calumet, probably Mandan**
61, p 59
North Dakota, early 1800s
Stem: 40 Bowl: 1¾ diam. Carved
catlinite with eagle feathers, beadwork,
horsehair. Tufts in eagle feathers
represent scalps.
Gift of the heirs of David Kimball, 1899.
PM/HU cat no 99.12.10
53100

* **759 Pipe Bowl and Stem, Pawnee**
Nebraska
Stem: 22¾ Bowl: 4 Carved stone
with carved and painted wood stem.
Bowl in shape of horsehead. Stem has
relief carvings of crescent, horseheads,
heart, steerheads, deerhead and turtle.
Collected by Albert Green Heath.
Purchased from Mrs. Emma Seizer.
LMA/BC cat no 30974

* **760 Pipe Bowl and Stem, Sioux**
ca 1870
Stem: 17½ Bowl: 3; 6 long.
Carved wood and catlinite.
COE

* **761 Pipe Bowl, Sioux**
8¾ x 1¾ x 4½ Carved catlinite
with lead inlay.
Collected 1926.
MHSM cat no 6585/8

* **762 Pipe Bowl, Sioux**
7¼ x 1½ x 2 Carved catlinite.
Represents an owl or eagle claw.
Collected 1919.
MHSM cat no E286

* **763 Pipe Bowl, probably Sioux**
Plains
4¾ x ¾ x 3½
Catlinite.
Collected from White Swan, in
Standing Rock, 1884.
MHSM cat no 6090

* **764 Pipe Bowl and Stem, Sioux (Eastern)**
Stem: 19 Bowl: 3 x 4 Carved wood
with quillwork, horsehair, mallard feathers.
SHSW cat no 1961.249.3a

* **765 Pipe Bowl, Sioux (probably Eastern)**
53, p 53
Lake Minnetonka, Minnesota
6¼ x 9½ x 1½
Catlinite. Moses Adams portrait pipe.
MHSM cat no E342/3325

* **766 Pipe Bowl and Stem**
Plains
Bowl: ¾ x ½ Carved catlinite bowl
with wood stem. Bowl represents a
bird's claw.
Gift as a memorial to Dr. Harlow Brooks.
BM cat no 43.201.255

* **767 Pipe Bowl and Stem**
Northern Plains
3¼ ; 6¼ long. Carved catlinite
with lead. Represents a horsehead
with incised decoration.
SMM cat no 1-622

* **768 Pipe, Haida**
Alaska
2¼ ; 9¾ long. Carved argillite.
MAI/HF cat no 6492

* **769 Pipe, Tlingit**
Angoon, Admiralty Island, Alaska
5 x 2¾ x 2¾ Carved wood.
MAI/HF cat no 9227

* **770 Pipe, Tlingit**
Kake, Alaska
7 x 1¾ x 3 Carved wood.
Represents a spirit figure below,
land otter giving birth above.
MAI/HF cat no 1
2918

* **771 Pipe, Tlingit**
Takokakaan, Alaska
8 x 3½ x 5½ Carved wood with
shell inlay. Represents a spirit
canoe with a bear, an eagle and a
human figure with the head of a raven.
Ceremonial use.
MAI/HF cat no 2
9169

* **772 Pipe, Tlingit**
Alaska
6 x 3¾ Carved wood. Represents
air spirit.
MAI/HF cat no 3
2239

* **773 Pipe, Tlingit**
Tongass, Alaska
3½ x 1¾ x 3½ Porphyry
stone. Represents sea lions.
AMNH cat no 19/184

* **774 Pipe, Tlingit**
Prince of Wales Island, Canada
5¼ x 2 x 3¾ Carved wood with
brass, copper. Represents a shaman's
spirit.
AMNH cat no 19/699

* **775 Pipe**
Northwest Coast
4 x 1⅞ Carved and incised wood
with brass, shell. Frog effigy with
crosshatching on back.
LMA/BC cat no 1560

* **776 Pipe, Eskimo**
Point Barrow, Alaska
1¼ ; 11½ long. Carved ivory.
MAI/HF cat no 5
                3142

* **777 Pipe, Eskimo**
Alaska
17½ x 2½ Carved and incised
ivory.
Collected by Frank G. Speck, 1929.
NMM cat no IV-E-960

* **778 Pipe, Eskimo**
Bering Sea Coast, Alaska
1¾ ; 17 long. Carved and
engraved walrus ivory.
Collected by Lieut. G. T. Emmons, December, 1918.
NMM cat no IV-E-929

* **779 Pipe, Eskimo**
Wrangell, Alaska
2½ x 2; 4 long. Carved wood
with brass. Represents a fish head.
AMNH cat no E/1528

Pottery

* **780 Water Jar, Pueblo (Acoma)**
Acoma Pueblo, New Mexico
10 x 10¼ x 5¾ Painted pottery. Bird
and flower motifs, with terraced designs.
Top rim shallowly scalloped.
Collected by Dr. H. J. Spinden's museum
expedition, 1912-23.
AMNH cat no 50.1/3654

* **781 Olla, Pueblo (Acoma)**
Acoma Pueblo, New Mexico
11½ x 13½ x 7 Painted pottery.
Geometric and curvilinear designs and
line patterns.
Collected by Dr. H. J. Spinden's museum
expedition, 1912-23.
AMNH cat no 50.1/6739

* **782 Pot, Pueblo (Acoma)**
Acoma Pueblo, New Mexico, 19th century
11 x 6½ Painted pottery. Geometric
designs.
WAC cat no x.2987

* **783 Pot, Pueblo (Acoma)**
Acoma Pueblo, New Mexico, early 20th century
11 x 7 Painted pottery. Floral and geometric
designs.
WAC cat no x.2988

* **784 Pot, Pueblo (Acoma)**
Acoma Pueblo, New Mexico, 19th century
12 x 6¼ Painted pottery. Geometric designs.
WAC cat no x.2990

* **785 Pot, Pueblo (Acoma)**
Acoma Pueblo, New Mexico, 19th century
10½ x 7¼ Painted pottery. Geometric design.
WAC cat no x.2985

* **786 Pot, Pueblo (Acoma)**   *177*, p 115
Acoma Pueblo, New Mexico, 1890-1910
8¾ x 11 Painted pottery. Geometric
designs.
MNM cat no 11014/12

* **787 Pot, Pueblo (Acoma)**
Acoma Pueblo, New Mexico, 1890-1910
12½ x 10½ Painted pottery. Geometric
designs.
MNM cat no 12005/12

* **788 Pot, Pueblo (Acoma)**
Acoma Pueblo, New Mexico, 1890-1910
10¾ x 9 Painted pottery. Geometric
designs.
MNM cat no 12026/12

* **789 Jar, Pueblo (Acoma)**
Acoma Pueblo, New Mexico, post 1960
4½ x 6½ Painted pottery. Geometric designs.
Made by Marie Chino, based on prehistoric
designs.
MNM cat no 25830/12

* **790 Medicine Jar, Pueblo (Acoma)**
Acoma Pueblo, New Mexico, 1961
4¾ x 6½ Painted pottery. Geometric design.
Made by Marie Chino.
MNM cat no 25831/12

* **791 Pot, Pueblo (Hopi)**   *178*, p 115
Hopi Pueblo, Arizona, 1900-1920
8¾ x 12⅝ Painted pottery. Abstract
bird pattern.
Made by Nampeyo.
MNM cat no 11020/12

* **792 Jar, Pueblo (Hopi)**
Arizona
8; 14¼ diam. Painted pottery.
MAI/HF cat no 19/4354

* **793 Tile, Pueblo (Hopi)**
Arizona
8 x 5 Painted pottery. Design
represents a kachina.
MAI/HF cat no 19/4370

* **794 Tile, Pueblo (Hopi)**
Arizona
6 x 4 Painted pottery.
MAI/HF 5/8171

* **795 Jar, Pueblo (Laguna)**
Laguna Pueblo, New Mexico, 1910-1920
12 x 13⅛ Painted pottery.
MNM cat no 18821/12

* **796 Pot, Pueblo (San Ildefonso)**
San Ildefonso Pueblo, New Mexico, late 19th century
11 x 7½ Painted pottery. Geometric design.
Style of San Ildefonso before the innovations
of Maria Martinez.
WAC cat no x.2977

* **797 Pot, Pueblo (San Ildefonso)**
San Ildefonso Pueblo, New Mexico, 1890-1910
10 x 12 Painted pottery. Geometric designs.
MNM cat no 11095/12

* **798 Pot, Pueblo (San Ildefonso)**
San Ildefonso Pueblo, New Mexico, 1920-1940
15 x 13 Painted pottery. Geometric design.
Made by Tonita Roybal.
MNM cat no 18782/12

* **799 Pot, Pueblo (San Ildefonso)**   *6*, p 11
San Ildefonso Pueblo, New Mexico, 1900-1910
16½ x 10 Painted pottery. Geometric designs.
Made by Maria Martinez, decorated by
Julian Martinez.
MNM cat no 18785/12

* **800 Water Jar, Pueblo (San Ildefonso)**
San Ildefonso Pueblo, New Mexico
9½ x 12 x 8½ Painted pottery. Bird
and leaf motifs with curvilinear patterns.
Collection of Dr. H. J. Spinden.
AMNH cat no 50.1/3356

* **801 Pot, Pueblo (San Ildefonso)**
San Ildefonso Pueblo, New Mexico
7½ x 7½ Painted pottery. One side
terraced.
Collection of Dr. H. J. Spinden.
AMNH cat no 50.1/3536

* **802 Water Jar, Pueblo (San Ildefonso)**
San Ildefonso Pueblo, New Mexico
9 x 11 x 8 Painted pottery.
Geometric designs.
Collection of Dr. H. J. Spinden.
AMNH cat no 50.1/3379

* **803 Plate, Pueblo (San Ildefonso)**
San Ildefonso Pueblo, New Mexico, 1963
2 x 11¾ Polished black pottery. Feathered
pattern first used by Julian Martinez. Signed Maria
Martinez. Made by Maria Martinez and her
son, Popovi.
Gift of Mrs. Popovi Da.
WAC cat no 72.18

* **804 Olla, Pueblo (San Ildefonso)**
San Ildefonso Pueblo, New Mexico, 1962
9 x 6 Polished black pottery. No decoration.
Signed Maria Poveka (Maria Martinez's
Tewa name).
Gift of Mrs. Popovi Da.
WAC cat no 72.19

* **805 Pot, Pueblo (San Juan)**
San Juan Pueblo, New Mexico, 19th century
11½ x 8¼ Polished and matte black pottery.
WAC cat no x.2975

* 806 **Pot, Pueblo (Santa Ana)**
Santa Ana Pueblo, New Mexico, 1925-1940
9 x 6¾ Painted pottery. Geometric designs.
MNM cat no 18951/12

* 807 **Jar, Pueblo (Santa Clara)** *3, p 10*
Santa Clara Pueblo, New Mexico, 1961
7¾ x 6¾ Burnished black ware. Three
incised bear-paw designs. Made by Severa
Tafoya.
MNM cat no 25833/12

* 808 **Pot, Pueblo (Santo Domingo)**
Santo Domingo Pueblo, New Mexico, 1880-1890
20 x 19 Painted pottery. Geometric designs.
MNM cat no 45611/12

* 809 **Olla, Pueblo (Santo Domingo)**
Santo Domingo Pueblo, New Mexico
11 x 10 x 8¼ Painted pottery. Naturalistic
designs.
Collection of Dr. H. J. Spinden.
AMNH cat no 50.1/5037

* 810 **Pot, Pueblo (Santo Domingo)**
Santo Domingo Pueblo, New Mexico
5⅛ x 5¼ Painted pottery. Geometric
design.
Gift of Amelia E. White, 1937.
AMNH cat no 50.2/4115

* 811 **Pot, Pueblo (Santo Domingo)**
Santo Domingo Pueblo, New Mexico, 1930-1940
10 x 6½ Painted pottery. Made by Monica Silva.
MNM cat no 11101/12

* 812 **Olla, Pueblo (Zia)**
Zia Pueblo, New Mexico
13 x 14 x 7½ Painted pottery. Bird,
deer and flower motifs.
Collected by George H. Pepper, 1903.
AMNH cat no 29.0/142

* 813 **Pot, Pueblo (probably Zia)**
New Mexico, early 20th century
11½ x 7½ Painted pottery. Geometric
designs.
WAC cat no x.2979

* 814 **Pot, Pueblo (Zuni)**
Zuni Pueblo, New Mexico, late 19th century
11½ x 8¼ Painted pottery. Geometric and
naturalistic designs. Two bands show deer
enclosed by arches, a narrower band is
filled with birds.
WAC cat no x.2981

* 815 **Pot, Pueblo (Zuni)**
New Mexico, 19th century
11 x 7 Painted pottery. Banded
geometric design.
WAC cat no x.2991

* 816 **Pot, Pueblo (Zuni)**
Zuni Pueblo, New Mexico, 1890-1910
9⅜ x 12 Painted pottery, geometric
design.
MNM cat no 11037/12

* 817 **Pot, Pueblo (Zuni)**
Zuni Pueblo, New Mexico, 1910-1924
14 x 9 Painted pottery. Geometric designs.
MNM cat no 12076/12

* 818 **Pot, Pueblo (Zuni)**
Zuni Pueblo, New Mexico, 1890-1910
19 x 9¼ Painted pottery. Geometric designs.
MNM cat no 12086/12

* 819 **Pot, Pueblo (Zuni)** *70, p 68*
Zuni Pueblo, New Mexico
3½ x 9¼ Painted pottery. Terraced rim with
geometric, butterfly and frog designs.
Gift of Philadelphia Museum of Art, 1949.
AMNH cat no 50.2/5653

* 820 **Pot, Pueblo (Zuni)**
Zuni Pueblo, New Mexico
4¼ x 11⅜ Painted pottery.
Curvilinear design.
Collected by Stephen Dennison Peet before 1890.
LMA/BC cat no 15523

* 821 **Priest's Jar, Pueblo (Zuni)**
Zuni Pueblo, New Mexico
8¾ x 11 x 7½ Painted pottery. Four
terraces jutting out at right angles from
top rim. Frog pattern.
Collected by A. L. Kroeber and Leslie
Spier expedition, 1916.
AMNH cat no 50.2/238

Weapons

822 **War Club, Iroquois**
Wagner, South Dakota
20 Carved wood with leather thong,
wolf head, turtle incisions on handle.
From Eddie Little Chief (Sioux).
Collected by Milford G. Chandler, 1919.
CIS cat no 3691

823 **Club, Ottawa**
Michigan
20 x 1½ Carved wood with buffalo tail.
MAI/HF cat no 14/3458

824 **Club, Winnebago**
Wisconsin
31¼ x 2½ Carved wood with metal studs.
MAI/HF cat no 2/5314

825 **Ball-head Club**
Woodlands
25 Carved wood with brass tacks. Ball and
handle in one piece with figure of otter on top.
LMA/BC cat no 1826

826 **War Club** *179, p 115*
Great Lakes
25¹⁄₁₆ x 5½ Carved wood. Otter
figure on round surface.
Gift of heirs of David Kimball, 1899.
PM/HU cat no 52985

827 **Shield, Cheyenne**
18½ diam. Painted cowhide and deerskin,
stroud cloth, feathers. Depicts a buffalo
cow with crescent moon and sun.
Collected by George W. Moffet.
DAM cat no PChy-19-P

828 **Shield, Comanche**
Texas
25 diam. Painted rawhide with buckskin
straps, feathers. Design represents a bison
head, two mountain lions.
LMA/BC cat no 6788

829 **Shield, Crow**
Plains, early to mid-1800s
54 diam. Painted buffalo hide with cow
tail hair. Design represents a bull.
Gift of Charles Peabody, 1915.
PM/HU cat no 15.34.10/86249

830 **Shield, Crow**
Montana
20 diam. Painted hide, feathers, hawk
skin, rawhide medallion. Pictograph of
hawk.
Gift of Lewis H. Farlow, 1905.
PM/HU cat no 05.7.10/64948

831 **Shield, Crow** *54, p 54*
Montana
21 diam. Painted buffalo hide with feathers.
MAI/HF cat no 12/7779

832 **Shield, Crow**
Montana
20 diam. Painted hide with feathers.
Represents confronting animals.
MAI/HF cat no 2/4426

833 **Shield, Crow**
Montana
19¾ diam. Bison hide with feathers,
flannel, beads. Single deer design depicting
tracks, visions, waves.
Collected by J. T. Allen.
CIS cat no 7530

834 **Shield, Crow** *20, p 23*
23 diam. Painted buffalo hide and buckskin.
Owned by Big Bear. A bear is shown charging
into a fusilage of bullets.
Collected by S. C. Simms, 1902.
FMNH cat no 71832-1

835 **Club, Iowa**
Iowa
19½ x 1½ Carved, painted and incised
wood, metal spike.
MAI/HF cat no 19/5086

836 **Shield and Cover, Pawnee**
Nebraska
20 diam. Painted rawhide.
Bequest of Victor J. Evans estate, 1931.
NMNH/SI cat no 359,060/113,605

837 **Shield, Sioux**
16½ diam. Buffalo hide with eagle
feathers, buckskin fringe. Netted discs
on front; geometric design on back.
Collected by Amelia E. White, 1912-1937.
CIS cat no 627

838 Shield, Sioux
Painted hide with feathers. Representations
of birds, lizard. Geometric designs.
Collected by Colonel Smith, Cheyenne Reservation.
Collection of Colonel George Smith, Swampscott,
1909.
PM cat no E26065

839 Shield, probably Sioux
20 diam. Painted rawhide with feathers, bells.
Depicts a horse painted for war, wearing a face mask.
Collected 1918.
MHSM cat no E110

840 War Club, Sioux
19½ x 7¼ Carved stone, wood, beadwork.
Buffalo head on bead-wrapped handle.
DAM cat no OS-69

841 Medicine Club, Sioux
Standing Rock Indian Agency, North Dakota
32½ Carved and incised wood with inlaid
clear glass and cloth, thumb tacks. Hand,
sword and rifle designs; bird and human heads
represented on tip.
Collected by Bradley, ca 1883.
CIS cat no 4170

842a Club, Sioux (Teton)
North Dakota
35 x 2¼ Carved and painted wood with
horsehair, hide. Represents a horse head
with a leg. Carried by one whose horse was
killed under him in battle.
MAI/HF cat no 14/1566

842b Club
Northern Plains
Incised wood with feathers, stone.
ROM

843 Shield, Navajo
24 diam. Painted hide with feathers, cloth.
Made by Many Horses, as replica of his own
shield. Bow and arrow, deer design within
crescent.
Collected by J. M. Johnson.
CIS cat no 3872

844 Shield, Pueblo (Santa Ana)
Santa Ana Pueblo, New Mexico
23 diam. Painted buffalo hide.
MAI/HF cat no 12/2508

845 Shield, Pueblo (Santa Ana)
Santa Ana Pueblo, New Mexico
21¼ diam. Painted buffalo hide.
MAI/HF cat no 20/1529

846 Shield, Pueblo (Santa Clara)
Santa Clara Pueblo, New Mexico
21½ diam. Wood hoop with painted muslin,
buckskin.
Collected by Fred Harvey.
TM/CSFAC cat no 7509

847 Shield, Pueblo
New Mexico
23 diam. Painted buffalo hide with feathers.
MAI/HF cat no 2/9349

848 Club, Coast Salish
British Columbia
23½ x 2½ Incised bone.
MAI/HF cat no 11/1320

849 Slave Killer, Kwakiutl
Vancouver, British Columbia
12½ x 3¼ Carved stone. Ceremonial use.
MAI/HF cat no 5/5054

850 Fighting Knife, Tlingit   *181,* p 115
Alaska, 19th century
14⅝ x 1 x 2⅝ Ivory, abalone
shell, iron, leather thongs.
MPA cat no 59.103

851 Dagger, Tlingit
Klukwan, Alaska
21¾ x 2½ Copper, abalone shell, fur, baleen.
Collected by G. B. Gordon, 1905.
UMUP cat no NA1287

852 Fighting Knife, Tlingit
15⅜ x 2⅛ Carved ivory with human hair
and skin, iron blade. Represents a mythical
bear with a man pressed to his body, a
fish and a raven's head.
AMNH cat no E/2067

853 Fighting Knife, Tlingit
18 x 2⅝ Metal blade, carved wood with
leather, string, abalone shell inlay. Represents
a bear.
AMNH cat no E/1545

854 Knife, Tlingit
Sitka, Alaska
20¾ x 2½ Carved wood with shell inlay,
metal. Handle represents a thunderbird.
MAI/HF cat no 9311

855 Knife, Tlingit
Alaska
17 x 1½ Carved wood, shell, metal. Handle
represents a raven.
MAI/HF cat no 19/7446

856 Knife, Tlingit
Cross Sound, Alaska
20 x 1¼ Carved wood with shell, metal.
Handle represents a killer whale.
MAI/HF cat no 9305

857 Throwing Stones, Eskimo
Alaska
1¾ x ⅞ Stone with incised pictographs,
fiber binding. Used for killing small game
and birds.
Collection of A. F. Jonas, M.D.
Gift of Mrs. A. F. Jonas, 1951.
JAM cat no 1951.494

Additions to Catalogue

858 Interior Housepost, Kwakiutl
Nawhitti, Hope Island, British Columbia, before 1899
99 Carved and incised wood with paint.
Represents a bear, raven, bird and the face
of a man. From Chief George's house.
Collected by C. F. Newcombe, 1899.
NMM cat no VII-E-408

859 Figure
Northwest Coast, before 1900
118 Carved and painted wood.
Represents a man holding a child.
Collected by Lord Bossom, ca 1900.
NMM cat no VII-G-610b

860 Pueblo (Hopi) Motsin (Disheveled) Kachina
North central Arizona
12½ x 4 Carved and painted wood with feathers,
hair. Case mask, cloth mouth, beard, rope.
Fred Harvey Foundation, Fine Arts Collection.
HM cat no 822-C-1

861 Shield, Sioux (Oglala)
17 diam. Painted rawhide.
Made by Wanyaka Nompa.
Collection of V. J. Evans.
NMNH/SI cat no 359059

862 Dance Stick
Northwest Coast, before 1869
54 Carved wood. Represents human figures.
Collected by George Hunt and Franz Boas, 1869.
AMNH 16/942

North American Indian
Tribal Locations
19th Century

North American Indian

Tribal Locations

20th Century

ARCTIC COAST

Eskimo

NORTHWEST COAST

NORTHERN
ATHABASCAN

Tlingit

Kaskaskia

Athabascan

Tsimshian

Haida
Sitka
Bella Bella
Bella Coola
Cowichan
Cowlitz
Niska
Kwakiutl
Nootka

Lillooet

Chipewyan

Cree

Naskapi

Algonkian

WOODLANDS

Micmac

Penobscot

Passamaquoddy

Pennacock

Makah

Skokomish

Kutenai

Gros Ventre

Klikitat
Wishram
Yakima
Wasco
Nez Perce

PLATEAU

Flathead

Blackfeet Assiniboin

Cree

Arikara
Hidatsa Teton
Mandan

Plains
Ojibwa

Ojibwa

Ottawa

Mohawk

Dene

Northern
Cheyenne

Sisseton

Menomini

Huron

Onondaga

Klamath

Achomawi

GREAT
BASIN

Shoshoni

Arapaho

Sioux
Brule

Oglala

Iroquois
Cayuga
Seneca

*Pueblo Tribes
Acoma
Cochiti
Santa Ana
Taos
San Ildefonso
Zia
Santa Clara
Santa Domingo
Zuni

*Oklahoma Tribes
Creek
Cherokee
Sauk & Fox
Osage
Ponca
Miami
Seminole
Potawatomi
Choctaw
Southern Cheyenne
Pawnee
Oto
Arapaho
Caddo
Kiowa
Comanche
Delaware
Illinois

Yurok
Karok
Hupa
Shasta

Pomo

Washo

Shoshoni

Panamint

Paiute

Ute

Yankton
Santee
Ponca
Winnebago

Sauk & Fox

PLAINS

Kickapoo
Potawatomi

Kickapoo
Iowa

Tulare

Miwok
Yokuts

Chumash
Cahuilla

Mohave

Chemehuevi

Paiute

Yuma

Hopi

Navajo

Apache Jicarilla

SOUTHWEST

*Pueblo Tribes

*Oklahoma Tribes

SOUTHEAST

Cherokee

Cocopa
Papago
Pima

Chiricahua

Mescalero

Choctaw

Creek

Chitimacha

Seminole

Bibliography

This bibliography is organized to correspond with the order in which the catalogue sections appear, beginning with general references, followed by references to the various essays. Two additional bibliographical sections are included: references to the art of the Southeast and California, topics not covered by catalogue essays.

General

Boas, Franz. *Primitive Art.* New York, Dover, 1927.

Christensen, Erwin O. *Primitive Art.* New York, Viking Press, 1955. (out of print)

Curtis, E. S. *The North American Indian.* 30 Vols. Cambridge, Massachusetts, Harvard University Press, 1903-1930. (reprinted 1970 by Johnson Reprint)

* Devel, Thorne. *American Indian Ways of Life.* Springfield, Illinois State Museum, 1968. (out of print)

Dockstader, Frederick J. *Indian Art in America.* Greenwich, Connecticut, New York Graphic Society, 1961.

Douglas, Frederic H., and D'Harnoncourt, Rene. *Indian Art of the United States.* New York, Museum of Modern Art, 1941, 1970.

* Driver, Harold E. *Indians of North America.* Chicago, University of Chicago Press, 1969.

Feder, Norman. *North American Indian Painting.* New York, Museum of Primitive Art, 1967.

——*Art of the American Indian.* New York, Harry N. Abrams, Inc., 1971.

——*Two Hundred Years of North American Indian Art.* New York, Praeger Publishers in association with The Whitney Museum of American Art, 1971.

Harding, Anne and Bolling, Patricia. *Bibliography of Articles and Papers on North American Indian Art.* Washington, D.C., Department of the Interior, Indian Arts and Crafts Board, 1938. (Kraus Reprint)

Jenness, Diamond. "The Indians of Canada," *Bulletin* No. 65, Ottawa, National Museum of Canada, 1932.

Josephy Alvin, M., Jr. *Indian Heritage of America.* New York, Knopf, 1968.

Jopling, Carol F. (ed.) *Art and Aesthetics in Primitive Societies; a Critical Anthology.* New York, E. P. Dutton & Co., 1971.

Kroeber, Alfred Lewis. "Cultural and Natural Areas of Native North America," *Publications in American Anthropology and Ethnology,* Vol. 38, Berkeley, University of California Press, 1939.

Murdock, George Peter. *Ethnographic Bibliography of North America.* 3rd ed. New Haven, Connecticut, Human Relations Area Files Press, 1960.

Musee de l'Homme. *Masterpieces of Indian and Eskimo Art from Canada.* Paris, Societe des Amis du Musee de l'Homme, 1969.

Tschopik, Harry, Jr. *Indians of North America.* New York, American Museum of Natural History, 1952. (out of print)

Underhill, Ruth M. *Red Man's America.* Chicago, University of Chicago Press, 1956, 1971.

Whiteford, Andrew Hunter. *North American Indian Arts.* New York, Golden Press, 1970.

* Willey, Gordon R. *An Introduction to American* Archaeology. Vol. 1, Englewood Cliffs, New Jersey, Prentice-Hall, Inc., 1966.

Rock Art

Gebhard, David. *Prehistoric Rock Art of the Seminole Canyon Area, Val Verde County, Texas.* Santa Barbara, Art Galleries, University of California, 1965.

——"The Shield Motif in Plains Rock Art," *American Antiquity,* Vol. 31, July, 1966, Norman, Oklahoma, University of Oklahoma, pp 721-732.

——*The Rock Art of Dinwoody, Wyoming.* Santa Barbara, Art Galleries, University of California, 1969.

Grant, Campbell. *Rock Art of the American Indian.* New York, Crowell, 1967.

——*The Rock Paintings of the Chumash.* Berkeley, University of California Press, 1965.

Grant, Campbell, Baird, James W. and Pringle, Kenneth J. *Rock Drawings of the Coso Range.* China Lake, California, Maturango Museum, 1968.

Heizer, Robert F. and Baumhoff, Martin A. *Prehistoric Rock Art of Nevada and Eastern California.* Berkeley, University of California Press, 1962.

Schaafsma, Polly. *Early Navajo Rock Paintings and Carvings.* Santa Fe, New Mexico, Museum of Navajo Ceremonial Art, 1966.

Siegrist, Roland. *Prehistoric Petroglyphs and Pictographs in Utah.* Salt Lake City, Utah Museum of Fine Arts, 1972.

Steward, Julian H. "Petroglyphs of California and Adjoining States," *Publications in American Anthropology and Ethnology,* Vol. 24, Berkeley, University of California Press, 1929, pp 47-238.

Turner, Christy G. II. "Petroglyphs of the Glen Canyon Region," *Bulletin* No. 38, Flagstaff, Museum of Northern Arizona, 1963.

Architecture

Cosgrove, H. S. and C. B. "The Swarts Ruin; A Typical Mimbres Site in Southwestern New Mexico," *Peabody Museum Papers,* XV, No. 1, Cambridge, Massachusetts, Peabody Museum, 1932.

Hamilton, Henry W. *The Spiro Mound.* Columbia, Missouri, The Missouri Archaeological Society, 1952.

Holmes, William Henry. "Aboriginal Pottery of the Eastern United States," *Annual Report* XX, Washington, D. C., Bureau of American Ethnology, 1899.

Klemen, Pal. *Mediaeval American Art.* New York, Macmillan, 1943, 1956. (out of print)

Martin, Paul S., Quimby, George I. and Collier, Donald. *Indians Before Columbus: Twenty Thousand Years of North American History Revealed by Archaeology.* Chicago, University of Chicago Press, 1947.

Moorehead, Warren K. *The Stone Age in North America.* New York, Houghton Mifflin Co., 1910. (out of print)

Scully, Vincent. *Pueblo Architecture of the Southwest: A Photographic Essay.* Austin, University of Texas Press, 1971.

Shetrone, Henry Clyde. *The Mound Builders.* New York, Appleton, 1930. (out of print)

Smith, Watson. "Kiva Mural Decorations at Awatovi and Kawaika-a," *Peabody Museum Papers,* Vol. 37, Cambridge, Massachusetts, Peabody Museum, 1952.

Woodlands

Alberts, Robert C. "Trade Silver and Indian Silver Work in the Great Lakes Region," *The Wisconsin Archaeologist,* Vol. 34, No. 1, Milwaukee, 1953.

Densmore, Frances. "Chippewa Customs," *Bureau of American Ethnology Bulletin* 86, Washington, D. C., Smithsonian Institution, 1929, pp 1-204.

* Dewdney, Selwyn and Kidd, K. E. *Indian Rock Paintings of the Great Lakes.* Quetico Foundation, Toronto, Ontario, University of Toronto Press, 1967.

Fenton, William N. "Masked Medicine Societies of the Iroquois," *Annual Report* 14, Washington, D. C., Smithsonian Institution, 1940.

* Fowler, Melvin L. (ed.) "Explorations into Cahokia Archeology," *Illinois Archeological Survey Bulletin* No. 7, Urbana, Illinois, University of Illinois Press, 1969.

Hoffman, Walter James. "The Menomini Indians," *Bureau of American Ethnology Annual Report* 14, Washington, D. C., Smithsonian Institution, 1896, pp 11-335.

* Johnson, Elden. *The Prehistoric Peoples of Minnesota.* St. Paul, Minnesota Historical Society, 1969.

Lyford, Carrie A. *Iroquois Crafts.* Lawrence, Kansas, Haskell Institute, 1945.

——*Ojibwa Crafts.* Lawrence, Kansas, Haskell Institute, 1945.

Morgan, Lewis H. *The League of the Ho-De-No-Sau-Nee or Iroquois.* Edited by U. M. Loyd. Two Vols. New York, Dodd, Mead & Co., 1902. (B. Franklin Reprint, 1971)

Parker, Arthur C. "Secret Medicine Societies of the Seneca," *American Anthropologist* (n.s.) Vol. XI, 1909, pp 161-185. (Available in *Parker on the Iroquois,* W. N. Fenton (ed.) Syracuse, New York, Syracuse University Press, 1968.)

* Quimby, George I. *Indian Life in the Upper Great Lakes; 11,000 B.C. to A.D. 1800.* Chicago, University of Chicago Press, 1971.

Radin, Paul. "The Winnebago Tribe," *Bureau of American Ethnology Annual Report* 37, Washington, D. C., Smithsonian Institution, 1916, pp 35-560.

Ritzenthaler, Robert E. "Iroquois False-Face Masks," *Publications in Primitive Art,* No. 3, Milwaukee, Milwaukee Public Museum, 1969.

——"The Potawatomi Indians of Wisconsin," *Bulletin,* Vol. 19, No. 3, Milwaukee, Milwaukee Public Museum, 1953.

* ——*Prehistoric Indians of Wisconsin.* Milwaukee, Milwaukee Public Museum, 1953. (out of print)

Ritzenthaler, Robert E. and Pat. *The Woodland Indians of the Western Great Lakes,* New York, The Natural History Press, Doubleday and Co., 1970.

Skinner, Alanson. "Material Culture of the Menomini," *Indian Notes and Monographs (Miscellaneous),* No. 20, New York, Museum of the American Indian, Heye Foundation, 1921.

Speck, Frank G. "The Double Curve Motif in Northeastern Algonkian Art," *Memoir,* No. 52, Ottawa, National Museum of Canada, 1941.

——"The Iroquois," *Bulletin* No. 23, Bloomfield Hills, Michigan, Cranbrook Institute of Science, 1955.

——"Montagnai; Art in Birch-bark, A Circumpolar Trait." *Indian Notes and Monographs,* Vol. XI, No. 2, New York, Museum of the American Indian, Heye Foundation, 1937.

West, G. A. "Copper, Its Meaning and Use by the Aborigines of the Lake Superior Region," *Bulletin* Vol. 10, No. 1, Milwaukee, Milwaukee Public Museum, 1929.

Plains

Ewers, John C. *Plains Indian Painting.* Stanford, California, Stanford University Press, 1939. (out of print)

——*Blackfeet Crafts.* Washington, D.C., Office of Indian Affairs, 1945. (out of print)

Feder, Norman. *Art of the Eastern Plains Indians.* New York, The Brooklyn Museum, 1964.

La Barre, Weston. *The Peyote Cult.* Hamden, Connecticut, The Shoe String Press, 1970.

Lowie, Robert H. *Indians of the Plains.* New York, AMS Press, Inc., 1954.

Lyford, Carrie A. *Quill and Beadwork of the Western Sioux.* Lawrence, Kansas, Haskell Institute, 1940.

Marriott, Alice. "The Trade Guild of Southern Cheyenne Women," *Bulletin of the Oklahoma Anthropological Society,* Vol. IV, April, 1956, pp 19-27.

Mooney, J. "The Ghost Dance Religion," *Bureau of American Ethnology Annual Report,* Washington, D. C., Smithsonian Institution, 1896.

Wildschut, William and Ewers, John C. *Crow Indian Beadwork; A Descriptive and Historical Study.* New York, Museum of the American Indian, Heye Foundation, Vol. XVI, 1959.

Wissler, Clark. "Decorative Art of the Sioux Indians," *Bulletin* XVIII, Part 3, New York, American Museum of Natural History, 1904, pp 231-278.

Southwest

Adair, John. *The Navajo and Pueblo Silversmiths.* Norman, Oklahoma, University of Oklahoma Press, 1944.

Amsden, Charles Avery. *Navajo Weaving; Its Technic and History.* Santa Ana, California, The Fine Arts Press, 1934.

——*Prehistoric Southwesterners from Basketmaker to Pueblo.* Los Angeles, Southwest Museum, 1949.

Bunzel, Ruth L. "The Pueblo Potter," *Contributions to Anthropology,* VII, New York, Columbia University, 1929.

Chapman, Kenneth M. "The Pottery of Santo Domingo Pueblo," *Memoir* I, Santa Fe, New Mexico, Laboratory of Anthropology, 1939.

Colton, Harold S. *Hopi Kachina Dolls with a Key to Their Identification.* Albuquerque, University of New Mexico Press, 1959.

Dockstader, Frederick J. "The Kachina and the White Man," *Bulletin* No. 35, Bloomfield Hills, Michigan, Cranbrook Institute of Science, 1954.

Earle, Edwin and Kennard, Edward. *Hopi Kachinas.* New York, Museum of the American Indian, Heye Foundation, 1971.

Fontana, Bernard L. *Papago Indian Pottery.* Seattle, University of Washington Press, 1962.

Goddard, Pliny E. "Indians of the Southwest," *American Museum of Natural History Handbook Series* No. 2, New York, American Museum of Natural History, 1931.

Kent, Kate Peck. "The Cultivation and Weaving of Cotton in the Pre-Historic United States," *Transactions of the American Philosophical Society.* (n.s.) Vol. 47, Part 3, Philadelphia, 1957, pp 457-733.

Kluckhohn, Clyde, and Leighton, Dorothea C. *The Navajo.* (rev. ed.) New York, Natural History Press, 1971.

McGregor, John C. *Southwestern Archaeology.* Urbana, Illinois, University of Illinois Press, 1971.

Marriott, Alice. *Maria; The Potter of San Ildefonso.* Norman, Oklahoma, University of Oklahoma Press, 1948, 1971.

Matthews, Washington. "The Night Chant: A Navajo Ceremony," *Memoirs of the American Museum of Natural History,* Vol. VI, New York, American Museum of Natural History, 1902.

Maxwell, Gilbert S. *Navajo Rugs.* Palm Desert, California, Best-West Publications, 1963.

Mera, Harry P. "Pueblo Indian Embroidery," *Memoirs of the Laboratory of Anthropology,* Vol. IV, Santa Fe, University of New Mexico Press, 1943.

——"The 'Rain Bird': A Study in Pueblo Design," *Memoir* II, Santa Fe, New Mexico, Laboratory of Anthropology, 1937.

——"Style Trends of Pueblo Pottery in the Rio Grande and Little Colorado Cultural Areas," *Memoir* III, Santa Fe, New Mexico, Laboratory of Anthropology, 1939.

Mills, George. *Navajo Art and Culture.* Colorado Springs, The Taylor Museum of the Colorado Springs Fine Arts Center, 1959.

Speck, Frank G. "Decorative Art and Basketry of the Cherokee," *Bulletin* 2, Milwaukee, Milwaukee Public Museum, 1920, pp 53-86.

Underhill, Ruth M. *Pueblo Crafts.* Washington, D. C., Bureau of Indian Affairs, 1944.

Woodward, Arthur. "A Brief History of Navajo Silversmithing," *Bulletin* 14, Flagstaff, Museum of Northern Arizona, 1938.

Plateau/Basin

Haines, Francis. *The Nez Perces, Tribesmen of the Columbia Plateau.* Norman, Oklahoma, University of Oklahoma Press, 1955. (out of print)

Spier, Leslie, and Sapir, Edward. "Wishram Ethnography," *Publications in Anthropology,* Vol. 5, No. 3, Seattle, University of Washington Press, 1930.

Strong, Emory. *Stone Age on the Columbia River.* Portland, Oregon, Binfords & Mort, 1960.

Northwest Coast

Adam, L. "Nordwest-Amerikanische Indianerkunst," *Orbis Pictus,* Vol. XVII, Berlin, E. Wasmuth, 1929.

Barbeau, Marius. "Totem Poles," *Anthropological Series* No. 30, *Bulletin* 119, Vols. I and II, Ottawa, National Museum of Canada, 1950.

——"Haida Carvers," *Anthropological Series* No. 38, *Bulletin* 139. Ottawa, National Museum of Canada, 1957.

Boas, Franz. "The Decorative Art of the Indians of the North Pacific Coast," *Bulletin,* Vol. IX, New York, American Museum of Natural History, 1897, pp 123-176.

Davis, Robert T. *Native Arts of the Pacific Northwest.* Stanford, California, Stanford University Press, 1949. (out of print)

Drucker, Philip. "Indians of the Northwest Coast," *American Museum of Natural History Handbook Series* No. 10, New York, McGraw-Hill, 1955.

Duff, Wilson, Holm, Bill and Reid, Bill. *Arts of the Raven — Masterworks by the Northwest Coast Indian.* Vancouver, B. C., Vancouver Art Gallery, 1967.

Emmons, George T. "The Chilkat Blanket," *Memoirs of the American Museum of Natural History,* Vol. III, New York, American Museum of Natural History, 1907, pp 239-400.

Ernst, Alice. *The Wolf Ritual of the Northwest Coast.* Eugene, Oregon, University of Oregon Press, 1952. (out of print)

Feder, Norman and Malin, Edward. "Indian Art of the Northwest Coast," *Denver Art Museum Quarterly,* Winter, Denver, Denver Art Museum, 1962.

Garfield, Viola. *The Tsimshian: Their Arts and Music.* New York, J. J. Augustin, 1951. (out of print)

Gunther, Erna. *Art in the Life of the Northwest Coast Indians.* Seattle, Catalogue of the Rasmussen Collection at the Portland Art Museum, 1966.

Gunther, Erna and Haeberlin, Herman. "The Indians of Puget Sound," *Publications in Anthropology,* Vol. 4, Seattle, University of Washington Press, 1930.

Hawthorn, Audrey. *Art of the Kwakiutl Indians and Other Northwest Coast Tribes.* Seattle, University of Washington Press, 1967.

Holm, Bill. *Northwest Coast Indian Art: An Analysis of Form.* Seattle, University of Washington Press, 1965.

Inverarity, Robert Bruce. *Art of the Northwest Coast Indians.* Berkeley, University of California Press, 1950, 1967.

Krause, Aurel. *Tlingit Indians: Results of a Trip to the Northwest Coast of America and the Bering Straits.* English edition translated by Erna Gunther. Seattle, University of Washington Press, 1956, 1970.

Michon, Marion Johnson. "Masks of the Northwest Coast," *Publications in Primitive Art,* No. 2, Milwaukee, Milwaukee Public Museum, 1966.

Niblack, Albert P. "The Coast Indians of Southern Alaska and Northern British Columbia," *United States National Museum Report,* Washington, D. C., 1888, pp 225-386.

Siebert, Erna, and Forman, Werner. *North American Indian Art.* New York, Tudor, 1967. (A catalogue of Northwest Coast art in Russian museums.)

Wardwell, Allen. *Yakutat South: Indian Art of the Northwest Coast.* Chicago, Art Institute of Chicago, 1964.

Eskimo Art

Birket-Smith, Kaj. *The Eskimos.* New York, Crown, 1971.

Hoffman, Walter James. "The Graphic Art of the Eskimos," *United States National Museum Annual Report,* Washington, D. C., 1895, pp 739-968.

Meldgaard, Jorgen. *Eskimo Sculpture.* London, Methuen & Co. Ltd., 1960.

Rainey, Froelich G. "Eskimo Prehistory: the Okvik Site on the Punuk Islands," *Anthropological Papers of the American Museum of Natural History,* Vol. 37, Part 4, New York, American Museum of Natural History, 1941, pp 453-569.

Ray, Dorothy Jean. *Artists of the Tundra and the Sea.* Seattle, University of Washington Press, 1961.

——*Eskimo Masks: Art and Ceremony.* Photographs by Alfred A. Blaker. Seattle, University of Washington Press, 1967.

Swinton, George. *Eskimo Sculpture.* Pennsylvania, Dufour Editions, Inc., 1965.

Southeast

Foreman, Grant. *The Five Civilized Tribes.* Norman, Oklahoma, University of Oklahoma Press, 1934, 1971.

Fundaburk, Emma Lila, and Foreman, Mary Douglas. *Sun Circles and Human Hands: The Southeastern Indians, Art & Industries.* Luverne, Alabama, Fundaburk Publishers, 1957.

——*Southeastern Indians Life Portraits: A Catalogue of Pictures 1564-1860.* Metuchen, New Jersey, Scarecrow Press, Inc., 1969.

Lorant, Stefan. *The New World.* New York, Hawthorne Books, Inc., 1965.

Rights, Douglas L. *The American Indian in North Carolina.* Durham, North Carolina, Duke University Press, 1947. (out of print)

Speck, Frank and Broom,L. *Cherokee Dance and Drama.* Berkeley, University of California Press, 1951. (out of print)

Swanton, J. R. "Indians of the Southeastern United States," *Bureau of American Ethnology Bulletin* No. 137, Washington, D. C., Smithsonian Institution, 1946.

California

Barrett, S. A. "Pomo Indian Basketry," *Publications in American Anthropology and Ethnology* VII, No. 3, Berkeley, University of California Press, 1908, pp 133-309.

Dixon, Roland B. "Basketry Designs of the Indians of Northern California," *American Museum of Natural History Bulletin* 17, Part 1, New York, American Museum of Natural History, 1902, pp 1-32.

Kroeber, Alfred L. "Handbook of the Indians of California," *Bureau of American Ethnology Bulletin* No. 78, Washington, D. C., Smithsonian Institution, 1925.

Kroeber, Theodora. *Ishi in Two Worlds: A Biography of the Last Wild Indian in North America.* Berkeley, University of California Press, 1961.

Latta, F. F. *Handbook of Yokuts Indians.* Bakersfield, California, Merchants Printing and Lithographing Co., 1949. (out of print)

Acknowledgments

The organization of the exhibition **American Indian Art: Form and Tradition** involved the efforts, counsel and support of many individuals and institutions. Members of the Indian Art Association, a newly formed group representing a number of regional Indian organizations, worked with the staffs of Walker Art Center and The Minneapolis Institute of Arts in developing related educational and community programs. Ron Libertus, assisted by Ellie Banks, served as liaison with the Indian Art Association. Gerald Vizenor worked on statewide community programs, under a special grant from the Minnesota State Arts Council. Yvonne Warhol developed the exhibition of Indian children's art at Northern States Power Company, with the help of June Schultz. Paul Day, of the Indian Art Association, and Eddie Benton, of the American Indian Movement, St. Paul, worked on related programs.

In organizing the exhibition we had the counsel of various specialists who worked closely with us during the selection process. Dr. Frederick J. Dockstader, Director of the Museum of the American Indian, Heye Foundation, New York, was an important consultant and a large number of loans were selected by him from that distinguished institution's collection. Norman Feder, Curator of Native Arts and American Indian Arts, The Denver Art Museum, assisted during the exhibition's early planning stages. Richard Conn, Curator, The Denver Art Museum, reviewed catalogue entries and provided supplementary information on attributions and use. Timothy Fiske, Assistant Director/Curator of Anthropology, Science Museum of Minnesota; John Garrigan, Associate Curator, Department of Architecture and Design, Museum of Modern Art; Betty Toulouse, Curator, Laboratory of Anthropology, Museum of New Mexico; and Mitchell A. Wilder, Director, Amon Carter Museum of Western Art, consulted on various aspects of the exhibition's organization.

Objects were selected by the staffs of Walker Art Center and The Minneapolis Institute of Arts: Martin Friedman, Mildred Friedman and Richard Koshalek of the Art Center; and Ron Libertus and David Ryan of the Institute. Gwen Lerner, assisted by Carolyn Farndell, coordinated the shipping and registration of borrowed objects for both institutions. The exhibition was designed by Richard Koshalek, assisted by Hideki Yamamoto. The Institute's installation was coordinated by David Ryan, with the cooperation of Evan Maurer and Merribell Parsons; its technical crew consisted of Vernon Blanck and Irwin Lucius. The Art Center's technical crew included Terry Fisher, Eldor Johnson and Stuart Nielsen. The catalogue was prepared and edited by Mildred Friedman, Dean Swanson and David Ryan, with the editorial assistance of Pamela Barclay; secretarial assistance came from Joan Benson, Linda Erickson, Donna Gale and Betsy Petersen. The publication was designed by James E. Johnson, with assistance from Carol Evans; Eric Sutherland made the majority of catalogue photographs, assisted by Tom Arndt and Steven G. Jensen; additional catalogue photographs were made by Carroll T. Hartwell, or supplied by the lenders or by the authors. Public information was the responsibility of Ann Mason and Margaret Otis; events related to the exhibition were coordinated by Phoebe Hansen, Molly LaBerge, Philip Larson, Tom Le Blanc, Tim Shepard, Dean Swanson, Bonnie Wallace and Suzanne Weil.

Educational programs were coordinated by Roger Mandle and Theresa Thorp.

The exhibition was supported with grants from the National Endowment for the Arts in Washington, D.C., a Federal agency created by Act of Congress in 1965, and from the Dayton Hudson Foundation. The Ford Foundation sponsored four internships for Indian graduate students in art and art history who worked on various aspects of the exhibition program: Carl Gawboy, Trudy Griffin, Gary Hood and David Ripley. A grant from the Minnesota State Arts Council provided funds for activities related to the exhibition. The Agricultural Extension Service of the University of Minnesota provided personnel and funds for the exhibition of Indian children's art held at, and partially funded by Northern States Power Company. The University of Minnesota Department of American Indian Studies sponsored a series of lectures by specialists in Indian art held in conjunction with the exhibition; these were arranged by George Morrison. The Downtown Council of Minneapolis helped sponsor the public information program for the exhibition and public bus transportation for visitors to the exhibition sites.

To these many individuals and institutions, and to all others who worked on this large project, we express our gratitude.

Walker Art Center
Indian Art Association
The Minneapolis Institute of Arts

Photo Credits

Credits refer to the illustration numbers in italics before each photo caption

Eric Sutherland: all photographs not otherwise credited

Carroll T. Hartwell: *52, 53, 56, 58, 74, 75, 76, 113, 119, 122, 148, 169, 170, 173, 179*

Alfred A. Blaker, courtesy The University of Washington Press, from Ray, Dorothy Jean, *Eskimo Masks: Art and Ceremony: 103-108*

Courtesy The Brooklyn Museum: *7, 67, 126, 129, 152, 180*

Courtesy The Detroit Institute of Arts: *89, 95*

G. T. Emmons, courtesy British Columbia Provincial Museum, Victoria, B.C.: *84*

David Gebhard: *22, 23, 26-32*

Courtesy M. Knoedler & Co., Inc.: *21*

Courtesy The Milwaukee Public Museum: *48, 49*

Courtesy The Museum of the American Indian, Heye Foundation: *25*

Courtesy The Museum of New Mexico: *35, 36, 42*

Courtesy The National Museum of Canada: *94*

Courtesy The National Museum of Natural History, Smithsonian Institution: *138*

Courtesy The National Park Service: *39*

Courtesy The Nelson Gallery of Art: *90*

C. F. Newcombe, courtesy British Columbia Provincial Museum, Victoria, B.C.: *86*

Courtesy The Portland Museum of Art: *102*

Vincent Scully: *33, 37, 38, 40, 41*

Courtesy Mr. and Mrs. Morton I. Sosland: *96, 118*

F. Sweet: *24*

Charles Uht, courtesy The Museum of Primitive Art: *120, 121, 123, 131, 132, 136, 150, 159, 171, 174, 181*

Courtesy Yale University Art Library: *34*

Colophon

Printing: Kolorpress Inc.
Binding: Midwest editions Inc.
Text type: 10 point Helvetica, Andersen Typesetting Inc.
Paper: Cover, 8 point Mark I; Text, 100
      pound Mead Enamel.
Color separations: Colorbrite Inc.